Object Relations and Relationality in Couple Therapy

The Library of Object Relations
Series Editors: David E. Scharff and Jill Savege Scharff

The Library of Object Relations provides an expanding body of theory for understanding individual development and pathology, human interaction, and new avenues of treatment. They apply to realms of experience from the internal world of the individual to the human community, from the clinical situation to everyday life, and from individual psychoanalysis and psychotherapy, to group therapy, couple and family therapy, and to social policy.

Titles in the Series

Object Relations and Relationality in Couple Therapy

Exploring the Middle Ground

James L. Poulton

JASON ARONSON
Lanham • Boulder • New York • Toronto • Plymouth, UK

Published by Jason Aronson
A wholly owned subsidiary of The Rowman & Littlefield Publishing Group, Inc.
4501 Forbes Boulevard, Suite 200, Lanham, Maryland 20706
www.rowman.com

10 Thornbury Road, Plymouth PL6 7PP, United Kingdom

British Library Cataloguing in Publication Information Available

Library of Congress Cataloging-in-Publication Data

Library of Congress Cataloging-in-Publication Data Available
ISBN 978-0-7657-0894-6 (cloth : alk. paper)

Library of Congress Cataloging-in-Publication Data

Poulton, James L., 1950-
Object relations and relationality in couple therapy : exploring the middle ground / James L. Poulton.
p. cm.
Includes bibliographical references and index.
ISBN 978-0-7657-0894-6 (cloth : alk. paper)
1. Couples therapy. 2. Marital psychotherapy. I. Title.
RC488.5.P68 2013
616.89'1562--dc23
2012032049

♾   The paper used in this publication meets the minimum requirements of American
National Standard for Information Sciences Permanence of Paper for Printed Library
Materials, ANSI/NISO Z39.48-1992.

Printed in the United States of America

To my family and friends, who have taught me the true value of the relational world.

"God, how we get our fingers in each other's clay."
—Ray Bradbury, *Dandelion Wine*.

Contents

Acknowledgments

Although the title page of this book identifies only one author, this project required the contributions of many individuals, without whose guidance, encouragement, feedback, and support it would have been neither begun, nor completed. There are many people I wish to thank; first on the list is my wife and partner, Donna Poulton. No words are powerful enough to describe the debt of gratitude I owe to her. Her coaching, editing, and loving encouragement have been invaluable; above all else, she has been the prime mover in my life and career.

Next I would like to thank David Scharff, who has played a particularly essential role in the creation of this book. As coeditor, with Jill Scharff, of the Jason Aronson Library of Object Relations, David encouraged me to imagine this project, and convinced me that my experiences and thoughts about treating couples were of sufficient value to be shared. In addition, David and Jill are the cofounders of the International Psychotherapy Institute (IPI), under whose auspices I have found a professional home and a group of colleagues, including faculty, staff and students, with whom I have had countless thoughtful and energizing discussions about the topics covered in this book.

This book also would not have been completed without the help of my friend and colleague, Charles Raps, whose gracious and intelligent reviews and edits of my work have been immensely valuable, and have helped me to clarify and formulate my thoughts. For similar reasons, I wish to thank the members of my reading group—Merritt Stites, Ruth Manville, Mitch Koles, Bill Fulton and Penny Jameson—for their thoughtful comments on drafts of some of the book's chapters.

I am also grateful to a number of people who have reviewed portions of this manuscript or who have discussed its ideas with me. These include: Richard Billow, who, along with Charles Raps, is my skiing buddy and with

whom every lift ride is an opportunity for in-depth discussion of psychoanalytic ideas; Julia Ting, who catalyzed the development of my thoughts about
the "cultural third" and cultural transferences; Michael Stadter, whose unique
perspectives on object relations and relational theory have been a continuing
source of enlightenment; Sheila Hill, whose interest in the work of Ferro,
Bolognini and others has stimulated my own; Charles Ashbach, Karen Fral-
ey, Paul Koehler and Michelle Kwintner, with whom I have had many fascinating discussions about the nature of sacrifice and its role in relationships;
and Carl Bagnini, with whom I have discussed many aspects of the treatment
of couples. My gratitude also to Geoff Anderson (current director of IPI),
Janine Wanlass, Colleen Sandor, Jane Prelinger, Judy Rovner, Sharon Dennett, Doug Dennett, Lea Setton, Caroline Sehon, and all of the other faculty
members of IPI who have encouraged me in my writing and who have
tolerated my absences while I tried to get my thoughts down on paper. I have
also deeply appreciated the support and tolerance offered to me by faculty
members of my local IPI group, including Karl Seashore, Becky Bailey,
Stephen Morris and Audrey Rice.

The editorial staff of Rowman and Littlefield Publishers, especially Sa-
mantha Kirk, Amy King, and Lindsey Frederick have played a central role in
the creation of this book. They deserve a special note of gratitude for their
patience, expert advice and skill in putting this book together.

Finally, I want to thank my patients, whose courage and patience in the
face of daunting challenges and seemingly insuperable conflicts have been a
constant source of inspiration.

PERMISSIONS

I would like to gratefully acknowledge the following publishers, who have
granted permission for my use of the following literary works quoted in this
book:

Something Wicked This Way Comes, by Ray Bradbury, reprinted by permission of Don Congdon Associates. Copyright © 1962, renewed 1990 by
Ray Bradbury.

"Agamemnon," from *The Oresteia* by Aeschylus, translated by Robert
Fagles, translation copyright © 1966, 1967, 1975, 1977 by Robert Fagles.
Used by permission of Viking Penguin, a division of Penguin Group (USA)
Inc. Also reproduced by permission from Sheil Land Associates Ltd.

Who's Afraid of Virginia Woolf? by Edward Albee, reprinted with the
permission of Scribner, a Division of Simon & Schuster, Inc. Copyright ©
1962 by Edward Albee. Copyright renewed © 1990 by Edward Albee. All
rights reserved.

"Ithaka," from Cavafy, C. P.; *C. P. Cavafy*. Copyright © 1972 Edmund Keely and Philip Sherrard. Reprinted by permission of Princeton University Press.

"Poetics," from *The Selected Poems, Expanded Edition* by A. R. Ammons. Copyright © 1969 by A. R. Ammons. Used by permission of W. W. Norton & Company, Inc.

Preface

During the course of psychotherapy with couples, the practicing clinician frequently faces problems and issues that can seem nearly insoluble. These impasses can threaten the therapy itself, and at the least they challenge the therapist's sense of competence and effectiveness. When problems like this arise, the therapist casts about for theories that offer guidance—i.e., that explain what is actually happening and why, and provide effective steps for resolving the impasse and getting the therapy moving again.

In this book, I survey some of the more intractable problems couple therapists are likely to encounter, and I suggest a therapeutic approach that offers the richest conceptual tools for understanding them. This approach draws upon the innovations from two distinct but interrelated theoretical traditions—object relations and relational theory. Although these two traditions have at times clashed, both over foundational assumptions and specific points of technique, they are also deeply committed to the same field of investigation: the role relationships play in forming and shaping the individual, and the role individuals play in creating their relationships.

These two theories have approached relationships from very different directions. While object relations theory has explored them in terms of their individual participants, and has developed extensive conceptual tools for understanding the interactions between individuals, relational theory has focused more exclusively on the relationship itself, describing those aspects of interactions in which the psychic material from both participants becomes sufficiently intertwined that a new dimension of experience—the relational dimension—emerges that functions as a "third" subjectivity between them, a unified entity operating according to its own principles. Although some controversy has surrounded the question of how foundational this dimension is, many analytic writers, from both object relations and relational perspectives, have recognized the value of treating both "individual" and "relational" concepts as equally foundational. These theorists have thus explored the middle ground between the two theories, and have borrowed the best ideas from both to begin to formulate an integrated therapeutic approach.

In my view, this middle ground perspective is uniquely suited to provide the therapist with the most comprehensive and effective ideas for working with couples. With this book, I hope to add to the growing literature that explores this middle ground. In doing so, I will provide extensive case material—both to illustrate the wide variety of concepts available to the therapist from this approach, but also to offer specific examples for how to translate those concepts into actual interventions.

In order to familiarize the reader with object relations and relational theory, chapter 1 presents an overview of their core concepts. In this chapter, I also describe some of the controversies that have at times set the two theories in opposition to each other, and I describe in detail the value of the middle ground approach.

Chapter 2 explores the middle ground's perspective on the kinds of transferences the couple therapist is likely to encounter, both between the members of the couple, and between the couple and the therapist. In this chapter, I also describe how focusing both on individual transferences and joint transferences, created by the relationship itself, deepens the treatment and facilitates the development of both individual responsibility and an empathetic connection between partners.

In chapter 3, I discuss a particular aspect of blended psychic experience that can occur within the couple. When two partners share similar internal objects, they will be likely, through repeated interactions, to create a "shared object," i.e., an object that is held in the relational dimension between the two, and that is fed, reinforced and augmented by the continuing contributions from both. Shared objects have a tendency to create escalating cycles of anxiety that both partners are desperate to avoid.

One of the more controversial techniques to arise out of relational theory is the intentional use of therapist self-disclosure. In chapter 4, I consider the theoretical arguments for and against self-disclosure, and suggest that, from the middle ground perspective, self-disclosure is not prohibited, but neither does middle ground theory endorse its unexamined or unlimited use. In this chapter, I suggest specific principles to guide the therapist in determining when and whether self-disclosure is appropriate.

In chapters 5 and 6, I consider two kinds of issues that are particularly difficult for couple therapists to manage. Chapter 5 discusses the "narcissistic couple," i.e., the couple whose interactions are controlled by the tendency of one or both partners to utilize narcissistic defenses against the relationship itself. In chapter 6, I describe a way of conceptualizing the impact of intergenerational trauma on the couple, and offer suggestions for therapeutic interventions that are specifically designed to help couples free themselves from the limitations imposed on their relationship by the traumas of their parents or grandparents.

Emotional violence between partners of a couple is another issue that confronts the couple therapist both with the fragilities of each partner and the durability of their defenses against them. In chapter 7, I describe a case in which both partners used emotional violence as a means of sacrificing the other, through which the sacrificing partner was able to gain temporary relief from internal persecutions. These partners had in effect created a "joint personality"—i.e., a co-constructed pattern of interacting—in which they not only traded sacrifices, but also took care to repair each other when they had been too injured by the sacrifices.

Chapter 8 considers another dimension in which relational interactions— this time at the cultural level—impact and determine the course of the couple relationship. This chapter describes a case in which the two partners grew up in families with diametrically opposed political affiliations. Because both partners identified with specific aspects of their political and cultural environments, and disidentified with others, they had developed "cultural transferences" through which each saw the other in polarized and unidimensional terms.

Finally, chapter 9 discusses an issue that has perplexed theorists from both object relations and relational perspectives, but that has been particularly examined by relational theory: the nature and value of truth in the therapeutic enterprise. Because relational theorists have argued that therapists' access to truth is compromised by their intimate involvement in the relational dimensions of experience between themselves and their patients, they have questioned how helpful truth can be as a therapeutic principle or concept. In this chapter, I explore a middle ground approach to this question, and discuss the means by which patients can be helped to establish a new relationship with the unconscious sources of both truth and illusion in their lives.

A final note: *For purposes of confidentiality and privacy, the names and details of all of the couples described in this book have been disguised.*

Chapter One

Shared Ground

*Commonalities in Object Relations and Relational
Approaches to Couple Therapy*

The relationship between members of a couple is a kaleidoscopic play among
a myriad of variables, all pressing for expression on the multiple axes of
conscious and unconscious experience. From one perspective, the interactions between the two partners, whose minds are joined together by intimacy
and long-term familiarity, may appear to be well defined and to have clear
meaning. But because the deeper implications of those interactions often lie
in the murky and seemingly impenetrable depths of each partner's unconscious, couple therapists perpetually remain in a disconcerting position of
uncertainty—never knowing whether they have fully explored all of the dimensions that would explain the couple's behaviors.

Indeed, it is difficult to pin down, with precision, *what* is happening in a
couple interaction, let alone *why* it is happening. The interplay between the
two partners takes place on so many levels and from the standpoint of such
varying perspectives, that tracking those elements of the interaction that will
be *useful* to the therapist—and ultimately to the couple—becomes a daunting
task.

In this chapter I will explore two related approaches to couple therapy,
one derived from object relations theory and the other from relational or
intersubjective theory, that cast the farthest light into the recondite corners of
relationships. Although these two theories have at times inspired contentious
disagreements between their more extreme advocates, each theory has advanced ideas and techniques that, when integrated into a consistent therapeu-

tic approach, provide a broad foundation for conceptualizing couple interactions and for designing interventions that facilitate the couple's growth. The approach that integrates the best ideas from each theory—which has been called the "middle ground" by those writers who have explored the commonalties and continuities, rather than the discontinuities, between the theories—is particularly suited to couple therapy because it provides tools necessary for addressing the tensions between the individual and the relational, the intrapsychic and the interpersonal, that arise in all relationships.

In what follows, I will review some of the central contributions object relations and relational theories have made to psychoanalysis and psychoanalytic psychotherapy, and I will discuss in detail the reasons the middle ground approach offers the modern clinician the widest range of options for working with couples. In order to demonstrate the utility of this approach, I will present a clinical case of a couple whose relationship had become incapacitated by the mutual influence of each partner's unresolved childhood conflicts.

TANYA AND MICHAEL

Tanya and Michael were a professional couple with every outward appearance of success. They lived in a coveted part of town, their two children excelled in college, and they seemed, to a casual observer, to enjoy a solid and durable marriage. And yet, something was wrong at the heart of their relationship. They had grown distant from each other, they said, but each had a different explanation for why this happened. Tanya said over the years she grew tired of Michael's "wishy-washiness," and a few years ago decided to take more control because he wouldn't. Michael said Tanya didn't respect him anymore and had abandoned her prior role as an understanding partner who loved him in spite of his weaknesses. Both partners then described a pattern of interaction that had recently occurred more frequently. It began when Michael wavered in his expression of an opinion or desire. Tanya, frustrated with his wavering, would say something Michael experienced as contemptuous. Michael then would retreat, injured, and Tanya would become even more judgmental because of his retreat.

An example of this occurred near the end of our first session. Tanya had enumerated Michael's failings. As she did so, she seemed cool and disdainful, and her tone reminded me of a mother disciplining her misbehaving child. When Michael then listed the ways Tanya hurt him, he seemed tentative and anxious, and tears were in his eyes. He said, "I'm tired of it. I've reached a point where I need it to change, or I'll . . . " He paused and didn't finish the sentence. Tanya, who had beens starring straight-ahead and seemed to have only partially listened, looked up when she realized he had stopped.

She saw he was crying, but her expression remained disdainful. "Or you'll what?" she asked, and her tone now implied accusation and smug satisfaction—I assumed because she just caught Michael in his weakness. Michael saw her expression and averted his eyes. With an air of defeat, he said, "I don't know what I'd do." They then looked at me with differing expressions. In Tanya's look I saw dissatisfaction with her husband's lack of forcefulness and an expectation I would join her in criticizing, even mocking, his performance. From Michael, I felt a similar expectation that I should see the unfairness in Tanya's behavior, but I also saw a child-like dependency on me to protect him from his hurtful wife.

OBJECT RELATIONS THEORY AND COUPLE THERAPY

How can we understand a pattern like this in an otherwise successful couple? Why did Michael place himself in a passive and indecisive position, which only drew Tanya's contempt? Why did Tanya dismiss and criticize Michael in a cold and disconnected manner, which only intensified his anxieties? And why did each partner turn to me, at the end of the session, with the implicit expectation that I would join them in their criticisms of each other?

For many years in the history of psychoanalysis, there were few answers to questions like these, since couple therapy as a mode of treatment was actively, and sometimes scathingly, discouraged by mainstream psychoanalysts. The arguments psychoanalysts marshaled against couple therapy generally fell into one of three categories. First, because Freudian theory was largely a theory of the individual that focused on the drives, conflicts, defense mechanisms, resistances, etc., that arose within the relatively contained functioning of the intrapsychic system, it could not—and should not, according to many early Freudians—guide the therapist in the complexities of couple interaction. Second, Freudian theory had asserted that therapeutic change could only occur through the analysis of transference, which, to be analyzable, required the protected environment of an individual psychoanalytic relationship. It wasn't that early detractors of couple therapy believed transferences would be absent in the treatment of couples; only that couple transferences would "so confound the therapeutic transference relationship that the conscious unraveling of fact and fantasy would be impossible" (Prochaska & Prochaska, 1978, p. 16). Finally, because psychoanalysis had, as a theory of both illness and health, endorsed the individualistic biases of *fin de siècle* Europe and devoted itself to encouraging the fullest development of the *individual's* potential, it simply lacked the conceptual foundations to offer guidance as to what the goal and purpose, let alone the technique, of couple treatment might be (Sander, 1978).

What a difference a few decades make. Although a few writers in the 1930s and 1940s attempted to adapt, with only modest success, traditional psychoanalytic theory to the treatment of couples (Oberndorf, 1938; Mittelmann, 1944, 1948), by the 1960s it had become clear that if psychoanalysis was to going to provide a model for couple therapy at all, it had to develop a new set of theoretical ideas and clinical techniques that took the relationship between individuals as a primary object of study. Fortunately, several analytic writers accepted the task (Bannister & Pincus, 1965; Dicks, 1967; Friedman, 1962; Main, 1966; Pincus, 1960). Drawing upon the relatively new and rapidly evolving theory of object relations, these writers created the foundation for a new approach to the treatment of couples based on a fuller appreciation of the conscious and unconscious pathways of communication and mutual influence within relationships.

"Object relations theory" is a term that refers to an amalgam of concepts and techniques unified by a few central ideas advanced by influential theorists (J. Scharff, 1995). Those theorists, who included Winnicott (1989), Fairbairn (1952), Guntrip (1961, 1969), Klein (1946, 1952a, 1957), Bion (1962b, 1965), M. Balint (1965, 1979) and others, held that each individual has a fundamental need for attachment and interaction with other human beings, and that the personality is structured, in its patterns of emotions, behavior and thoughts, as a consequence of the vicissitudes of prior and present relationships. Object relations theory thus places the individual's internal structure squarely in a social context, emphasizing the role of interpersonal interaction in both the *development* of the personality in the context of relationships with early caregivers, and in the *creation* and *maintenance* of ongoing psychological and behavioral patterns within the contours of current relationships with family, friends or partners.

CORE OBJECT RELATIONS CONCEPTS

Perhaps because of its unique emphasis on the effects of relationships on the individual, object relations theory, from its inception, has attracted many adherents who have introduced a wide array of loosely related concepts and clinical techniques. While many of these ideas proved to be useful to the newly emerging field of couple therapy, a few, such as *transference, countertransference, projective and introjective identification* and *containment*, formed the core around which the rest of the theory was built. In this and the following section, I will briefly review these concepts and illustrate their application to the case of Tanya and Michael.

A central tenet of object relations theory is that the structure of the personality is built up through the gradual internalization, from birth onward, of interactions with primary figures in the interpersonal environment, resulting in internalized representations not only of those figures (which the theory terms "objects"), but also of the self and the interactions among them. This process of internalization is not a one-on-one mapping of external events onto internal representations. Instead, it is distorted, especially in the early developmental years, by multiple mechanisms. A primary source of distortion lies in the propensity of the infant's mind to utilize *splitting* as a central mechanism of defense (Fairbairn, 1940, 1943, 1944; Klein, 1935, 1946). As the infant interacts with its caregivers, it experiences a full range of drive-related emotions, such as hate, love, envy, aggression and idealization. Because the infant's hateful emotions are experienced as threatening to its loved objects, it initially internalizes separate, or split, representations of those objects. That is, the actual external object is internalized—along with the infant's experiences of it—as both a "good" object (i.e., one that is satisfying, loved and loving) and a "bad" object (i.e., one that is frustrating, hated and persecuting), and these two sides of the object are kept separate, internally, so that the infant can feel it is keeping its loved objects safe from its own hateful attacks.

This splitting of the infant's internal objects, which is characteristic of what Klein called the "paranoid-schizoid position" (1946), will eventually be healed if the infant has "good-enough" experiences with its caregivers and is not burdened by an overage of aggression in its temperamental makeup. If the infant can heal its internal splits, its internal objects will become "whole objects," in which their satisfying and frustrating aspects are held together in the same representation (characteristic of the "depressive position"—Klein, 1935). If, however, the infant is unable to bridge those splits, its objects will remain polarized, thereby not only misrepresenting the actual external object, but also creating an internal world in which unresolved conflicts, unmoderated emotions and extremized representations of both self and object predominate.

The infant's internalization of its experiences with objects, whether whole or split, does not result in static representations of object and self, but rather of the two in a dynamic relationship, which thereafter links them with the original emotions, desires, drives, perceptions and attitudes that once were felt to characterize their actual interactions (Ogden, 1983). Fairbairn (1944, 1946) termed this internalized complex of self, object and the relationship between them the *internal object relationship*. As soon as these internal object relationships are created, they begin to function in their primary role: as sources of implicit models for understanding, predicting and responding to experiences with others (Bowlby, 1977; Lyons-Ruth, 1999). When a husband, for example, who as a child developed an angry-mother/frightened-self internal object relationship, experiences marital conflict, his internal structure will not only distort his understanding of the meaning of the conflict and of the roles played by himself and his wife, but it will also provide him with a limited range of options for how to feel and what to do next. In object relations theory, the tendency of an internal object relationship to mold current experience according to its own parameters is the foundational mechanism underlying transference, countertransference, and projective and introjective identification (Ogden, 1983).

According to object relations theory, *transference*, which occurs both between partners and between patient and therapist, is the result of the activation and projection of aspects of internal object relationships, formed in the arena of past interactions, into the current relationship (Heimann, 1956; Joseph, 1985; Klein, 1952a). Transference can become complex rapidly, for two reasons. First, *either* side of the internal object relationship (viz., the self or the object) can be projected into the other; and second, the person doing the projecting may then also internally identify with either the self's or the object's role. That is, the projecting individual is not restricted to identifying only with the self's position in his internal object relationships, but may also identify with the object's position. Thus, the husband with an angry-mother/frightened-self internal configuration may project either anger or fear into his wife, but may also then feel *either* angry or fearful in relationship to her. Regardless of the form transference takes, however, the subsequent interactions between the two individuals will follow, because of the dual processes of projection and internal identification, the narrative line of the projecting person's internal object relationship.

In contrast to transference, which depends upon one partner's projection of unconscious material into the other, *countertransference* occurs when the partner who receives those projections unconsciously identifies with them and enacts them (Heimann, 1950; Racker, 1968; Tower, 1956). Countertransference can thus function as something like a mirror of the first partner's original transference projections, although this mirror can often be distorted by the receiving partner's additions, from their own unconscious sources, to their countertransference responses. Finally, *projective identification*, in its most common form (for a more extensive discussion of projective identification, see chapter 2), is similar to transference in that it begins with the projection of aspects of an internal object relationship, but contains an added element: an unconscious attempt, on the part of the projector, to *coerce* or *induce* his partner into identifying with his projections (via *introjective identification*) and thereby, again, enacting them (Bion, 1962b; Dicks, 1967; Grotstein, 1981; Heimann, 1952; Klein, 1946, 1952b; Ogden, 1979, 1982; J. Scharff, 1992). When both partners engage in processes of projective and introjective identification, they can produce sequences of transference and countertransference interactions in which each partner is both the inducer and the induced.

We'll see in the next chapter that transferences, countertransferences and projective and introjective identifications abound in the context of couple treatment. For our present purposes, we need only recognize that because these phenomena are based on internal object relationships that are often distorted, polarized, and laden with infantile emotions and imagery, they are likely to fuel the primary sources of conflict in any couple relationship (Dicks, 1967; Graller, 1981; Ruszczynski, 1992; Scharff & Scharff, 1991; Willi, 1982).

A final concept from object relations theory that is fundamental to working with couples is *containment* (Bion, 1962b, 1963), which refers to the mother's capacity to identify with the unmoderated sensory and affective experiences the infant has projected into her. Once the mother identifies with those experiences, she then reflects upon, mentalizes and moderates them so she can return them to the infant in a more tolerable and digestible form. The infant's reinternalization of these moderated experiences not only allows it to then claim and acknowledge them as its own, but it also provides the infant with the psychic resources necessary to develop its own tools for working through difficult and primitive emotions. In the object relations approach to therapy, the therapist is thought to occupy a similar position as the mother: the therapist listens to the patient, takes in their unmoderated and unconscious material, and reformulates it so it is more tolerable and comprehensible to the patient, and less likely to be enacted or split-off and projected through transferences or projective identifications. In couple therapy, the therapist provides containment for each individual as well as for the couple as a whole, and the coordination between these two levels of containment is a primary method for helping the couple understand and work through the unconscious material each contributes.

AN OBJECT RELATIONS VIEW OF TANYA AND MICHAEL

We'll see throughout the chapters in this book that in couple interactions the partners' internal object relationships often seem to be tailor-made for each other. This common phenomenon originates in the fact that when choosing partners in the first place, each individual unconsciously seeks others whose internal worlds complement their own. The internal object configurations at work in Tanya and Michael's interactions were no different. Michael, who was the only son of a single mother, described his mother as beautiful, engaging, and powerful in social circles, and critical and prudish in her relationship with him. She avoided speaking of sex with him and actively attempted to exclude from their relationship any aspects of his body or personality that reminded her he was male. He said, for example, she punished him for his attempts to assert himself as the male in the household and she once viciously attacked him for having a visible erection. As a result, Michael was unable to internalize a strong male object and instead developed an internal object relationship in which he, with hidden resentment and anger, felt required to submit to a judgmental and castrating female in order to preserve her good will, the loss of which created the same anxiety he felt as a child during his mother's attacks.

Tanya reported she was raised in an intact family, but with a mother who was debilitated by fear that the outside world contained unavoidable disasters and a solicitous father who tried to help his wife by negotiating many of the family's obligations (school meetings, arranging for plumbers, etc.) without her knowledge. The impact on Tanya was that she became disdainful of her mother's inability to face responsibilities and frightened her father would fail in protecting the family from the disasters her mother's anxieties predicted. Out of these dynamics she developed dual internal object relationships in which she was angry at her internalized incompetent mother, but also afraid her internalized father would fail to be powerful enough to protect her, both in the abstract and in everyday matters.

As Tanya and Michael explored their childhood experiences in treatment, the roles played by their internal object relationships in creating emotional conflicts became increasingly clear. For example, in one session, which occurred midway through treatment, Tanya began by saying she wanted to discuss Michael's handling of a cable representative's failure to appear for a scheduled repair. They had both waited for the representative for several hours. When it was clear he wasn't coming, Tanya asked Michael to call the company and complain. Michael made the call, but failed, in Tanya's eyes, to be forceful enough. She took the phone from him and demanded the company either compensate them or send someone out immediately.

In session, Tanya described this event with accompanying contempt for Michael. When he defended himself, saying he would have eventually gotten to the same solution she did, she dismissed him and said he was weak and would always be weak. She added bitterly that she now knew she was alone in the marriage. Michael seemed devastated and tried to talk her out of her mood by saying he was working on his problems, and he would be better in the future. But Tanya stopped talking to him, and sat staring at me, furious. I asked if she could tell me what exactly in Michael's behavior triggered her anger. She said it was his inability to perform a simple task so she wouldn't have to do it. I asked what it meant to her if she had to do the task. She said it meant she'd been abandoned and she had to face everything by herself. I said it seemed underneath her anger there may be fear—of being alone or of having to negotiate things without support. She was surprised, but agreed and said she didn't know where her fear came from. I said I wasn't sure either, but we were in familiar territory, since what she was afraid of—Michael's inability to manage tasks—was similar to her descriptions of her mother, and her need for Michael to be competent was analogous to her need for her father to negotiate the outside world for her and her mother.

At this point, Michael interrupted to say Tanya always wanted him to be "hard and uncompromising" when talking to service people, but she herself "never" wanted to initiate contact with them. "So I try," he said pleadingly, "but she always takes over." I asked him how she accomplished taking over. He said she terrified him and he wasn't about to stand in her way when she was in a mood like that. I said when she was "in a mood like that," he seemed to see her as so powerful his only option was to submit to her. He said yes and then realized the similarities to his childhood. "Just like with my mother," he said with a pained look.

In these interactions, we can discern the transferences, countertransferences, and projective and introjective identifications—all arising out of internal object relationships—that saddled Tanya and Michael with emotionally intense conflicts stimulated by, but only indirectly related to, the actual events occurring between them. In Tanya's transference toward Michael, she interpreted his submissiveness as the equivalent of her mother's incompetence, which she then felt was as intolerable as her mother's. This led her to experience the same disdain she felt toward her mother, as well as the same urgency she felt in her need for her father's power, and she utilized both to demand Michael be strong. In addition, Tanya's countertransference identification with the maternal power and judgment Michael projected into her—an identification facilitated by its compatibility with her image of herself as justifiably judgmental of anyone incompetent—further reinforced her sense of herself as powerful and competent, and of Michael as deserving condemnation. Along similar lines, the net impact of Michael's transference, in which he experienced Tanya as the equivalent of his powerful and angry mother, and his simultaneous countertransference identification with the incompetence she projected into him, was that both his fear and his need to submit to her—as a way of securing his safety—were reinforced and intensified.

The final unconscious mechanisms contributing to Tanya and Michael's conflicts have to do with the coercive and role-enactment aspects of their projective and introjective identifications. These mechanisms, which were grounded in each partner's need for the other to stay in the roles their projections assigned to them, were in contradistinction to their conscious expressions of what each wanted from the other. Tanya, for example, clearly stated she wanted Michael to become more competent, but unconsciously she needed him to remain incompetent, because within the emotional logic of her internal object relationships, this allowed her to assume the self-comforting role of disdainful critic. In the above interaction, Tanya's statement that Michael would always be weak can be interpreted as an indicator not just of her fear, but also of an unconscious pressure she was putting on him not to change out of his assigned role. Similarly, although Michael was forceful in saying he wanted Tanya to change, he unconsciously needed her to play his critical mother, since this justified the use of his childhood method of using submission to secure safety. When Michael interrupted Tanya's and my exploration of the link between her current behavior and her experiences with her parents (which had been accompanied by a softening of her tone) to remind us of her harshness (she "always" wanted him to be hard and uncompromising), he was unconsciously pressuring her to behave as his projected internal object was expected to behave.

This session occurred at a point in Tanya and Michael's treatment at which they had already achieved some awareness of the link between their past and current experiences, and had begun to work through the crises and difficult emotions that characterized their childhoods. When Michael said "Just like my mother" and seemed pained after I pointed out how similar his views of his mother and Tanya were, it indicated he was beginning to re-experience painful childhood events, and he understood he needed to find new ways to resolve them. This was borne out in the following session, when Michael returned to a theme we had often discussed—the impact his mother had on his comfort with making decisions—and said he felt anxious about making decisions even in simple situations, like when Tanya asked him what movie he wanted to see. When I said this suggested he was still frightened of his mother's attacks on his attempts to be both male and strong, Michael responded, "But *why* would she do that to me!?" The anger and grief in Michael's voice, I thought, indicated both his willingness and his beginning capacity to face the emotional consequences of his upbringing. He went on to speak, in sorrow and anger, of the losses his mother's behavior had imposed on him. Near the end of the session, he said he realized he was feeling different about his mother (who was still alive): "I'm more aware," he said, "of how much I didn't get from her, and I'm not as afraid of how much I won't get from her in the future." He then turned to Tanya, who was paying close attention (in contrast to our first session) and apologized for imposing his "drama" on their relationship.

The containing role of the couple therapist from an object relations perspective consists first in identifying and understanding those aspects of each partner's internal world that contribute to relationship conflicts, then offering responses (which may include interpretations, mirroring reflections, gestures of acknowledgement, etc.) to highlight and illuminate those contributions, and finally provide an environment in which the unresolved emotions associated with past events can be re-experienced, thought about, and worked through in more mature ways. Often this process requires one or both partners to actively grieve past losses in order to arrive at a new way of managing their internal legacy. The net effect of this process is a gradual liberation of the relationship from the grip of projections anchored in archaic internal object relationships, as each partner develops an increasing capacity to understand and tolerate not only their own painful history, but their partner's as well.

FURTHER CONTRIBUTIONS FROM OBJECT RELATIONS THEORY

As psychoanalytic writers began to construct an object relations approach to couple therapy, the core concepts of the internal object relationship, transference, countertransference, projective identification and containment created a scaffolding through which they could peer into the inner workings of a couple and understand not only why their interactions occurred the way they did, but also how to replace those interactions with healthier patterns. These, however, weren't the only concepts that proved to be helpful. Others included the *internal couple* (Ludlam, 2007), the *holding environment* (Winnicott, 1960), mechanisms of *object choice* (Dicks, 1967), and the couple relationship as a recapitulation of the psychosomatic partnership between mother and child (Clulow, 1993; Scharff & Scharff, 1991). An additional group of ideas are worth mentioning in more detail here, because they in particular underscore the commonalties between object relations theory and the relational approach. These include the *joint personality, shared illusions,* and *mutual projection* (Bannister & Pincus, 1965; Dicks, 1967; Friedman, 1962; Main, 1966; Meissner, 1978; Nadelson, 1978; Pincus, 1960).

Each of these concepts emphasizes the tendency of interpersonal interactions to blend psychic material from all participants so that unconscious emotions, beliefs and desires become coordinated around central, shared themes and goals. The joint personality in a couple relationship, for example, is created by the division of function that results from the mutual projections (Main, 1966; Meissner, 1978; Nadelson, 1978) entailed in the cycle of projective and introjective identification. In these cycles, each partner projects and then seeks the lost half of their internal object relationship in the other, much as the bifurcated people in Plato's *Symposium* sought the lost halves of their once complete bodies. If the other partner identifies with those projections, they in effect "complete" the first partner—at least within the confines of their internal object relationship (Dicks 1967). When the internal object relationships of both partners become coordinated by similarities of roles and themes—as occurred between Tanya and Michael—each partner ends up playing one side of what becomes effectively a single self-and-object relationship. Thus, Michael's internal object (his critical mother) was the same figure, more or less, as Tanya's disdainful self; and Tanya's internal object (her incompetent mother) effectively matched Michael's frightened, submissive self. Their joint personality thus could be seen as functioning as a single entity, organized around the couple's complementary internal object relationships.

It is important to note that joint personalities are not set in stone, and that a couple is not fated to create only one kind of joint personality over the course of their relationship. Rather, a couple may: (1) develop more than one joint personality at a time (or their joint personality may be very "fluid"—see chapter 5), since each partner possesses many internal object relationships that may find simultaneous matches in the other partner's internal world; and (2) those joint personalities may transform over time, since they are responsive not only to the varying internal structures of each partner, but also to changing circumstances. A couple, for example, whose relationship is new will most likely create very different joint personalities than a couple who has endured years of chronic frustration or who is experiencing "empty nest syndrome" (Amos & Balfour, 2007).

Shared illusions (or fantasies) are related to joint personalities in that they also develop out of the mutual processes of projective and introjective identification (Bannister & Pincus, 1965). When a relationship is first forming, both partners unconsciously negotiate how their internal object relationships will fit together. As they do so, they begin to settle on a shared unconscious narrative that remains as faithful as possible to the stories told by their individual internal object relationships, but that also reflects the merging of material from both individuals. Because this shared narrative is founded on each partner's internal world and its inherent distortions, it often contains illusions that each partner has in essence agreed to believe, or at least not to dispute openly. In Tanya and Michael's case, the shared narrative created by their mutual projections contained the illusions that Michael's indecisiveness was tantamount to unbearable incompetence and Tanya's anger was too frightening to confront. As with joint personalities, shared illusions also tend to transform over time and with changing circumstances.

THE BASIC ASSUMPTIONS OF OBJECT RELATIONS THEORY

The object relations concepts I've presented, including those of the joint personality and shared illusions, all make a common set of assumptions about the nature of individuals and their place in relationships. These assumptions state that the individual and the relationship are *equally* foundational concepts, in the sense that while both are required to explain psychological phenomena, they are still theoretically independent of each other and can be described in relatively self-contained terms. The imprint of these assumptions can be found in almost any clinical vignette written from an object relations standpoint, in which patients are described in terms of (1) the early relationships that first formed their individual, intrapsychic worlds, (2) the specific contents of those intrapsychic worlds (internal object relationships, drives and affects, primary defenses, etc.) and (3) the ways in which those contents now affect current relationships. Descriptions like this not only assume that individuals and their relationships can be differentiated, but also that meaningful psychological observations can be made in both realms.

For a number of years, these assumptions went relatively unchallenged. Object relations theory grew, after all, out of classical psychoanalytic theory, whose individualistic bias was unapologetically defended. If object relations theory retained the language of the individual, even while it elevated the relationship to a central function, few theorists were going to object. With the rise, however, of relational theory in the past thirty to forty years, the individualistic underpinnings of some of object relations' central concepts have come under new scrutiny. In order to appreciate the full meaning of this scrutiny, it will be necessary to first review the major tenets of relational theory.

FOUNDATIONS OF RELATIONAL THEORY

Relational theory has been described by Aron as "not so much a unified theoretical system as . . . a community of psychoanalysts who share a common clinical and theoretical sensibility" (1996, p. 31). For this reason, relational theory is difficult to summarize, as it reflects the views of many psychoanalysts who have approached the theory from a wide variety of perspectives. Still, relational theory does have something of a theoretical center, and most if not all analysts who think of themselves as "relational" would agree with at least a few basic assumptions. Of those assumptions, two are the most indicative of the basic thrust of the theory: (1) in any interaction, there is an important level of experience (we'll see that relational theorists disagree as to how universal this level is) at which the mental processes of each participant are continuously and reciprocally permeated by those of the other participant(s)—in such a way that it can become impossible to isolate and identify the "individuals" involved; and (2) the proper subject of psychoanalytic inquiry and treatment is not the isolated individual mind, but the larger system created by the "mutual interplay between the subjective worlds of patient and analyst" (Stolorow & Atwood, 1992, p. 1; see also Aron, 1996; Fiscalini, 2004; Hoffman, 1991; Mitchell, 1988, 1997; Renik, 1993; Stolorow, Brandchaft & Atwood, 1987).

Because of relational theory's diverse origins, the development of even these basic assumptions has followed a long and complex path. In general, however, the relational perspective can be traced to two primary sources. The first was relational theorists' dissatisfaction with the major tenets of classical psychoanalysis and it's American cousin ego psychology, which had in effect established "hegemony" (Wallerstein, 1988) over analytic theory in the decades prior to the 1970s. Those tenets, which formed the basis of what has been called a "one-person" psychology, assumed that both patient and analyst were stand-alone, solitary and autonomous entities, and that, because of the analyst's superior knowledge of the human mind, he or she was able to both understand and provide interventions to the patient from a neutral, objective and disengaged position. In its assertion of these tenets, relationalists argued, classical analysis had become complacently overconfident in analysts' capacity to achieve such neutrality and objectivity, and had consequently fostered an unfounded and indefensible image of the analyst as an authoritarian presence who was presumed to be the final arbiter of whatever truths were discovered about the patient.

The second source of ideas contributing to the development of the relational perspective lay in relational theorists' assimilation of concepts from a wide variety of philosophical, psychoanalytic and political movements, which, taken as a whole, were representative of the mid-twentieth century paradigm shift away from traditional conceptualizations—not only of the individual and his or her relationships with others, but also of epistemology, ontology, language, and the nature of truth and consciousness. For example, from the philosophic theories of deconstructionism (Derrida, 1978; Fairfield, 2001), phenomenology (de Bernardi, 2008, p. 89; Merleau-Ponty, 1962), linguistic analysis (Frie, 1999; Wittgenstein, 1969), social constructivism (Hoffman, 2002), hermeneutics (Schafer, 2002; Spence, 1993), postmodernism (Carlisky & de Eskenazi, 1997b; Fairfield, 2001) and Hegelian dialectics (Benjamin, 1988, 1997), relational theory borrowed such concepts as the dialectical interplay between subject and object, the decentering of the subject (i.e., the "I") because of its embeddedness in other minds and in the community of language, the social construction of meaning, the relativity of truth to prevailing conditions, and the dependence of individuals on social relationships for the formation and expression of desire and affect. From other psychoanalytic theories, such as Kohut's self-psychology (1971, 1977), Sullivan's interpersonal theory (1953), Lacan's neo-Freudianism (Bernet, 1996), Loewald's neo-ego psychological perspective (1980) and object relations theory, relational theorists developed such ideas as the dependence of drives (both in form and content) on interaction with others, the creation of the self within an interpersonal field, the dependence of the cohesiveness of the self on relationships with others, and the inescapable interdependence between transference and countertransference (see below). Finally, from feminism and other diversity movements, relational theory incorporated critiques of hierarchical power structures in the psychoanalytic relationship, as well as the ideas of the social origins of racial, cultural and gender identity, and the constitution of all aspects of the psyche by broad cultural influences (Benjamin, 1988; Bodnar, 2004; Garner, Kahane & Sprengnether, 1985; Gilligan, 1982; Mitchell, J., 1974; Walls, 2004).

Utilizing the best ideas from all of these theoretical perspectives, relational theorists created an intellectual foundation from which they could not only criticize those analytic concepts and techniques that depended too heavily on individualistic assumptions, but also offer new concepts, techniques and attitudes toward the analytic enterprise that bore the imprint of the relational sensibility. For example, relationalists challenged classical theory's assumption of the therapist's neutrality and objectivity by noting that because the therapist's subjectivity is in continual interplay with the patient's, he or she is prevented from achieving the neutral coign of vantage from which to be "objective" (Boesky, 1990; Fogel, et al., 1996; Renik, 1996; Spezzano, 1993; Wachtel, 1986). Similarly, relationalists questioned the therapist's authority to hold him or herself out as an expert because the contextual nature of truth and the interrelatedness of knowing create uncertainties and indeterminacies in the therapeutic relationship that the therapist's expertise cannot resolve (Tubert-Oklander, 2006a; Wolstein, 1983b, 1992).

The real value of relational theory, however, particularly in terms of its applicability to couple therapy, lies not so much in its critique of classical theory as in its exploration of new ways of conceptualizing relationships and in its development of techniques and attitudes toward the therapeutic process that take full account of the implications of the relational foundations of experience. Whereas object relations theory emphasized the centrality of relationships in the life of the individual, relational theory has provided the conceptual tools with which to understand those aspects of interactive experience in which the unconscious mind of one partner not only affects and influences the mind of the other, but intertwines with it so that the two minds together create a mutual experience that is more than the sum of the parts.

Perhaps the most central concept relational theorists have proffered has been variously referred to as the *relational* or *intersubjective field* (Barranger, Barranger & Mom, 1983; Ferro, 1999), the *relational unconscious* (S. Gerson, 2004, 2006; Tubert-Oklander, 2006a, 2006b; Zeddies, 2000), the *relational matrix* (S. A. Mitchell, 1988) or the *analytic third* (Ogden, 1994a, 1994b). The essential intuition underlying these terms is not only that "the mind is inherently dyadic, social, interactional and interpersonal" (Aron, 1996, p. x), but that in any interaction each individual involved occupies a dual role. On the one hand their contribution helps to shape the course of the interaction; on the other, they are also shaped by the interaction because they are continuously subjected to the interplay between their own subjectivity and that of the other person. This dialectic between the active and passive aspects of relationships implies, first and foremost, that "individuals" in relationships cannot always be counted on to function solely as individuals. At some point the psychic material from both participants becomes so blended and the outlines of their individuality so blurred, that it begins to make more sense to analyze them from two divergent perspectives—as individuals, yes, but also as a relational unity, that is, as a whole or single entity that displays emergent and supra-individual properties of its own (Ogden, 1994b).

In working out the implications of these intuitions, relational theorists have not so much offered a spate of entirely new concepts, but have instead embarked on a project of reconceptualizing basic psychoanalytic concepts so they reflect a more relational sensibility. Thus transference, which in the object relations perspective is defined as the projection of aspects of one's internal object relationships into a current relationship, has been redefined as an event codetermined by the two partners in the relationship, meaning that because of the "reciprocal mutual influence" (Stolorow, 2001, p. 532) between the two partners what appears to be one partner's transference is actually co-created by both. And countertransference, from the relational perspective, does not arise from the therapist's identification with the patient's projections, but is instead a product of the joint contributions made by each to the "transference-countertransference matrix" that operates unconsciously between them (Ogden, 1991). The implications of this view are that in the therapeutic relationship transference and countertransference are interdependent events, rendering the relationship between therapist and patient significantly more symmetrical than classical analytic theories had imagined. Other psychoanalytic concepts as well, such as projection, projective identification and resistance have undergone similar reconceptualizations, in order to emphasize that their deepest origins lay not in individuals, or even individuals in interaction, but in the stratum of experience in which the relational predominates (Baranger & Baranger, 1966; Bromberg, 1995; Fiscalini, 2004; Wolstein, 1983a).

Perhaps even more influential, and in some cases more controversial, than their reconceptualizations of traditional analytic concepts have been relational theorists' suggestions of new techniques and attitudes toward the therapeutic enterprise. While these are too numerous and complex to consider fully here, a few, particularly those relevant to couple therapy, may be reviewed. Of course, the most foundational shift in technique proposed by relational therapists has been to elevate the realm of relational phenomena to a primary focus of therapy. Although this elevation has sometimes been recommended at the expense of an equivalent focus on the individual contributions to interactions (M-J. Gerson, 2001), most relational theorists have argued that patients' interests are best served if both dimensions are held equally in mind (Boesky, 1990; Burch & Jenkins, 1999; Pizer & Pizer, 2006). Pursuant to this re-orientation toward the mutual, however, relational theorists have also recommended a more controversial alteration in technique: the therapist's use of self-disclosure of their countertransference responses. If therapists, these theorists have argued, are already unavoidably engaged within and revealed by their interactions with patients, and if therapists' emotional responses within those interactions are indicators not only of their own unconscious but of unconscious aspects of patients as well, then the more authentic and effective policy would be to make those engagements explicit. The complex issues involved in the question of self-disclosure will be discussed in detail in chapter 4.

Two other alterations in therapeutic technique that should be mentioned here pertain to the therapist's relationship with uncertainty. In the relational perspective, participants in interactions are subject to influences from two general sources—each participant's individual unconscious and the relational field between them—that are effectively unknowable, at least in their entirety and at least in the moments in which the interaction is occurring. Because of this, relational therapists have recognized that they must both accept and incorporate acknowledgment of uncertainty—and the indeterminacy of interactive phenomena (S. Gerson, 2006; Hoffman, 1987; Renik, 1993)—into their therapeutic technique. This embrace of uncertainty has, in turn, led relational therapists to attempt to create a cooperative treatment atmosphere in which patients and therapist equally participate in a *process* of investigation, rather than in a hierarchical search for true or right interpretations (Moore, 1999), and in which patients' perspectives are valued, even if they contradict the therapist's, as potential means of access to as yet unexplored (and uncomprehended) interactive dimensions (Hoffman, 1996).

THE APPLICATION OF RELATIONAL THEORY TO COUPLE THERAPY

A therapist utilizing relational theory in couple therapy will, much of the time, employ techniques that are similar to those of an object relations therapist. Both, for example, will acknowledge the role of the relationship in forming and shaping each partner's individual experience, and both will emphasize the contributions each partner makes to the relationship from their own individual internal worlds. Relational therapists, however, will distinguish themselves by focusing more consistently on relational phenomena— i.e., the emergent supra-individual patterns that neither partner could have created on their own—and attempting to link individual phenomena to the relational and perhaps (depending on the extent of the therapist's zeal for relational concepts) even subsuming individual phenomena under the relational. Moreover, as noted above, the relational therapist will be more likely to utilize self-disclosure, and to foster an atmosphere of mutual cooperation, in which all three parties accept there are no "right" answers, but that through a joint process of openness and exploration the couple may discover new ways of being in a relationship (M-J. Gerson, 2001). Thus, a couple therapist utilizing relational concepts would, after mapping the topography of each partner's individual worlds, call their attention not only to how those individual worlds interact, but also to how they blend together, become embedded in each other, and thereby create a layer of shared experience in which neither partner can define what precisely is their own contribution and what is their partner's. We'll see below, in an example of my treatment with Tanya and Michael, how such a relational focus can be pivotal in helping the couple take responsibility for and work toward resolving the conflicts arising both from their internal worlds and from the relationship they have jointly created.

RELATIONAL THEORY'S COMPLEX RELATIONSHIP WITH OBJECT RELATIONS THEORY

Relational theory has always stood in a complex and often incongruous relationship with object relations theory. On the one hand, relational theorists recognize their debt to object relations, particularly because the latter, in its response to and modification of the original views of Freud, was the first theory to question the intrapsychic drive model and to systematically insist on the importance of relationships in the formation and maintenance of psychological structure and behavioral patterns. Moreover, object relations theorists' explorations of the interactive aspects of transference and countertransference effectively created the early versions of the relational model, since these explorations were among the first "to question whether the individual self ought to be considered the sole source and engine of experience" (Stern, 1996, p. 281). However, because object relations theory has retained some of the individualistic bias of classical psychoanalysis, it too has become, at least for some relational theorists, the target of the same criticisms that have been leveled against classical theory (Greenberg, 1991). In these theorists' view, because object relations theory has remained a one-person theory, or at best a "one-person-in-a-relationship" theory, it is not only unable to fully account for relational phenomena, but it has also committed some of the same excesses as classical analysis, such as relying too heavily on the authority, neutrality and objectivity of the analyst.

In effect, relational theory has become divided within itself over this issue. On the one hand are those theorists who endorse, or seemed to endorse, the more radical project of eliminating individualistic concepts altogether and establishing a purely "two-person" psychology that interprets every psychological phenomenon from a relational perspective and that radically alters psychoanalytic technique accordingly. On the other hand are those theorists who believe that individualistic and relational concepts can be effectively utilized side by side, both in theory and in analytic practice. A representative of the latter theory is Aron, who suggests that the relational perspective should approach traditionally held distinctions dialectically, attempting to maintain a balance between internal and external relationships, real and imagined relationships, the intrapsychic and the interpersonal, the intrasubjective and the intersubjective, the individual and the social. (1996, p. ix)

Although the views of Aron and others (Baranger & Baranger, 2008; Billow, 2003; Ferro, 1999, 2006a; Ogden, 1994b, 2004; Spezzano, 1996b; Tubert-Oklander, 2006c; Walls, 2004; Zeddies, 2000) represent the majority of relational theorists, the radical trends in relational theory have at times been the most visible and have drawn some of the most energized responses from the rest of psychoanalysis. I use the term "trends" because within the relational oeuvre many of the more radical assertions have been made only intermittently by writers who have otherwise endorsed a more inclusive perspective similar to Aron's—suggesting that the radicalism in their assertions is less an indication of theoretical commitments and, perhaps, more a function of exuberance or of the limitations imposed by language on descriptions of complex relational phenomena. Spezzano, for example, has been particularly articulate in describing his inclusion of the individual and the relational as equal dimensions of a broader dialectic (1996a, 1996b; see also Elliott & Spezzano, 1996), but he has nevertheless made statements that imply he defines the individual in terms of the relational, thereby making the relational the more foundational dimension. In 1995, for example, he suggested that in the relational perspective, "consciousness . . . is viewed as, inherently, the creation of minds in interaction" (p. 24). Similarly, Mitchell was explicit in bringing together concepts of both the individual and the interpersonal under the overarching framework of the relational matrix, but at times his writings reveal the zeal of a revolutionist (Aron, 1996). He has argued, for example, that because the contents of any apparently individual mind are the result of a mixture of minds at a level of "fundamental and fluid interactional reality" (1988, p. 19), the concept of the individual must be regarded as a "secondary" construction that is superimposed on the more real aspects of experience.

The radical trend in statements made by relational theorists had not only focused on the rejection or demotion of individualistic concepts. Other statements implied relational theory constitutes a new paradigm in psychoanalysis that preempts all prior theories—including object relations. While many of these assertions have also been made by theorists who otherwise take a more inclusive approach (Greenberg & Mitchell, 1983; Mitchell, 1988, 1993; Renik, 1998a, 1998b, 2004; Spezzano, 1996a), it is important to acknowledge that a small group of writers has launched a more extended and consistent defense of this position. These theorists thus cast the choice between relational theory and other theories that harbor concepts of the individual in uncompromising terms. In arguing against any analytic system that recognizes the individual, for example, Orange, Atwood and Stolorow stated:

> But we are making a more serious and radical claim, namely that the whole conception of psychoanalysis as technique is wrongheaded . . . and needs to be rethought . . . [because] it relies on an assumption that one Cartesian isolated mind, the analyst, is doing something to another isolated mind, the patient, or vice versa. (1997, p. 21)

The difference between the radical and non-radical interpretations of relational theory pertains to the extent to which each theorist is willing to accept and work within the parameters of the dialectic described by Aron. If theorists embrace such a dialectic, they have available to them the explanatory power of both individual and relational constructs, which in turn translate into a variety of clinically effective interventions. If they reject the dialectic, however, they are forced by their own dichotomies to choose *only* the two-person approach, and to utilize only the concepts and techniques derived from that perspective. Thus, the radical trend in relational theory, if put into practice, would lead to the use of radical techniques as well, and it is these that have elicited the strongest reaction from other psychoanalysts.

REACTIONS TO THE RADICAL TREND IN
RELATIONAL THEORY

The reaction to these radical positions, among both object relations theorists and those relational theorists who disagree with their colleagues' more extreme assertions, has been forceful. These theorists have argued that the radical elevation of the relational at the expense of the individual would inescapably lead to a nihilistic position in which the therapist is robbed of all tools that make treatment effective. If, for example, as some relationalists suggest, the therapist cannot achieve objectivity because the meanings of a therapeutic interaction are "never 'fixed'" and instead "shift along with the mental states of analyst and analysand" (Bass, 2003, p. 664), then the therapist is denied the ability to establish even basic facts about patients (Kernberg, 1996; S. Gerson, 2006; Stern, 1991). Under this perspective, the therapist could presume no specific knowledge of patients "other than what evolves jointly" (Kernberg, 1996, p. 140) in their here-and-now transactions (Meissner, 2000), and could therefore offer patients nothing generalizable from treatment, since generalizations rely on patients having understood that they transport their own internal conflicts from relationship to relationship (Kernberg, 2007).

Similarly, some relationalists have suggested that because of the interdependence of transference and countertransference, the roles of therapist and patient are effectively symmetrical and "interchangeable" (Wolstein, 1983b). In the eyes of critics, this perspective not only calls into question the therapist's professional authority, but also eliminates the therapist's capacity to advise or guide patients, since the presumption of expertise, under conditions of symmetry, is *prima facie* inauthentic (Frederickson, 2005; Mills, 2005; Wolstein, 1983b). And finally, those same presumed symmetries have led some relational theorists to at least implicitly endorse the use of unlimited and even unexamined therapist self-disclosure, which in effect resurrects Ferenczi's controversial idea of mutual analysis, in which the therapist reveals as much to the patient as the patient does to the therapist (Bass, 2009). Critics of the radical trends in relational theory point out that these practices would threaten to alter psychoanalytic practice beyond both recognition and usefulness (Blechner, 1992; Fiscliani, 2004; Frederickson, 2006; Hirsch, 1992).

THE MIDDLE GROUND

Although the radical trends in relational theory have drawn heated attention and created many controversies, the larger proportion of relational theorists have continued to explore and develop a more moderate and balanced theory. Theorists like Aron and others, for example, who disagree with the positions of their more radical colleagues, have effectively endorsed a mixed or middle ground perspective, in which they recognize the equal value of the individual and the relational in explaining psychological phenomena and in guiding clinical interventions. In exploring this middle ground, these theorists have wedded concepts of the individual that are already in place in psychoanalytic theory with the unique formulations of the relational derived from their own theoretical tradition.

But the middle ground is not just the bailiwick of relational theory. As I've described above, object relations theory has, from the beginning, taken as its object of study the individual in relationships, and many of the concepts it has utilized to describe those relationships (such as the joint personality, mutual projection, shared illusions and the intermixture of transference and countertransference) were already moving analytic theory toward relational intuitions. It is for this reason that relational theorists recognize their debt to, and their kinship with, object relations theory. It is also for this reason object relations theorists are rarely entirely opposed to relational ideas, and tend to see them as attempts to elaborate on phenomena that are already the central focus of the object relations perspective. The disagreements object relations writers have had with relational theory primarily focus on the latter's radical trends.

In a real sense, then, moderate relational theory and object relations theory have explored the same middle ground, the interface between the individual and the relational, even though they emphasize different aspects of that interface. Because object relations theory approached the relational from the highly individualistic perspective of classical analysis, it retained well-developed intrapsychic concepts, which it folded into its formulation of relationships. Relational theory, on the other hand, was empowered by developments in philosophy, linguistics, social movements, etc. to explore the relational on its own terms, and to develop means of conceptualizing it that emphasized its unique qualities. But the two theories together have been somewhat analogous to the blind men inspecting the elephant: although they have approached their object of inquiry from very different directions, they each have made essential contributions to understanding its overall structure.

The commonalities between moderate relational and object relations theories have led, over the years, to a gradual intertwining between the two, so that, like a couple, their mutual contributions have enriched and informed each other. This blending of ideas has played a significant role in the consolidation of the more moderate relational perspective that has been careful to free itself from some of relational theory's more radical assertions (Aron, 1996; Boesky, 1990; Zeddies, 2000). More generally, however, it has led to a gradual development, among theorists from both perspectives, of an increasingly unified theoretical approach that uses the best ideas from both theories. In recent years, for example, it has become commonplace to find theorists employing concepts from both perspectives to create broadened views of such issues as transference and countertransference (Meissner, 2000; Tubert-Oklander, 2006b), the sharing of psychic material and the creation of an interpersonal unconscious (Scharff & Scharff, 2011), the dynamics of groups (Billow, 2003, 2010), the interpersonal foundations of dreams and waking dreams (Ferro, 2002, 2006a), and the selective use of therapist self-disclosure (Bollas, 1987; Cooper, 1998; Jacobs, 1991; Meissner, 2002; Renik, 1995). In my view, this gradual development of integrated models is a natural result of both theories' shared commitment to explore the middle ground between them, and to use individual and relational concepts together, not only to extend our understanding of a complex topic, but also to deepen our treatment of patients and to discover more accurate and effective interventions to help them.

THE MIDDLE GROUND APPROACH IN COUPLE THERAPY

Putting the middle ground approach into practice requires, on the part of therapists, a carefully developed awareness and appreciation of the many possible phenomena that may confront them when sitting face-to-face with patients. The conscientious development of this appreciation is all the more necessary for couple therapists, who must track the complexities of not one relationship, but three (one between the partners and one between each partner and the therapist) and perhaps even four (if the relationship between the therapist and the couple's joint personality is included, as some couple therapists have suggested). The value of the middle ground approach in couple therapy, however, is manifold. Not only does it expand the therapist's capacity to conceptualize couple interactions and formulate more effective interventions, but it also creates a field of investigation in which relational and individual perspectives inform and enrich each other, allowing both therapist and patients to develop a more penetrating view of the entire phenomenon under consideration. The following brief example from my work with Tanya and Michael illustrates some of the ways in which the relational and the individual illuminate each other.

I've already described some occasions in my treatment of Tanya and Michael in which I addressed the individual transferences each had toward the other. An occasion when I turned the couple's attention toward the relational had to do with the pattern of interaction we saw in the first session, when both partners turned to me with expressions that asked me to help them with their partner's failures. I thought at the time that each partner treated me not just as a therapist, but as a father they sought out to settle a fight between siblings. As my understanding of their histories and internal worlds improved, I realized they were instead asking me, as a father, to solve the problem presented by their mothers. Over several sessions, we discussed this in terms of individual transferences: Each partner had projected into me a wished-for, powerful father who would safeguard against an incompetent (Tanya) or critical (Michael) mother. Over time, however, it gradually became clear Tanya and Michael's anxieties were also co-constructed, in that each partner's fears of dangerous mothers had blended together to create a shared transference (see chapter 2), originating as much from them as a unit as from them as individuals, in which each unconsciously carried the other's anxiety in such a way that their own was augmented or intensified.

Because this shared transference recurred many times, we were able to address it in a session early in the second year of treatment. Michael had just described Tanya's criticism of the way he handled a financial issue with one of their children, saying to me she was "so contemptuous" and she wasn't trying to change. Tanya didn't respond verbally, but looked at me, rolled her eyes and shook her head. I said, repeating a theme that had become familiar, that each of them treated me as if I was going to be the father who allied with them against their "bad mother-partner." "That again?" Michael said. "That again," I said, adding that perhaps this kept cropping up because they were supporting each other in holding onto it. Tanya asked how they were doing that. I said, "Because you're each afraid of being hurt by a dangerous mother,

I think you may be feeling not only your own fear, but your partner's as well. The addition of that extra fear has fed and intensified your own, so you've become more frightened as a couple than you actually are as individuals." They were puzzled but curious. Michael asked what made me think this was happening. I answered, "The repetition of this moment, when you both look to me to rescue you. I think fear drives you to do that, but I suspect that if you were two individuals who had never met, you wouldn't be as afraid as you are, and you'd be more able to consider other options for managing it."

They now seemed to grasp this idea. Tanya said, "You mean that I get more worried about Michael being like my mother because he's worried about me being like his mother?" I nodded. Michael said, "And so we both turn to you to save us from our terrible mothers." I said, "The fears you share have created a dominating fantasy that your mothers are too frightening or incompetent to bear, and the only way to be safe is to find a dad, me, who will shelter you."

It was a new way of thinking for Tanya and Michael, but over time the idea took hold. As they realized they were forced by their shared fears into staying trapped in repetition, they began to search for independent solutions to those fears, which then played a role in moderating the acrimony in their conflicts. At a later point in treatment, Tanya looked back on these shared patterns. "We were like two little kids lost in the woods," she said. "We could only think of one thing to do."

CONCLUSION

My use of the middle ground approach in the treatment of Tanya and Michael was what ultimately allowed us to break through the paralysis created by their shared fear. Their breakthrough depended upon our analysis of their interactions from both individual and relational perspectives, and from using each perspective to elucidate the other. The dual-faceted foundations of the middle ground approach, I believe, make it uniquely suited for use in couple therapy. In the remainder of this book, I will explore a wide variety of tangled relationships the couple therapist is likely to encounter, for which the middle ground approach offers effective tools to both understand and unravel.

Chapter Two

Negotiating Individual and Joint Transferences in Couple Therapy

In chapter 1, we saw that the middle ground approach to couple therapy underscores the importance of addressing both individual and relational phenomena in helping the couple resolve the conflicts that bring them into treatment. This balance between the individual and the relational is nowhere more paramount than in the clinical management of the multiple transferences couples present in therapy. In this chapter, I will consider three types of transference the couple therapist is likely to encounter: *individual transferences*, *transference-countertransference entanglements*, and *shared transferences*. Because projective and introjective identification are integral to the formation of these transferences, I'll discuss these mechanisms in detail. I'll then describe the roles these same mechanisms can play in helping the couple resolve their internal and interpersonal conflicts. To illustrate these points, I'll introduce a couple whose many layers of projective and introjective identifications created a continually shifting landscape of transferences directed toward each other, the therapist and the therapy itself.

RICK AND NANCY

Rick and Nancy were referred by a family friend because their marriage of two years had not yet recovered from a difficult beginning. The difficulty started in the couple's courtship. When they met in college, Nancy—who by her description had been promiscuous and unfocused in terms of career and long-term commitments—was just getting serious about her education. Rick, in contrast, was already successful as a student and about to begin a lucrative career. When she met Rick, Nancy realized he represented "something different, someone who would always be stable and supportive." The two felt an immediate connection with each other, but for Nancy it was more like a connection with a brother. She was not physically attracted to Rick, she said, because he was "just not very good looking." In high school and college, Nancy had been a cheerleader and part-time model and she described herself as "very body conscious."

Prior to meeting Nancy, Rick had not been in a serious relationship, had not had intercourse, and rarely masturbated. His upbringing was, as he put it, "pretty awful." His father was emotionally disengaged from the family for as long as he could remember and his mother turned to Rick as a substitute husband. His mother's behavior, according to Rick, bordered on sexual abuse and included embraces in which she pressed against his genitals, moments in which she seemed to plan that he would see her naked, and intrusive curiosity about his sexual development, experiences, and fantasies. At the same time, Rick, the oldest child, was asked to discipline his younger brothers and sisters. He resented these responsibilities, as well as his parents who imposed them, but he didn't rebel against them. Instead he displaced his anger at his parents onto his siblings and developed an insensitive and sometimes hostile style of controlling their behavior.

When Rick met Nancy, he was taken by her physical attractiveness. Although he was aware of her prior promiscuity and checkered school record, he believed she was now committed to accomplishing her goals and thought she would make a good wife. As their courtship proceeded, Nancy revealed she was not attracted to him, although she professed to love him. In response, Rick started a forceful lobbying campaign. He could not believe, he said, that the mere fact of his not being good-looking enough was a sufficient reason to prevent their relationship from moving toward marriage—especially when they loved each other. It would be a shame, he said, to break up just because she wasn't physically attracted to him. Besides, he was certain Nancy would come to love him physically as well.

Although she felt pressured and controlled by Rick, Nancy agreed to marry him—in large part because he represented the stability she was looking for. Nancy reported she also had a difficult childhood, with a father who was well meaning but largely unable to understand the concerns and issues she faced, and a hyper-critical and controlling mother who "never gave me reason to believe she loved me or was proud of me." As a result, Nancy entered her adult years feeling both distrustful of other people's affections and angry that she felt so devalued. The combination of these two emotions, in turn, led to a personal style in which she undermined her relationships and other commitments by being irresponsible and rebellious. The fact that Rick persisted in pursuing her even after she revealed her lack of attraction to him had deeply impressed her.

Ostensibly for religious reasons (although other dynamics were also at work), the couple did not have sex prior to marriage. The traumatic aspects of their physical relationship, then, were not revealed until their honeymoon. In a week-long series of attempts, they failed to have satisfying sexual relations. In the years since their honeymoon, their sexual relationship hardly improved, and because the injuries each suffered still cast a long shadow, they argued frequently.

One such argument occurred in the days prior to our first session, and Rick and Nancy spent much of that session describing it. The argument began when Rick criticized Nancy for forgetting to pick up his clothes at the cleaners. Almost as an aside, Rick said he "should have known" she would forget. Nancy asked what he meant and Rick said he knew she didn't care about him—if she cared, she'd find a way to enjoy having sex with him. Nancy then accused Rick of being self-centered and uncaring about *her* feelings. Rick dismissed these complaints and told Nancy she was only interested in what *she* wanted, not what he wanted. Nancy then reminded Rick he pressured her into marrying him; and Rick said she should just go find someone else to marry who wasn't so ugly.

As Rick and Nancy described this argument in session, their emotions varied widely. At times they were calm and rational and were able to provide a coherent overview both of their argument and of their history. They also, though, devolved into exchanges of contempt and recrimination that not only revealed their most profound insecurities, but also seemed to trap them in a collapsed interpersonal space in which they could think of nothing else to do but continue to fight. When they intermittently emerged from this space, they would apologize to me and express embarrassment that they had let themselves "go."

THE FOUNDATIONS OF THE COUPLE RELATIONSHIP

A relationship is a field in which battles and truces, deceits and covenants, separations and mergers take place, often simultaneously, at multiple levels. These dramas are typically the result of each partner playing out, in the interpersonal landscape, split off or disavowed psychic conflicts lodged in their internal worlds. Both partners bring to the relationship the legacies of their childhoods, encapsulated in internal object relationships. When any part of one partner's internal world is too difficult to bear alone, he or she will project it into the relationship in the unconscious hope that a solution may be found—either in the simple act of projection or in the interactions that follow from it. Such solutions may take many forms: the partners might find ways to heal, soothe, hide, eliminate, enact, compensate for or hold in safety any aspect of the projecting partner's internal world that is felt to be unmanageable. These projections, of course, occur unconsciously, so that neither party understands why the relationship has followed the course it has. But they are all the more compelling because they are unconscious, and when linked to primitive or polarized emotional states, they dominate the relationship and limit the courses of action available to the partners.

The couple relationship is the most fitting container for these projections because it replicates two predominant modes of relating, the psychosomatic and the psychological, that characterized each partner's early interactions with primary caregivers (Zavattini, 1988). In the most foundational mode of relating, the psychosomatic, the skin-to-skin intimacies of the couple recapitulate the "psychosomatic partnership" (Winnicott, 1971; Scharff & Scharff, 1991) between infant and caregiver, which in turn reawakens the rudimentary emotions, often located in body experience, that punctuated that partnership. At a higher level of organization, but building upon the psychosomatic mode, is the psychological relationship (Scharff & Scharff, 1987). In the caregiver-infant bond, this mode of relating adds *meaning* to the psychosomatic partnership through the gradual development of patterns of interaction in which caregiver and infant take on increasingly differentiated roles. When the adult couple attempts to define their psychological relationship, the patterns and role differentiations from childhood are also revived and guide both partners in determining what roles each will play. The tendency of these two modes of relating to reactivate childhood experiences in couple interactions is what led Thompson to suggest the couple relationship is "the most direct heir" of the primary relationships of childhood (1960, p. 3).

"ONE-PERSON" PROJECTIVE IDENTIFICATION

The most common mechanism by which the legacies of childhood enter into the couple relationship is projective identification, along with its complementary mechanism of introjective identification. Although there is some controversy about whether projective identification should be regarded as a "one-person" or "two-person" event (Goretti, 2007; Grotstein, 1981; Meissner, 1980; J. Scharff, 1992), my view is that both perspectives are helpful in deciphering the varying phenomena couples present. In its one-person form, the individual attempts to eliminate unacceptable or disavowed parts of self—i.e., self- or object-representations, drives, impulses, fears, desires, hatreds, abilities, ideals, etc.—by projecting them into another and then perceiving the other "as having acquired the characteristics of the projected part of self" (Segal, 1964, p. 126). This form thus occurs as "strictly an intrapsychic phantasy" (Grotstein, 2000, p. 108) that is independent of any characteristics the target of the projection, the other person, may actually possess. Under the most extreme conditions (for example when the projecting individual's reality testing is severely compromised) one-person projective identifications may generate psychotic phenomena (Rosenfeld, 1952; Searles, 1963). In less extreme conditions they are one of the primary mechanisms responsible for the formation of individual transferences (Bollas, 1987; Malin, 1966).

As many theorists have pointed out, the term "individual transferences" is something of a misnomer, since once a projective identification has entered into a relationship, it is difficult, if not impossible, for the other partner not to identify with it and respond emotionally (Bollas, 1987; Grinberg, 1962; Ogden, 1994b; 2004; Racker, 1957; Renik, 1995). In couples, this implies that while individual transferences may occur at times, they rarely remain anchored solely in the circumscribed arena of one-person projective identifications. Instead, the partners tend to become engaged in mutual, co-constructed transactions that revolve around the theme of the original projection but that go beyond it to create a matrix of interlocking transference and countertransference responses (Ogden, 1994a).

Similarly, when individual transferences arise between a partner of a couple and a therapist, the therapist is typically unable to avoid at least *some* level of identification with the patient's projections. Rather than regarding this as problematic, modern therapists recognize that their countertransference reactions are sources of information about the patient's inner world, and therefore strive to remain as receptive to them as possible (Heimann, 1950). Because the therapist, however, resists enacting their countertransference with patients (Compton, 1990), the transferences a patient may have toward the therapist differ in form and intensity from similar transferences as they function within the couple. To mark this differentiation, it is common practice to use the term "individual transferences" to refer to those un-enacted and un-entangled transferences either partner has toward the therapist (cf., Shapiro, et al., 1977; Waska, 2008).

With these considerations in mind, I'd like to describe an individual transference Rick developed toward me, which was linked to a powerful emotional entanglement within the couple that was centered on themes of devaluation and helplessness. Rick's transference arose as we were discussing his mother's sexually inappropriate behavior and his emotional reactions to it—which included anger that she had used him for her own needs, fear of sexual contact and intimacy, and a pervasive feeling that he had not been important enough for her to protect. As we explored these issues, Rick started to feel that the treatment had become focused on him, which then activated a deep feeling of shame that he was the dysfunctional partner. This, in turn, led him to project the shaming part of himself into me, thereby creating an individual transference in which he felt I was disdainful of him for being afraid and inexperienced in sex. In a moment, after I've discussed the two-person form of projective identification, I'll describe a session in which Rick's transference toward me merged with his transference entanglements with Nancy to create moments of paralysis and despair for both partners.

"TWO-PERSON" PROJECTIVE AND INTROJECTIVE IDENTIFICATION

The two-person form of projective identification adds two essential features to the one-person version. First, the projecting partner, rather than leaving his or her projection in one-person space, unconsciously attempts to induce or coerce the other partner (whom I'll call the "receiving partner") into taking the projection in, making it their own, and enacting it in whatever form that is available to them (Goretti, 2007; Laing, 1962; Ogden, 1986; Sandler, 1976; J. Scharff, 1992; Segal, 1956; Steiner, 2000; Zinner & Shapiro, 1972). Second, the receiving partner, having experienced the induction, cooperates with it, introjectively identifies with the projected material, and proceeds with its enactment (Boesky, 2000; Heimann, 1950; Jacobs, 1986, 1991; Lyons-Ruth, 1999; Maroda, 1991; Smith, 1997). This process of induction can only be successful if the receiving partner already has characteristics within his or her personality that resonate with the other partner's projections. That is, the content of the projection must meet with aspects of the receiving partner's personality that (1) are *already accepted* within that partner's psychic repertoire (Klein, 1955; Zavattini, 1988), and (2) are not overly defended against (in which case they would be unavailable to be activated by the projection). When these two requirements are met in the receiving partner's personality, he or she is said have a *valency* (Bion, 1961; Gabbard, 1995; Poulton, Norman & Stites, 2006) for the projection. Valencies, of course, depend upon the approvals and prohibitions of psychic experience that were internalized during the receiving partner's own psychological development.

Once introjective identifications activate emotions and other unconscious content already present in the receiving partner, that content enters into the stream of unconscious exchanges occurring between the partners and merges with the material already present from the other partner's projections (E. Balint, 1993; Cleavely, 1993; Meltzer, 1981). This merging of unconscious material from both partners is characteristic, to some degree, of all couple interactions, but its form and content will vary depending upon its function within the relationship. The most general function of these mergers is to establish deep layers of emotional communication and intimacy that allow each partner to feel they are not alone and that they are understood by the other (Ogden, 1982). More specifically, however, these mergers function either as mechanisms of defense or as vehicles for psychological growth and healing (Bion, 1962a, 1962b; Grinberg, 1962; Kernberg, 2003; Meltzer, et al., 1982). Because these two functions are pivotal in creating both healthy and dysfunctional interactions in the couple, I will consider them separately.

THE DEFENSIVE FUNCTION OF PROJECTIVE AND INTROJECTIVE IDENTIFICATION

When projective and introjective identification are used as mechanisms of defense, the primary goal of the projecting partner is to calm the internal anxieties associated with parts of self that cannot be accepted or acknowledged. These parts of self may actually be internally deemed to be either "good" or "bad" (Jaffe, 1968; Klein, 1946, 1955), but they still require projection because they are embroiled in internal conflicts that have rendered them too dangerous or toxic to be retained. Good or desirable parts of self, for example, may be projected if the partner is frightened of them or feels guilty for desiring them. Bad parts, on the other hand, are projected in order to avoid internal persecution or devaluation. In either case, once the projection is accomplished and the unacceptable material is located in the receiving partner, the projecting partner then injects all of the emotions associated with it into the couple, with the result that the relationship bears the mark of his or her internal conflicts (Jaffe, 1968; Zinner & Shapiro, 1972).

These kinds of conflicts were abundant in Rick and Nancy's relationship, particularly around issues of sex and control. Rick, for example, longed to find a way to feel more sexually adequate, but, as we've seen, he was frightened of sex because it elicited his emotional associations to his mother's inappropriate behavior. As a result, Rick projectively identified two parts of himself into Nancy—his wished-for sexual adequacy (a "good" but frightening part of himself) and his internal mother, in regard to whom he felt both angry and betrayed—which led him to see her both as a teacher who could help him develop healthy sexual desire *and* as a faithless and manipulative partner who, like his mother, threatened the stability of their relationship with unbridled sexual appetites.

For her part, Nancy possessed valencies that prepared the ground for her identifications with both parts of Rick's projections. These valencies were anchored in unresolved internal conflicts of her own, revolving primarily around themes of sexuality and control. One of the most volatile conflicts between Nancy and her mother had centered on her mother's critical and over-controlling reactions to Nancy's assertions of autonomy and independence. Although Nancy had responded with seemingly self-confident episodes of acting out, underlying them she felt both insecure and lonely. These conflicts created in Nancy an ambivalence toward anyone on whom she depended: on the one hand, she wanted to please them in order to feel loved and secure; but she also expected that they would eventually attempt to control her as her mother had. This ambivalence, in turn, appeared in her relationship with Rick in two ways. First, she projected both parts of it into him, with the result that she saw him as a source of love and stability, but also of control and abandonment. To defend herself against the latter, she had given him, from early in their relationship, preparatory warnings that she could abandon the marriage if it didn't suit her. Her lack of attraction to Rick, and the implicit threat that she may sexually act out, could both be seen in this light.

Second, Nancy's internal ambivalence was also intimately involved in her identifications with Rick's projections. Her feeling that she needed to please others in order to be loved and protected, for example, matched Rick's projected desire for her to teach him about sexuality (her greater experience and comfort with sexual matters also contributed to this match); and her fears of being controlled, and her rebellious defenses against it, were almost a perfect complement to Rick's projected fears of his mother's inappropriate behavior. Needless to say, Rick's internal conflicts also set the stage for his identifications with Nancy's projections (his feelings of inadequacy matched her need to please, and the controlling parts of his personality, anchored in his anger at his parents, matched her fear of control), with the result that highly charged emotional material from both partners' internal worlds merged and intertwined, augmenting their internal anxieties and intensifying the conflicts between them. Because of their escalating cycles of projective and introjective identification, by the time I saw them, both partners had become entrenched in distorted perceptions of the roles the other was playing in the relationship. Nancy, for example, had become certain Rick was trying to control her, and Rick was sure she had judged him and was on the verge of leaving—even though the actual emotions each felt for the other were significantly more complex and multifaceted.

As these entangled interactions between Nancy and Rick illustrate, one of the primary consequences of mutual systems of projective and introjective identification is that the couple's relationship becomes constricted around the themes of both partners' most compelling internal conflicts (Sander, 2004). These themes tend to dominate interactions the more each partner feels internal pressure to disown or eliminate parts of self, and the more they possess valencies for the other partner's projections. When high projective needs are matched with well-developed receptive valencies in both partners (as was the case with Rick and Nancy), the resulting projective-introjective processes become repetitive, inflexible and limited in scope, depleting the partners' internal resources (Klein, 1963b) and leaving them little room for creative or spontaneous problem solving (Dicks, 1967; Kernberg, 1995; Nadelson, 1978; Ruszczynski, 1993).

These constricted but mutually coordinated interactions, in turn, give rise to their own particular kinds of transferences in which both partners participate in equal measure. These joint or mutual transferences fall into one of two major categories, depending on what target, or object, they take. I'll use the term *transference-countertransference entanglements* (cf., Cooper, 2003; Greenberg, 1999) to describe joint transferences in which the object, for each partner, is the *other* partner. That is, in this kind of entanglement both partners' transferences and countertransferences are aimed at each other and remain entwined, ricocheting as it were, within the confines of the dyadic relationship. In Rick and Nancy's case, Rick's (transferential) distrust of Nancy's fidelity instigated Nancy's (countertransferential) threats of being unfaithful, while, at the same time, Nancy's (transferential) fears of being controlled instigated Rick's (countertransferential) distrust and subsequent attempts to control her. The term "transference-countertransference entanglements" does not simply refer to one partner's transference and the other's countertransference, but rather to a mutual, co-constructed system in which each partner experiences both transferences and countertransferences, and both partners are mutually reinforced by the other partner's actions and reactions.

Shared transferences, on the other hand, arise when both partners have similar transferences about a person or event outside of the couple (Ehrlich, Zilbach & Solomon, 1996; Stewart, et al., 1975). In this case, the mutual processes of projective and introjective identification blend the two partners' internal worlds so that they hold similar emotions or fantasies about that person or event, and each is reinforced in those attitudes by the other's contributions. Two of the shared transferences that emerged in my work with Rick and Nancy, which were directed toward me and toward the therapy in general, were rooted in the critical and rejecting aspects of each partner's internal objects. When these aspects were projected into me, they created fears in both partners that I would be critical or disappointed in them. This transference was somewhat in evidence in our first session, when Rick and Nancy were embarrassed for letting themselves "go," but as time progressed it deepened into a subtle but powerful undercurrent that dampened the couple's willingness to explore the less admirable emotions underlying their interactions. At the same time, each partner's expectation of the inevitability of criticism and injury created a second shared transference, toward the treatment process itself, in which both believed it would not be sufficient to help them solve their problems. Because these two shared transferences were inter-related, they reinforced each other, and together they led to a dispirited atmosphere in treatment in which problems were raised but not resolved, and in which expressions of futility were common.

Before I discuss the second, growth-enhancing use of the mutual processes of projective and introjective identification in couple relationships, I'd like to pause and describe a session with Rick and Nancy in which their defensive uses of those processes created individual and joint transferences that, when combined, constricted the couple's interactions to the point that they could find, at least at times, no other options but to remain in split-off and polarized psychic enclaves from which they could only view the other as a source of injury.

RICK AND NANCY IN SESSION

In this session, which took place in the second year of treatment, Rick and Nancy pick up on a conversation from the prior session, in which Nancy had told Rick she thought he was a good husband and she felt secure with him. Rick had reacted angrily and said he believed Nancy was being insincere and manipulative, because he "knew" she thought he was a "lousy" husband. Although we linked the intensity of Rick's emotional reaction to his transference (i.e., to his experiences with his mother, who he had also felt was shaming and manipulative), I didn't feel we gained much ground in helping him understand or contain it.

Nancy began the next session by reporting Rick had been "distant and cool" since the last session and she really didn't understand why. "What's wrong with telling him he's a good guy?" she asked in a critical tone. She then began to explain why she thought Rick was a good husband, but after several glances in his direction she seemed to realize he wasn't interested in what she was saying. She stopped talking, turned to him directly, and said, "I know you're just sitting there thinking what I'm saying is crap." Rick's response was intellectual and cold. "It just all sounds like manipulation to me," he said. "I don't really see how it can be anything different."

With these opening parries, Rick and Nancy defined their field of battle for the session. Both partners were frustrated because they viewed each other as motivated by singular, malevolent attitudes. These perceptions, on both partners' parts, were of course consequences of their transference-countertransference entanglements, but in the lived moments of their interaction their transferences convinced them that what they were seeing was the truth. Rick, for example, was convinced that Nancy's compliment could only amount to manipulation because he was also convinced that she had already decided to reject him. Accordingly, he not only refused to consider the possibility that she might harbor more complicated feelings, but he also blinded himself to his own contributions to the causes of her behavior. Similarly, because Nancy had decided Rick's distrust amounted to nothing more than his attempt to both control and criticize what she did and felt, she also couldn't see he had more complex motivations, or that some of his distrust was due to the injuries she caused him. Thus, within the first few minutes of the session, each partner had signaled to the other they were going to remain in rigid and uncompromising stances. The result was the rapid development of a deadened and restricted atmosphere in which neither felt they could make a move without provoking more conflict. After a few more angry exchanges, both partners seemed to lose energy for their fight. Rick then turned to me to say, with resignation, "It's no good even trying to talk about this."

I said it seemed to me that both partners were hurt because the other didn't understand them, but that this situation had arisen because each was presenting a polarized image of the other as though it represented the other's actual mind. I reminded them of our past discussions, in which we'd discovered that both partners' views of the other were rooted in painful past experiences that collapsed their ability to think beyond their own injuries. Finally, I said that because both experienced the other's misperceptions as a renewed injury, to which they responded with renewed accusations, together they had created a system that perpetuated their conflict and reinforced their polarized images of each other. Ultimately, this mutual system had led them to feel there was no room to move and they might as well give up trying.

I didn't say all of these things at once. Rather, they were delivered in smaller pieces over several minutes in which we tried to understand the paralysis that developed so quickly in the session. As we continued the conversation, Rick and Nancy became somewhat calmer. Eventually Nancy said, with a more conciliatory tone, that this all reminded her of their honeymoon. She then said, "Part of what bugs me is how Rick handled my difficulty having sex with him in the first place. When we first got married, I wanted to love him for who he is and I wanted to love him sexually as well. I didn't—and I don't—like this part of me that can get so focused on just the right appearance. The way Rick tells it, on our honeymoon I was brutal and told him that I didn't want to have sex with him because he wasn't attractive. That wasn't it. What I wanted was to talk to him about why I was having that difficulty. I wanted to be able to think about it with him, and get him to help me find a way to get past it. But as soon as I raised it, he reacted so strongly that he couldn't hear what I was really trying to say."

It seemed to me, with this statement, that Nancy was expressing her desire for Rick to play the stabilizing role to help her understand and manage her internal conflicts. I also thought, however, that it was possible her statement carried hidden aggression toward Rick, in that it once again reminded him how he failed her on their honeymoon. Rick's response was complex. While Nancy was talking, he seemed to be moved, at least to some degree, and as I watched him I felt a trace of sadness I thought might reflect what he was feeling. When she was done, he said, in a softened tone, "I don't know if you've ever put it that way before," to which Nancy responded that she tried to say it before, but she hadn't felt he was listening. Rick then looked at me and, still seeming saddened, asked, "This is what you're talking about? That I haven't been seeing this part of her?" I immediately felt cautious, because I wasn't sure I understood this exchange, and I thought there was still a possibility it contained hidden hostility. I said, tentatively, that it seemed the two were trying to feel their way into new territory and they weren't sure what they were going to find there.

My caution was rapidly confirmed. After a brief pause, Rick said, with a return of the coldness he'd shown at the beginning of the session, "It's almost funny that Nancy feels I don't understand her, when ever since I've known her I've felt invisible. All she's ever seen of me was that I'm not good enough for her." Nancy responded eagerly. "But that's what I was trying to say," she said. "That's how you saw me and some of it was right—but not completely. I was trying to . . . "

Rick interrupted her. "You were just trying to push me away," he said, "because I didn't match your idea of a beautiful man, or I wasn't sexy enough for you, or I was too afraid of sex." With this last statement, Rick looked at me with an expression that suggested he included me among those who had been critical of him for being afraid of sex. He then turned back to Nancy. "And that's how I feel now," he said, "when you tell me I'm a good husband. I just can't hear it as anything other than your manipulation." As Rick said these last words, his tone returned once again to what felt to me to be sadness, but now it also seemed to contain injury and despair. For her part, Nancy had been injured by Rick's reassertion that she was only being manipulative and, consequently, didn't hear the shift in his tone. Instead, she was now in a retaliatory mood. She said, simply, "This is why." Rick asked, "Why what?" "This is why," she said, "I don't know if I can go on."

The three of us sat in silence. The couple's unconscious interactions had come full circle. Both partners began this session in their entrenched perceptions of each other as the sole source of their misery. They then entertained the possibility of expanding their understanding of each other, but they now returned to their positions of individual and joint transferences, in which each was innocent, the other deserved condemnation, and nothing could be done about it. The return was triggered by Rick's angry outburst, in which he projected his shaming and devaluing internal mother into both Nancy (as part of their transference-countertransference entanglement) and me (his individual transference), but Nancy completed the circle by threatening, once again, to leave the relationship.

The atmosphere in the room was heavy and depressed and with it a wave of pessimism and futility also washed through me. Although I understood this was my countertransference, i.e., my identification with projected material from both partners, it nonetheless robbed me of words for a few moments. As I started to think again, I realized this was a moment in which all three of the couple's transferences (individual, shared and entangled) might be illuminated. I decided to begin carefully, focusing on the relationship as a whole. "You're both angry," I said. After a moment, Nancy responded, saying she didn't think Rick was ever going to "let go of this way of looking at me." I said, "And you despair over that." She said yes. I said, "I suspect that in your despair you go to your own locked-in feelings—the feelings you also had with your mother—that the situation is hopeless and that leaving is the only thing that's going to rescue you." She was now growing calmer, even contemplative, as she had been earlier in the session. She said, "I do feel hopeless, and I do feel like getting up and running out right now." I said, "That was what you did as an adolescent." She was silent for several seconds, then said, "And it never worked." After another brief silence, I said, "I know your threat of leaving is triggered by Rick's anger and distrust of you, but when you make those threats, they trigger fear in him, which solidifies, all the more, his distrust of you. The two of you then create a self-sustaining cycle—he distrusts you, you get angry, you threaten to leave, he gets scared, and he distrusts you even more. It's a dance whose steps you know so well, it's difficult not to do them automatically." This of course wasn't the first time I'd made a relational, interactive interpretation with this couple (I'd made one just after their paralysis earlier in the session), but with each repetition, I now realized, it was sinking in a little more. Nancy didn't respond, but she seemed to grasp what I said and was now thinking about it.

Rick, who had been intently scrutinizing this exchange, now said, "I don't know if I'm in that much despair." At first I thought he said this out of the defiance and anger he'd exhibited in the last few minutes, but as I looked at him I realized he at least appeared to be more thoughtful and introspective. I said, "Well, maybe not. But that seems to be what has been hanging here in the room. Nancy seems to feel you're going to continue to believe you're not good enough for her, and that you'll keep getting angry about it." Rick was quiet for a moment, then said, as though talking to himself, "I have been angry about it. It's been hard to think that she ever cared about me." At this moment, in what I took to be my countertransference resonance with Rick, I had a vivid internal image of his mother treating him without concern for the effect her behavior had on him. I also then felt he was, again, back in the sadness that now seemed to permeate the moment. I said, "You've had a lifetime of feeling like that," to which Rick nodded. A few more moments passed, in which Rick seemed to think about the whole of his life. I said, "The shame and unimportance you felt as a child shows up here, in your relationship with Nancy, and with me. Because of it, you feel Nancy can't care about you, and that I must be judging you as well."

Rick heard this, but didn't respond. He continued to stay in what looked like an internal space of self-reflection. Nancy too remained silent, looking at Rick with something approaching compassion and empathy. Finally, Rick turned toward her, but seemed to be addressing both of us. "It's weird," he said, "I hope I don't sound like I'm schizophrenic or anything, because I know what I've just been saying. But I don't think I've made myself clear, and I don't think you've really understood me." Nancy asked, "What haven't I understood?" Rick said, "I think you thought—and I understand why you did, I'm not saying you were all that wrong—that I was saying you hate me, and that I hated you in return for thinking I wasn't good or attractive or sexual enough. But . . . it's hard to say . . . but I don't think that's how I really feel. I reacted terribly when you told me I'm a good husband, but . . . I liked it when you said it. . . . I didn't know how to tell you, but I liked it."

Again the three of us were silent, but this silence had a very different feeling than the earlier one filled with paralysis or despair. Nancy reached out to touch Rick's hand, while he looked down with what seemed like a complex mood of confession, hope, anxiety, and grief.

THE GROWTH-ENHANCING FUNCTION OF PROJECTIVE AND INTROJECTIVE IDENTIFICATION

As I observed earlier, the mutual processes of projective and introjective identification can be used for both defensive purposes and for the promotion of healing and psychological growth. In this session, the interactions between Rick, Nancy, and me illustrate both of these uses. On the one hand, the couple's mutual projections of judgment, shame, and devaluation into each other, as well as both partners' subsequent introjective identifications with those projections, had trapped them in repetitive, rigid and constricted inter-actions that rapidly led them to despair and futility. On the other hand, Rick and Nancy, with help from me, were also able to utilize those same mutual processes to take at least small steps toward creating a relational atmosphere in which both partners could begin to withdraw their projections and work through the emotional consequences of reintegrating them into their senses of self. The exchange between them at the end of the session, for example, consisted first of Rick's attempt to reclaim ownership of his projections (which had painted Nancy as *only* hateful and shaming and him as only shamed and devalued), and second of Nancy's simple gesture of empathy, which effectively said, although not in words: *I understand your projection; I have harbored it in myself for a long time; I will help you grieve the losses from which it arose.*

When projective and introjective processes are used for growth-enhanc-ing purposes between the members of a couple, the primary mechanism of healing is not the elimination of the projecting partner's unacceptable parts of self (as in the defensive use of these processes), but rather the capacity of the receiving partner to temporarily house those projections in such a way that the projecting partner can eventually retrieve and reintegrate them back into the self (Bion, 1962a, 1962b; Cleavely, 1993; Kernberg, 2003; Klein, 1955; Malin, 1966; Meltzer, et al., 1982). This reintegrative process, which is the process of *containment* (see chapters 1 and 4), requires the appearance, at least at crucial moments, of a secure emotional atmosphere in which respect, tolerance, and a willingness to work with both the good and bad qualities of the projecting partner without being retaliatory or hypercritical are paramount. When this atmosphere is in place, as it was at the end of the session with Rick and Nancy, the partner who has received the projections is able to think about them and contextualize them—particularly in light of his or her understanding of the projecting partner's past—so that, when they are returned to the projecting partner, they are in a moderated and detoxified form. As the session illustrates, containment need not be a complex process: Nancy's empathy and simple touch were pivotal to helping Rick secure his ability to reclaim his projections. Because of Nancy's empathy (and also because of my attempts, throughout the session, to contain both partners' projections, which I will discuss in a moment), Rick then had the opportunity to reintegrate psychic contents that had originally been too toxic to acknowledge (Zavattini, 1988). It is this capacity of the members of a couple to function as containers for each other that has led many writers to call the relationship itself a "therapeutic institution" (Colman, 1993).

Because the healing function of projective and introjective identification provides a path for the reintegration of each partner's disavowed parts of self, its use within a couple diminishes their reliance on the defensive functions of those mechanisms. No couple, however, is free from at least some defensive use of projection and introjection, and for some couples the defensive function predominates. This was the case with Rick and Nancy. Although both partners clearly hoped for containment, and could take intermittent steps in that direction (as was demonstrated in the session), they had so far been unable to reliably move their relationship beyond their defensive uses of projective mechanisms. Ultimately, this was the unconscious reason they decided to seek treatment: because their own containment capacities were inconsistent and hadn't found stable purchase, they needed a therapist to provide an additional layer of containment for them (Brookes, 1991).

THE THERAPIST'S USE OF CONTAINMENT WITH THE COUPLE

The therapist's provision of containment requires similar conditions as those between members of a couple. That is, the therapist provides respect, tolerance, and a willingness to allow and watch for the development of introjective identifications with the patients' projections in an atmosphere of acceptance, thoughtfulness and non-reactivity (Feinsilver, 1989). When the therapist's introjective identifications form under these conditions, they are moderated by the conditions themselves, and thus become "partial" or "trial" identifications (Fliess, 1942; Reich, 1960) that are more transient and exert less pressure for enactments than those involved in the defensive uses of projective and introjective identifications.

Although trial identifications are less compelling than their counterparts, they are nevertheless the products of a channel of unconscious communication that serves to inform the therapist of the topography of the patient's unconscious, often in a more immediate and direct way than is possible through verbal exchanges. Because, however, those communications are unconscious, the therapist must use indirect means to identify and understand them. One of the most effective methods at the therapist's disposal is the analysis of his or her countertransference reactions to the patients' transferences, since those reactions often represent the conscious, though not always easily available, effects of introjective identifications (M-J. Gerson, 2001; Meadow, 1977). Although the clarity of the information that can be gained through analyzing the therapist's countertransference reactions is compromised by the potentially distorting influence of the therapist's own contributions to those reactions (Compton, 1990; McLaughlin, 1981), they can, if approached cautiously, still be an invaluable resource for the therapist.

Although the intricacies of countertransference analysis are beyond the scope of this discussion, we can summarize its essential elements. First, the therapist approaches the treatment in a calm and receptive manner, in order to make himself or herself available as the object of the patient's projective identifications (Searles, 1963). Second, the therapist utilizes numerous internal strategies, such as reverie (Bion, 1962b), "free-floating responsiveness" (Sandler, 1976), internal play, and "negative capability" (Grinberg, 1969), to feel his or her way into the often subtle and ephemeral countertransference responses within the mind or the body. Third, the therapist checks his or her countertransference experiences against "the form and content of the patient's material, the quality of the interaction between patient and analyst and all other information available" (Stein, 1991, p. 333) to determine whether the countertransference responses can be legitimately linked to the patient's projections.

If the therapist determines that the patient's projections are an active source of the therapist's countertransference, he or she then uses this information to formulate containing responses. The content of a containing response may vary: typically it is an interpretation, but it may also consist of a gesture, an act of mutual recognition or even of "mere enlightened encouragement" (Feinsilver, 1989, p. 442). Regardless of the form, to any act of containment the therapist appends two additional elements derived from his or her own internal resources: the cognitive capacity to think about the projected material, and the emotional capacity to experience it calmly without being overwhelmed. When the patient then reinternalizes his or her projections, after they have passed through the therapist's mind, he or she also internalizes the therapist's capacities to contain them, which over time helps to build the patient's own internal containment capabilities (Steiner, 1994).

In my session with Rick and Nancy, many of my interventions would classify as containing, although some were more facilitating of each partner's reintegration of projections than others. My brief statement to Rick, for example, that he'd "had a lifetime of feeling like that" seemed to me to have been more effective in helping him liberate himself from his projections than many of my more complex interpretations (although the two forms of intervention were probably interdependent). This statement arose out of a countertransference moment (my image of his mother) in which I believe I had listened to the unconscious channel of communication between us, and I had therefore been more attuned to the present moments of his internal world. My statement, then, was containing in that it communicated to Rick that I understood him, and it informed him that his internal conflicts (which he had just been projecting) were both thinkable and emotionally manageable.

WORKING BETWEEN THE INDIVIDUAL AND THE COUPLE

The middle ground approach to couple therapy recognizes the equal validity of individual and the relational contributions to the nature and quality of the couple relationship. One primary implication of this approach is that all forms of transference, whether they originate in one-person projective identifications or two-person, mutual processes of projective and introjective identification, are considered legitimate targets for the therapist's containing interpretations. Thus, in any session, the therapist may shift, sometimes often, between offering containment for individual transferences (in which case the focus is on one partner or the other) and shared or entangled transferences (when the focus is on the couple as a whole), depending on the material the couple presents in the moment and on the therapist's determination of which transference would be of most benefit, for the couple, to illuminate.

In chapter 4, I'll discuss the process of *relational containment*, in which the therapist's interpretations target the relational field between the partners, rather than the individual partners themselves. For now, we can observe that when the therapist offers interpretations of mutually constructed transferences, the partners are effectively asked to consider and contain not only their own contributions, but those of their partner as well. In the session with Rick and Nancy, for example, my interpretations that each partner's contributions to their mutual system of accusation and misperception had reinforced the other's polarized perspectives, provided both partners with a momentary opportunity to reabsorb their own projections *and* to become aware that their partner experienced fears and vulnerabilities similar to their own. Interpretations of the mutual processes between partners can thus create multiple acts of simultaneous containment: at the same time that both partners are contained in their own projections, they are also witness to, and participate in, acts of containment for the other partner.

A hallmark of dysfunctional couples is that both partners tend to inflexibly believe that what they have projected into the other actually constitutes the other's "true" nature, without being able or willing to investigate the projective mechanisms that have created their distorted perceptions, or to re-internalize and re-own the content of those projections (Morgan, 1995). The therapist's equal focus on individual, shared and entangled transferences counters this dysfunctional tendency, because it emphasizes, first, that both partners have contributed to the relational field from which the couple's difficulties have arisen, and second, that each partner is also capable of helping to resolve those difficulties by re-internalizing the parts of themselves they have projected into the other. Thus, a middle ground approach, in which all forms of transferences are subject to analysis and containing responses, underscores that individualities *and* mutualities make up the couple and that holding the two in equal balance facilitates the development of both individual responsibility and an empathetic connection between partners (Clulow, 2001; Zeitner, 2012).

The goals of the middle ground approach to couple therapy are to utilize the analysis of the couple's individual and shared states of mind to develop both partners' capacity to understand and contain their own and their partner's unconscious, and to tolerate those regressive moments, which occur in all relationships (Kernberg, 1995), when internal conflicts and psychic splits necessitate momentary projections. When a couple is able to meet these goals, the result is a relationship that is relatively free from repetitive conflicts, and that enjoys instead the fruits of synthesis and creativity that become possible when each partner is comfortable in their own skin, and in the "containing skin" of the relationship that surrounds them (Cleavely, 1993).

Chapter Three

Shared Objects, Amplified Fear

As described in chapter 1, the primary motivation for middle ground therapists to strike a balance between individual and relational concepts has been their recognition that relying on one group of concepts to the exclusion of the other, regardless of which group is favored, is unnecessarily limiting and restrictive, and leads to numerous problems, both in theory and technique. As part of their commitment to this balance, middle ground theorists have undertaken the project of re-examining many psychological phenomena that have been traditionally defined in one-person terms, to determine if they may also be conceptualized from a two-person perspective. In this light, such traditional one-person concepts as the unconscious (S. Gerson, 2004, 2006; Tubert-Oklander, 2006b), transference (Ehrlich, Zilbach & Solomon, 1996; Hoffman, 1983; Ogden, 1994a; McLaughlin, 1981;), countertransference (Jacobs, 1991; Levine, 2009; Maroda, 1991; McLaughlin, 1981) and resistance (Boesky, 1990; Bromberg, 1995) have all been reconfigured to include not only intrapsychic elements, but also the oftentimes hidden influence of relational modes of experience as well.

One core concept, however, that is still in the process of such a transformation is that of the internal object itself, even though the possibility of an interpersonally based, though still unconscious, object has been mentioned in the literature for several decades. In 1967, for example, Henry Dicks observed that the confused and confusing presentation of many disturbed couples may result from "fluidity of ego boundaries and identities" anchored in such mechanisms as mutual projection, projective identification, and role reversal. He suggested that through these blurred boundaries one could glimpse the "deeper unconscious bonds" that unite the couple in a joint personality, or "a unit around which some sort of joint ego-boundaries" should be drawn. The components of such joint personalities, according to Dicks, could be merged egos, joint resistances, a joint false self, or "shared objects" (1967, p. 68). In this chapter, I would like to elaborate on the concept of the shared object, and extend it against the backdrop of modern theories of object relations and relationality. I will use an example from psychoanalytic psychotherapy with a couple to underscore the clinical validity for such a conceptual extension.

MIKE AND LANA

Mike and Lana were an unmarried couple in their late-twenties who had lived together for four years. They entered treatment at the urging of a family member, but they made it clear from the beginning they were ambivalent about therapy and didn't know if it would help them with their problems. In the first session, they described their relationship as marked by "constant bickering," even though they also said they loved each other and wanted to stay together if they could. As I listened to them describe the details of their interactions, I found Lana's primary attitude toward Mike was wary and critical, while Mike's was defensive and aggressive. Lana's complaints about Mike, moreover, were about his selfishness and his "inability" to understand her perspectives or value her opinions. Mike, on the other hand, consistently complained Lana refused to see the good he contributed to the relationship. At one point in our first session, for example, he said: "Everybody in my family tells me that I've already done too much for this woman. But does she ever appreciate it? No."

The precipitating cause of the couple's decision to enter therapy was a fight, five weeks earlier, about how much time Mike spent with his family. During the fight, Mike raised his fist, as though to strike Lana. The action frightened both partners and Mike left their apartment and didn't return for three days. When he did return, they tried to patch over the conflict, but both partners agreed "something had changed" and their relationship seemed on a different footing now—one that made both partners uneasy. During those five weeks, they resumed their sexual relationship, which they said was "mostly" satisfying, but they also argued frequently. Their arguments were about multiple topics—not just Mike's relationship with his family—and Lana described them as "vicious," filled with accusations and expressions of contempt whose vehemence surprised both partners.

In our sessions Mike and Lana quickly established an unproductive pattern of trading criticisms and accusations about each other's behavior that mirrored their descriptions of their home life. Typically, this pattern began when Lana accused Mike, with angry and withering commentary, of some fault or failure. Mike then denied any fault and argued, with angry commentary of his own, that the transgression was Lana's. She then also refused to accept fault and again accused Mike of wrongdoing. With each accusation, the couple's anxiety escalated to the point where it was clear, to an outside observer, that each partner was afraid to accept any blame at all.

The foundation of their fear of blame lay in each partner's family history. Mike was raised in a family that convinced itself of a myth that it was a perfect, loving, caring, and unified group. The myth was not completely inaccurate, but underneath it a history of his older brother's intermittent but brutal violence, his mother's emotional fragility, and his father's narcissistic indifference functioned as an unconscious rebuttal. The impact on Mike was that he came to believe that *he*—or more to the point, his badness—was what explained the multiple fault lines he felt, but not quite understand, in the myth. The belief in his badness was thus linked to an accusing and critical internal object that utilized the family myth as a standard against which his failings were even more harshly judged. In his fear of this object, Mike developed a defensive narcissistic organization: criticism, especially Lana's, elicited in him highly energized anxiety around themes of shame and guilt, and in defense he utilized both denial and projective identification (as in the projection of his sense of badness into Lana).

Lana's history, though appreciably different than Mike's, yielded a similarly punitive internal object in regard to which she felt guilt, shame, and fear. Raised in a wealthy and politically connected family with, by her description, a disinterested self-absorbed mother and a controlling self-righteous father, who imposed strict expectations on her behavior, Lana rebelled against those strictures with drug use and promiscuity throughout her teenage years. Because her behavior disappointed her parents and threatened, in Lana's terms, the carefully crafted image of the family they tried to convey in social circles, it created an emotional rupture between her and her parents that had never fully healed. When Lana went away to college, she significantly reduced her drug use, partially in the hope she could repair some of the damage she felt had been done to her standing in the family. Her decision to move in with Mike, and to try to establish a stable relationship with him, had a similar motive. Her parents, however, were unresponsive to her overtures, and remained cool and distant, further entrenching her feeling that she had irreparably failed them. As a result of these experiences, Lana internalized a harshly accusing internal object, in whose presence she felt not only guilty and ashamed, but also doomed to irresolvable failure. To protect herself from these feelings, she utilized splitting and dissociation to immure herself from blame, and projective identification to then locate that blame in others—most commonly Mike.

SHARED OBJECTS

Research by Beebe, Lachmann, Jaffe and others (Beebe & Lachmann, 2002, 2003; Beebe, Lachmann & Jaffe, 1997) has shown that a fundamental characteristic of dyadic interactions is that, in response to any action given by one participant, the other immediately, automatically, and unconsciously adapts and adjusts his or her own actions, so the interactive sequence is one of continual reciprocal modifications of each person's behavior and experience. These reciprocal adjustments occur substantially in the unconscious arena, at the level of "implicit" or "enactive" knowing (Lyons-Ruth, 1999; Nahum, 2008), rather than explicit, verbal, or conscious understanding. This implicit, nonverbal dimension "provides a continuous background of moment-by-moment mutual influence" (Beebe & Lachmann, 2002, p. 141) in which the participants are capable, though not necessarily conscious, of altering each other's timing, spatial orientation, affect, arousal, thoughts, actions, and unconscious experience.

In an interactive sequence, each participant is both responding to the other person and making decisions about their own actions in literally split-second time frames—often at the rate of 1/12th of a second (Cohn & Beebe, 1990). These decisions, though rapid, are not made randomly. Instead, they are guided by two factors that limit the kinds of choices that can be made within the sequence.

The first limiting factor is each participant's unconscious endowment. When any person enters into an interaction, they bring with them the contents of their unconscious, and in particular their internal object relationships, by which I mean both the internal objects themselves and the self's emotional responses to them (Scharff & Scharff, 1992). These internal object relationships, as we know, supply the models by which that person will both interpret and respond to other people's behavior. In Mike's case, for example, his harsh, accusing internal object, in relation to which he was afraid and defensive, would often lead him to interpret Lana's anger as frightening because it exposed him, in his mind, to unbearable shame or guilt. In the moment-to-moment flux of their interaction, both his responses to her split-second behaviors and his decisions about his own actions were thus guided by that interpretation.

The second factor that limits the choices that can be made within an interactive sequence is the contour of the other's behavior. As Mike listened to Lana's expressions of anger, for example, the specifics of her behavior—her gestures, movements, postures, inflections, affective intensities, voice timbre, etc.—all functioned to implicitly inform him of her psychological and emotional attitudes. These in turn funneled his responses in certain directions. If he "read" in her behavior anxiety about having to bear responsibility for failure, his subsequent responses and actions (whether mollifying or accusing) would occur within the context of that recognition, even though he may not have been aware that he *had made* that recognition.

In the microsecond intervals of a real-time interaction, each participant's internal object relationships play an integral role in determining how that interaction proceeds. When Lana accused Mike, she engaged in behaviors that followed the models given to her by her internal object relationships. Her behaviors, in turn, elicited automatic and unconscious actions from Mike that were a response to her behavior but that also followed the rules of *his* internal object relationships. The couple's interactions thus proceeded in a circular fashion, with every action bearing the trace of both the actor's and the other's internal worlds.

As interactions like this are repeated over and over in a long-term relationship, the couple comes to "know," in the implicit, procedural sense of knowing, each other's internal object relationships and the models of response and action they supply. As the partners develop this implicit understanding, their behaviors and affective responses become more coordinated and synchronized. The process of synchronization follows the familiar steps of the cycle of projective and introjective identifications (Klein, 1946, 1952b, 1955; J. Scharff, 1992), and it is similar to Stern's concept of relational knowing (Stern, et al., 1998). As one partner utilizes projective identification to inject the contours of their internal object relationship into the interaction, the other resonates with those contours *because of the convergences between that internal object and their own.* On the basis of those convergences (which are similar to Bion's idea of valencies—1961), the receiving partner's internal object relationship is activated, preparing the ground both for their internalization of the other's material (via introjective identification), and for their own projective identifications in return.

Once this projective and introjective sequence is begun, each partner's original internal object relationship becomes more and more modified by material borrowed from the other's, with the result that the two internal objects drift toward each other and become increasingly similar. The implicit models the two objects engender become more and more coordinated around the same themes, and each partner's contribution reinforces the other's. Ultimately, the couple comes to implicitly know that their two objects have become identical, and that now the same object—a shared object—dominates both of their worlds. They are each now synchronized, in the assumptions they make about the interpersonal environment, their emotional responses to it, and their defensive strategies (if any) against it.

It is important to note that shared objects may not always require a convergence of the themes of a couple's internal objects. Rather, in some cases, it is possible a shared object can be forced upon one participant by the strength, intensity, and polarizing capacity of the other's internal object(s). In this case, the shared object is more complementary than convergent. A wife may, for example, be deathly afraid of an internalized critical object. In defense against this object, she may project blame with levels of viciousness to which her husband is unaccustomed. Over time, as the spiral of communications develops between them, the husband will begin to take on a similar fear of a critical object. Although the primary embodiment of the critical object is in the wife, a new critical object has been constructed between them, and the husband has been introduced to, or inculcated (or even intoxicated) with the emotional topography of this object. In this case, the shared object takes on a parasitic quality (see Baranger & Baranger, 1966), in that the husband is in a kind of thrall to the dominant traits of the wife's internal world.

It also must be noted that shared objects may be of either positive or negative emotional valence. Couples may develop shared objects around themes of love, holding, or containment (based in their individual internal "good" object relationships) as easily as around themes of accusation, shame, or fear. Beneficent shared objects most likely underlie couple relationships that are functional and satisfying, although it is possible—and perhaps even common—that such positive shared object phenomena are used pathologically, in defense, for example, against aggression, envy or other frightening psychic material. Still, "negative" shared objects (viz., those developed around themes of aversive emotional experience) are disproportionately responsible for the difficulties couples typically present in a clinical setting.

The shared object in Mike and Lana's case was punitive, accusing, and frightening. Because of the thematic convergence of their dominant internal objects, Mike and Lana's relationship was fertile ground for the development of such a shared object, and of each partner's implicit knowledge of shared fears of guilt and shame. Ultimately, their two feared objects became a dangerous shared object, whose frightening and punitive mien permeated both their internal and interpersonal worlds.

Shared objects are thus built up out of the slow accrual of microscopic coordinations—via projective and introjective experiences—of unconscious material. The net result is the erosion of the boundaries between the two partners and their internal worlds, which Henry Dicks first noted in 1967, and the formation instead of an interpersonal or relational unconscious environment that is sustained by the patterned interactions between the partners. The shared object and the implicit models that are coeval with it thus produce a bipersonal field (Baranger & Baranger, 1966; Langs, 1978, 1981) in which both partners are structured by the conscious and unconscious communications that arise "toward and from both centers" (Baranger & Baranger, 1966, p. 60).

Let's return to Mike and Lana to illustrate the kinds of interactions I believe are characteristic of such a shared object.

THE SHARED OBJECT IN ACTION

By the second year of therapy, it was becoming clear just how entrenched Mike and Lana were in their pattern of accusation, denial, and counter-accusation. Individual sessions with Mike led him to soften some of his defensive attacks and to display more insight into their origins, but Lana remained more injured by the history of Mike's behavior and, hence, distrustful of his overtures. They considered separating and went so far as to look at separate apartments, but they were unable to move any further. It was during this period they revealed to me that early in their relationship, just as they were getting to know each other and long before they moved in together, Lana had become pregnant. After briefly discussing their options, which they said, "lasted all of twenty minutes," they agreed to have an abortion, even though this violated both partners' moral and religious beliefs and upbringings. Mike made the arrangements and drove Lana to the doctor's office. After the procedure, he drove her back to her apartment in silence and, according to their report, they never spoke about it again.

The fact that Mike and Lana did not speak about this abortion and did not reveal it until nearly two years into their therapy, indicates its significance for each partner, individually—particularly in terms of their relationships with their internal objects—and also for the implicit patterns their interactions subsequently developed. Individually, each partner came to feel the abortion was proof of the validity of their internal objects' accusations. For Lana, it pointed to the same kind of behavior that caused the rupture with her family in her teenage years; and for Mike, it was another moral failure that proved his basic and irredeemable fault. In their interactions, the unavoidable "fact" of their guilt became a shared indictment that functioned as the pivot point, or as an anchor, which grounded them in a new and shared psychic space.

This new psychic space was the bailiwick of their shared object, augmented and sustained by each of their internal objects, but rotating around a guilt they both shared and yet neither could avoid. Their shared object, in turn, mobilized a coordinated set of moment-to-moment implicit procedures that always functioned in reference to the shared object, but also attempted to protect each from the unbearable weight of its accusations. The tension and conflict in their relationship—particularly the repeating pattern of accusation, denial, and counter-accusation—can be seen, in this light, as an elaborate implicit mechanism that, as long as it operates, defends both parties against their fear of guilt.

The following sequence occurred two sessions after the revelation about the abortion. In it, Mike and Lana attempt to talk about the early months of their relationship. Although Mike attempts an apology for his role (specifically, for pressuring Lana to have sex when they had no protection), Lana does not accept the apology and the two quickly regain their familiar pattern

of trading accusations. In this sequence, we can see how the patterned interaction between them, which has a scripted quality because of its repetitive-
ness, functions to defend both partners against their shared fears of a guilt-
inducing object.

Lana began by saying she wanted to talk to Mike about his role in the
events that led to the abortion. With a tone that clearly implied she saw, or
could see, no role of her own, she reminded him that he pressured her to have
sex, even though she resisted because she knew they weren't protected. Mike
responded with characteristic defensiveness, saying, as he remembered it,
she was as interested in sex as he was. Lana answered, with some anger, that
she wasn't "into it," and she only agreed because he pressured her. Mike,
now with increasing anger and defensiveness, said that wasn't how he remembered it. "I remember it very clearly," he said, "It's etched in my mind.
You wanted to have sex. You know you did."

At this point I suggested both partners were feeling anxious and that it
had to do with their guilt about the abortion and the events leading up to it. I
added that we were familiar with this pattern, and if it continued, each of
them would continue to blame the other, with the result that neither would
hear what the other was trying to say. They paused at this, and then Mike
continued in a less defensive tone. "You're right," he said to me. Then
turning to Lana he said, "I want to hear what you have to say." Lana, who
was also now somewhat less defensive, said the abortion bothered her ever
since it happened. She thought about it all the time, she said. She then
described the early months of their relationship. "I was really insecure and
scared," she said, "and all I wanted was for somebody to love me. I met you,
and I loved you almost from the beginning, but it seemed all that you wanted
from me was sex. You didn't want *me*. I felt like I had to have sex with you
or I would lose you. I don't think you were even thinking about me, or what
it meant to me. You were just thinking about yourself and you manipulated
me." Although Lana was in tears by the end of this, which revealed both the
fear and pain she felt about the abortion, her last sentence ended on a sharp
edge of accusation, conveying once again her anxieties about guilt and
blame.

Mike, however, didn't respond to Lana's accusation. After a long pause,
in which he began to tear as well, he said, "You're right. When I met you, I
was so lost. Susan [a prior girlfriend] had just dumped me because I was
drinking too much and I didn't really know if I was going to finish school. I
don't think I ever felt so low, so bad about myself. I couldn't think of a single
thing that made me worth anything at all. My family was furious at me
because I was wasting my life, but I couldn't talk to them about what I was
really feeling. I was so desperate to get it all behind me that I was willing to
do anything. And then I met you. And it seemed like you were the best thing
that had ever happened to me. You were beautiful and you loved me and I

couldn't understand it. But I was in this place where I would do anything to have you and in my screwed-up mind, at the time, that meant having sex. I know I manipulated you and I pressured you. And I am sorry. I am so sorry for all of the pain that caused you, and for the abortion, and for my inability to address it head-on and to come to you as a better man."

After Mike's speech, Lana was silent, but only for a brief interval. Then she asked why Mike hadn't been able to say all this before. He answered that he didn't think he understood it well enough before, and that he had been afraid to say it. She asked why he was afraid. He said, with a tone that seemed to carry a hint of anxiety about where this conversation might lead, that he was afraid of what she would think of him. Lana then seemed to pick up on Mike's anxiety, and with a note of impatience and perhaps accusation in her voice, asked, "And what *would* I think of you?" Mike's characteristic defensiveness was now returning. He said, "Why don't you tell me, Lana?" She answered that he manipulated her into having sex and he just admitted it. Mike said, "Yes. And . . . ?" Lana said, "Isn't that enough? You manipulated me. How could I ever trust you now?" Mike seemed taken aback by this. Lana continued, "How could I ever trust anyone who had done those things? You treated me like I was just some piece of fluff that you could have sex with because *you* needed it? And I had an abortion because of it!? And I'm supposed to accept your apology and say that everything's wonderful and we can just start our life again?" Mike asked angrily, "What would be wrong with that?" Lana shot back, "It's not going to happen, Mike!" Back in his full defensive mode, Mike then said, "OK. That's it. I'm done. I'm done with apologies. You don't even recognize when I'm trying to be as honest as I can be. You know what? To hell with it."

In this interaction, Lana and Mike were terrified of the same thing: being responsible for something that would mean they are too guilty, too bad, and, therefore, too far beyond recovery or redemption. Underlying this intense and shared fear was their shared object, which here operated like an angry and condemning presence whose accusing stare each partner tries to avoid. Although much of the affective intensity surrounding this shared object was due to each partner's internal object relationships, still a significant portion came from interactional sources: from the shared indictment of the abortion and from the conflagrational process of fear meeting fear, kindling even greater fear. Empowered by these processes, Mike and Lana's shared object became a truly formidable opponent. In defense against it, they developed a rigid set of implicit interactional rules that were clearly on display in this sequence: First, interpret all accusations as unbearable and impossibly oppressive; and second, respond to each accusation with denial and a reversal of blaming.

To be sure, Mike, following my intervention, did attempt to derail the implicit rules of their interactions by apologizing, in a way that seemed sincere, for his past behavior. His attempt, in essence, amounted to a turning-toward the shared object and an acceptance and even a containment of its accusations. Mike's capacity to do this, in the midst of an interaction that began with an accusatory tone, was evidence of his developing ability to regulate the anxieties associated with his own internal object and the sense of self-condemnation related to it, and to understand some of the relational origins of his interactions with Lana. As such, his apology represented a new relational moment—a bid or invitation to Lana to suspend the old determinants of their interactions and open up space for the emergence of new possibilities.

Mike's apology, however, was unsuccessful. Lana's immediate response was a spike in anxiety, which manifested itself in additional accusations and a refusal of the invitation implicit in his apology. Her refusal was an indication of an aspect of her internal world that was only to become fully clarified much later. Lana's fear of the couple's shared object (and of course of her internal object that gave rise to the shared object) was substantially greater than Mike's and, consequently, the defenses she erected against it were significantly more rigid and unyielding than his. When Mike, through his apology, opened at least a partial window on the origins of their shared object, Lana's fear intensified her projective defenses against that object in the form of escalating blaming and accusation, even to the point of irrationality. The intensity of Lana's response then overwhelmed Mike's capacity to manage his anxiety and, within seconds, he was back again, operating according to the old implicit rules that protected both from, and prevented each from confronting the shared object. Shared objects, in other words, possess a strength and inertia that can constitute a powerful, relational resistance to therapeutic progress.

FURTHER THOUGHTS ABOUT SHARED OBJECTS

Shared objects do not jump, but rather seep into existence. At first, the partners find a certain *union* in an emotional sequence, a pleasure of recognition and of being known at layers never *thought* possible. It is not just the unthought known, as Bollas has suggested, but the *unthought being known* that motivates them. The union grows with repetition; themes develop; implicit narratives are elaborated with subplots and subtexts. All the while the shared object grows in intensity as each partner reads every gesture the other makes, adds their own elaboration, and instantaneously responds to the other's response. Over time the implicit procedural models founded on individual internal objects become a single intersubjective model that both share. The result is a gathering of thematic gravity around a central theme. Every step is filled with all of the drives, anxieties, and presuppositions from the preceding steps, so the whole sequence seems like a gathering storm.

For much of the time, the shared object—much as other internal objects—does not discretely identify itself. Instead, it is experienced like an emotional atmosphere: it is felt as a presence, but it is just beyond the point where one can put one's finger on it. In this phase of its life, it functions like the gravitational pull from a planet not yet discovered, bending the content and tone of the interaction toward itself without ever really making itself explicitly known. If the shared object is persecutory, it will bend the interaction toward themes of safety and danger and the anxieties surrounding them; if it is critical, the relationship will revolve around questions of goodness and badness. For much of the shared object's life, its influence is unknown and the participants in the shared object are merely subject to its drives, assumptions, and anxieties.

At some point, though, the shared object *atmosphere* gathers itself into a discrete form, identifiable *as* a shared object. Most commonly, this occurs through the formation of transference. *Shared object transferences* are more complex than individual transferences and can underlie both transference-countertransference entanglements and shared transferences (see chapter 2). In shared object transferences, one partner may embody the shared transference, or the two may embody it together. Whether they arise in one partner or both, these transferences aim at multiple targets: the other partner, the self, the couple, the therapist, or the therapeutic environment. No matter what its form, when a shared object transference arises, it gathers into itself all of the intrapsychic associates (assumptions, expectations, affects, drives, etc.) of each partner's internal object relationships, as well as of the shared object that the couple has co-constructed. The gathering of all of this material then produces, in an unconscious dynamic symphony—the specific moments of shared object transference.

Shared object transferences are identifiable both by their intensity and their circularity. The interaction seems to spiral into a monotonous and tedious movement that all parties experience with frustration or boredom. Psychic growth is thwarted, as each partner settles into the comfort of a repetitive role. Unless worked with directly, these transferences will split off, conceal and camouflage important and potentially energizing material. A barricade or a "bastion" (Barranger & Barranger, 1966) will form that opposes progress and resists penetration into the couple's intrapsychic and intersubjective dynamics.

Because of their intensity, shared object transferences can easily engulf the therapist in his or her countertransference emotions. These emotions will be anchored in the therapist's own history, but they will also reflect, sometimes with surprising fidelity, the thematic currents of the shared object. If the therapist loses sight of his containment function in the therapeutic triangle, he will be drawn into an enactment (Jacobs, 1986) of the shared object drama. In such a case, all three individuals in the room will contribute to the creation of a bastion and therapeutic progress will grind to a halt.

Two examples of shared object countertransference emotions surfaced in me as I watched Mike and Lana re-engage, with perverse persistence, in their repetitive cycle after Mike's apology. On the one hand, I felt proud of Mike for having taken this unique step. On the other, I felt frustrated and angry with both partners—but especially with Lana—for their rapid reversal to the old implicit rules. Both of these responses reflected my resonance with the field of emotional meaning that was constructed by the couple's shared object. In my pride, I was an approving object for Mike via a counter-identification with the accusatory shared object. And in my anger, I was the momentary incarnation of the shared object itself. Because I did not enact these emotions, they were available to me instead as objects of analysis (Winnicott, 1949; Heimann, 1950; Little, 1951; Reich, 1951; Tower, 1956), through which I could see more deeply into the emotional contours of the shared object. Although working with couples in shared object transferences is oftentimes a protracted process, thorough analysis of the countertransference and the multiple manifestations of the shared object transference will often help the therapist to illuminate more accurately the unconscious foundations of the couple's interactions.

Two examples of shared object countertransference emotions surfaced in me as I watched Mike and Lana re-engage, with perverse persistence, in their repetitive cycle after Mike's apology. On the one hand, I felt proud of Mike for having taken this unique step. On the other, I felt frustrated and angry with both partners—but especially with Lana—for their rapid reversal to the old implicit rules. Both of these responses reflected my resonance with the field of emotional meaning that was constructed by the couple's shared object. I my pride, I was an approving object for Mike via a counter-identification with the accusatory shared object. And in my anger, I was the momentary incarnation of the shared object itself. Because I did not enact these emotions, they were available to me instead as objects of analysis (Winnicott, 1949; Heimann, 1950; Little, 1951; Reich, 1951; Tower, 1956), through which I could see more deeply into the emotional contours of the shared object. Although working with couples in shared object transferences is oftentimes a protracted process, thorough analysis of the countertransference and the multiple manifestations of the shared object transference will often help the therapist to illuminate more accurately the unconscious foundations of the couple's interactions.

Interventions in shared object phenomena, particularly in couple therapy, must be flexible enough to move back and forth between the individual and the intersubjective, constantly identifying and underscoring the links between them. Emphasis on one element to the exclusion of the other will have a deadening influence. If the therapist confines his or her interpretations to the intrapsychic elements, both the therapist and the couple will feel that the full volume of the emotional landscape has not been captured. Also, an intrapsychic interpretation of a shared object transference will feel like blaming to each of the partners, and will tend to embroil the therapist in patterns of accusation and counter-accusation that the shared object may already have created. If, on the other hand, the therapist attempts to interpret only the intersubjective aspects of shared object phenomena, the interpretations will appear ungrounded and without reference to the real affective and historical ground from which the shared object arose.

The following segment, from the session immediately after the one in which Mike apologized, illustrates the necessity of moving back and forth between transferences based on individual internal objects and shared transferences based on the shared object. Mike began this session by angrily criticizing Lana for not accepting his apology. After a brief exchange, Lana said to me, "He apologized all right. He apologized for manipulating me. How am I supposed to trust him after that? He didn't mean the apology at all. When he said he was done apologizing, I knew it was the same crap all over again. He apologized to try to manipulate me again." The two sources of Lana's transference were fairly obvious in this statement. On the one hand, she was performing one of the repeating acts of the shared object repertoire by striving once again to land responsibility for the problems in the relationship in Mike's lap. On the other hand, the anger and urgency in her words were also indicators of the difficult history of her relationship with her own accusing internal object. In this instance, I chose to focus on the shared object transference first, particularly because she and Mike both so clearly enacted it at the end of the prior session.

I said, "We're where we were when we left off last time, when both of you were trying to convince me that the other is guilty, not you. It seems you see me as either the arbiter of your guilt, or maybe as your accuser, but you both have been arguing your case as though making the other guilty in my eyes is the most important thing you could do." Lana responded first, saying she didn't feel guilty, and she didn't have anything to feel guilty about. I said to both partners that in the last few sessions they had tried to talk about events they hadn't talked about for years, and now both were trying to declare themselves blameless and to prove to me the other was guilty. I then added that the entire process seemed to suggest both were terrified of carrying any guilt at all. Mike now protested, saying, "Hey wait a minute. Didn't I take on all the blame last week?" I said yes, he made that offer, but he also quickly retracted it when he said he was done apologizing. Mike said, "Yeah—because Lana refused to hear any of it, and didn't believe me anyway." I said, "Right, and now you're saying it's Lana's fault that you gave up feeling guilty. Which is to say that you've again tried to pass the guilt to her."

Mike said he didn't know if he was trying to "pass the guilt" to Lana as much as he was trying to say she was guilty too. "I know I'm guilty," he added, "I know I've done some lousy things in this relationship." I said there were times, especially when Lana was angry at him, when he lost sight of that fact and just focused on how she was hurting him.

At this point, both partners became silent and Mike, in particular, seemed to be thinking through what was happening. I thought back to his last statement. It seemed genuine to me, and it implied he had again attempted to acknowledge his mistakes without blaming Lana. The feeling I had in regard to this statement was similar to what I'd felt after his apology: something like melancholy, which I thought was related to a process of grieving (of past misbehavior and of the failures of old objects) Mike was trying to work his way through. Because this process seemed to represent Mike's attempt to liberate himself from the shared object's patterns, I decided to focus now on his intrapsychic, internal object, in order to illuminate and help him contain its role in the creation of the shared object. I said, "I suspect you focus on Lana, and how she is hurting you, when your own guilt feels too big and too unmanageable—like you're a child again with that terrifying realization that you'll never be able to rectify your badness. That's when you try to eject the whole feeling of badness into Lana." Both partners were quiet for a moment, but Lana then said she could "feel" it when Mike was trying to make her the guilty one. "It's what he always does," she said, "That's why I can never talk to him. He always blames me." I asked if she felt Mike blamed her at that moment and she said yes. I then asked, "And last time, when Mike apologized?" Lana answered, "That wasn't an apology. He's never apologized! Why should I believe that one?"

The appearance of Lana's rigid defenses at this point in the session seemed to me to now require that I focus on her individual transferential contributions. Otherwise, I was concerned her defenses would obstruct any progress we might make—either for her, for the couple, or for Mike. I said to her, "I wonder if it's possible that you're holding Mike to a pretty rigid definition—Mike is the bad one in this relationship, Mike will never change—without leaving room for the possibility that maybe he *can* change." Lana said, "Maybe you don't know Mike the way I do. He *can't* change. That's who he is." I said, "I notice, Lana, that earlier you were kind of allied with me when it looked like you and I would be on the same page in being critical of Mike. But now, as I've raised the possibility he might change, I think you might be distancing yourself from me, as though I'm kind of suspect too." Lana didn't respond to my transference interpretation, but simply repeated it was impossible for Mike to change. I said I understood, but I also wondered if it was more than that. "I wonder," I said, "if the very idea that Mike might not be totally to blame raises anxiety for you—enough that if I suggest it, you need to push yourself away from me too."

Lana asked when she pushed me away. I said, "When you said that maybe I don't know Mike the way you do." She said, "Well, maybe you don't." I said, "Right. You might even be angry with me for suggesting that Mike may not be totally guilty." Lana now sounded increasingly angry, but also desperate. "But he *is* guilty," she said, "he's guilty for everything." I paused. After a moment I said, "I suspect you feel desperate about this, as though it's terribly important that you maintain the picture of him as guilty, and yourself as innocent, and that you convince yourself and him and me of it. . . . I wonder what could make it that important?" Looking caught and uncomfortable, Lana only answered, "I don't know. . . . I don't know."

Lana's "I don't know" seemed to me to rest on a complex set of emotions. On one hand, she was frightened and tried to manage her fear, according to pattern, by projecting blame. But there also seemed to be a thread of introspection in her "I don't know," as though my observations resonated for her at least momentarily. At this point, however, I also felt she needed space from me and that any further interaction between us ran the risk of my becoming overly identified as her frightening object, both internal and shared. Consequently, I decided to pull back from my interpretations of her internal world and focus instead on the connection we uncovered earlier between the internal object relationships of both partners, and on their roles in the creation of their shared object. In high-stress situations in couple therapy, a renewed focus on the commonalities between the partners can sometimes fulfill a soothing and containing function. I said, still speaking to Lana, "I think you may carry a set of assumptions about yourself that are very similar to Mike's. Something along the lines of: if you're guilty at all, it feels too big, too frightening, too impossible to recover from." I then turned to both partners and said, "And in that fear, you each can feel desperate enough that the only thing that saves you from impossible badness is to eliminate it within yourself, and tell yourself it only exists in your partner. It's a strategy you both have been using for a long time." The session was over and Mike and Lana left my office seeming thoughtful. How long that thoughtfulness would last, I didn't know, but I did know we would have more opportunities to confront, and attempt to contain, all of the consequences their shared object, which had taken firm residence in their relationship, had in store for them.

CONCLUSION

Flexibility in moving between the intrapsychic and relational elements of a shared object interaction requires the therapist to understand (1) each partner's individual internal worlds; (2) the points of convergence and divergence between those internal worlds (e.g., similarities or dissimilarities between internal objects, ego positions in regard to those objects, drives, drive derivatives, resistances, etc.); (3) the shared history which may contain, as in the case of Mike and Lana, events that create natural bridges between the individual internal object worlds; and (4) the patterns of interaction, in whose implicit rules the possibility of shared objects and shared affective reactions to those objects may be glimpsed. Once the therapist has all of these elements in hand, they are able to shift the focus of their interpretations—now on one partner's intrapsychic contributions, and now on both partners' co-construction of the shared interaction—so that slowly a system of understanding which 'takes into account all of the dimensions of the spiraling unconscious communicative interaction' (Langs, 1981, p. 212) is built up. It is only on the basis of this kind of real understanding that partners to a shared object can find their way out of the repetitive sequences that so burden their relationship.

Chapter Four

The Uses and Misuses
of Self-Disclosure

The Value of Countertransference in a Relational World

In 2006, Gediman suggested the debate over the value and usefulness of therapist self-disclosure, which was heated for many years, has moved from dichotomous and absolutistic positions to "a more harmonious realm of discourse" (2006, p. 241). Given that the primary advocates for the use of self-disclosure have been theorists committed to exploring the implications of the relational perspective, the moderation Gediman observes may be the result of an increasing integration of relational ideas into mainstream psychoanalysis. This integration, however, is clearly not complete, since discussions about the theoretical rationale for self-disclosure and its implications for other aspects of analytic technique have continued relatively unabated (Bonovitz, 2006; Farber, 2006; Kuchuck, 2009; S. Pizer, 2006; Shill, 2004; Sholes, 2005).

Because "self-disclosure" has been something of a catch-all term, used to describe a wide array of therapists' behaviors, it is important to differentiate among them. First are disclosures of characteristics of the therapist's personality that are so embedded in gestures, clothing, word choice, office decorations, etc., that they cannot help but be revealed. For this type of disclosure, the term *inadvertent self-revelation* (Frank, 1997; Levenson, 1996; S. Levine, 2007) is most applicable. Second are the problematic, unplanned and unexpected disclosures of the therapist's spontaneous and often polarized countertransference reactions, which are termed *countertransference enact-*

ments (Jacobs, 1986, 1991; Maroda, 1991; McLaughlin, 1991; Smith, 1997; Steiner, 2000). Third are the equally problematic *personal self-disclosures* of details about the personal life of the therapist (Menaker, 1990). And finally are the therapist's deliberate and planned disclosures, within an atmosphere free of enactments, of his or her countertransference responses that arise within the course of the therapeutic relationship. For this type of deliberate countertransference disclosure, Shill (2004) has suggested the short-hand term *elective self-disclosure*, which I will also use for the remainder of this chapter. It is elective self-disclosure that has been at the center of the controversy surrounding the use of disclosure as an analytic technique.

Essentially, two groups of relational theorists have argued in favor of the therapist's use of elective self-disclosure: the radical relationalists and the advocates of the middle ground approach. While both groups have utilized some of the same arguments, writers who adhere to the radical perspective have tended to describe and defend self-disclosure in provocative terms, giving the impression that they advocate its excessive and unexamined use. In contrast, middle ground advocates have taken a more cautious approach, suggesting that principles can be developed that both guide and limit the use of self-disclosure, and demonstrating the ways it can be integrated with other therapeutic techniques, including those addressing intrapsychic, in addition to relational, phenomena. In this chapter, I will explore the middle ground's arguments for elective self-disclosure, and attempt to extend them by offering specific criteria for determining when its use is warranted.

THE MIDDLE GROUND ARGUMENT FOR ELECTIVE SELF-DISCLOSURE

The theoretical rationale for the middle ground theorists' advocacy of elective self-disclosure relies on the concept of the interlinking relationship between the patient's transference and the therapist's countertransference. The origin of this view lies in an influential set of papers from early object relations theorists (Heimann, 1950; Little, 1951; Reich, 1951; Tower, 1956; Winnicott, 1949), who argued that the patient's transference is constructed by projective identifications that trigger, via unconscious channels of communication, introjective identifications and countertransference responses in the therapist that are significant sources of information about the structure of the patient's unconscious (Gorkin, 1987; Scharff & Scharff, 1998, 2005; Tansey & Burke, 1989). Although this view provides a powerful explanation for many therapeutic phenomena, middle ground theorists have noted that its core assumptions are individualistic. That is, in such a view, the primary means by which countertransference develops is through the projective identification of unconscious material *from* the patient *into* the therapist—making it an essentially *unidirectional* process between the intrapsychic unconscious arenas of two separate individuals.

As described in chapter 1, the guiding principle of the middle ground perspective is to merge both individual and relational concepts into an integrated approach. Consequently, middle ground theory acknowledges the value of unidirectional communications between patient and therapist, as well as the usefulness of those communications in illuminating elements of the patient's intrapsychic unconscious (indeed, as described in chapter 2, these kinds of communications underlie the therapist's ability to resonate with the patient's individual transferences). In addition, however, middle ground theory argues that the concept of a relational unconscious is of equal value, and that the two-way exchanges of psychic material that it implies create a mutually defined transference-countertransference matrix that operates side-by-side with other, more unidirectional communications. When both of these dimensions (i.e., the individual and the relational) are taken into account, the therapist's countertransference can be regarded as a potential indicator not only of the patient's (and therapist's) individual unconscious, but also of the unconscious relational field operating between the two (Aron, 1996; S. Gerson, 2006; Lyons-Ruth, 1999; Ogden, 1992, 1994a, 1994b, 2004; Tubert-Oklander, 2006b; Zeddies, 2000).

With these considerations as a background, middle ground theorists have offered several arguments for the use of elective self-disclosure. Of these, three are the most central. The first rests on the observation that because of the continuous mutual influence between therapist and patient, the therapist is, in essence, already revealed by his or her participation in the therapeutic process: "Self-revelation is not an option," says Aron, "it is an inevitability" (1991, p. 40). If the therapist is already revealed, then pretense to the contrary injects a "game-playing" (Shill, 2004, p. 151) atmosphere into treatment, in which the therapist attempts to conform to traditional, but impossible to achieve, ideals of neutrality, authority, and objectivity. Elective self-disclosure is a way of both countering this impression and acknowledging the more "real" aspects of the therapeutic relationship (Renik, 1998a). The second argument focuses on the value of elective self-disclosure in highlighting the relational dimensions that partially construct the patient's psychic reality and that are an inescapable aspect of the human condition. Through the use of disclosure, the therapist exposes the mutual influences operating between the two parties, and thereby helps the patient recognize, understand, accept and contain those aspects of experience that refer beyond the confines of the individual self (Cooper, 1998; Davis, 2002; Hoffman, 1991). Finally, elective self-disclosure can also be used to illuminate the patient's intrapsychic unconscious structures, since the joint examination of the therapist's countertransference can bring the patient's contributions into sharper focus (Aron, 1991). (These latter two uses of elective self-disclosure will be discussed in more detail below, in terms of their capacity to generate *relational insight*.) On the basis of these arguments and others, the use of elective self-disclosure has gained acceptance among a growing number of clinicians (Bollas, 1987; Burke, 1992; Frank, 1997; Greenberg, 1995; Jacobs, 1995; Menaker, 1990; Militec, 1998; Renik, 1999; Tansey & Burke, 1989). This is not to say, of course, that self-disclosure has not continued to be the subject of extended, and sometimes impassioned, criticisms.

THE PROBLEMS WITH ELECTIVE SELF-DISCLOSURE

The most common criticisms of elective self-disclosure have focused on the extent to which its underlying rationale deviates from mainstream analytic theory, as well as the extent to which it, as a technique, appears to replace other techniques that have proven effectiveness (Hanly, 1998). Shill (2004), for example, has argued that as a technique elective self-disclosure ignores the value of transference and resistance analysis, minimizes the patient's internal object world, bypasses instinct-based drives, and perpetuates an illusion that the therapeutic relationship is a reasonable model for relationships the patient will have outside treatment. Kernberg (1997, 2007), in addition, has argued that because of its implied abandonment of the therapist's role as a neutral authority, elective self-disclosure diminishes the therapist's capacity to help the patient work through intrapsychic conflicts—which, in Kernberg's view, is the primary means available to the therapist to help the patient generate insights that are generalizable beyond the particulars of the patient-therapist relationship.

These criticisms are founded, in large measure, on a specific impression self-disclosure's critics have formed of its advocates—that they use the technique excessively, to the point of crowding out many if not all other kinds of analytic intervention. This impression cannot be said to be woven out of whole cloth. Indeed, some advocates of elective self-disclosure, particularly those endorsing the more radical tenets of relational theory, not only suggest that it should be employed as a regular part of analytic technique, but have at least appear to advocate using it spontaneously and without subsequent attempts to interpret or link it to the patient's intrapsychic dynamics, or even to integrate it with other conventions of formal technique (Ehrenberg, 1992; Hoffman, 1994; Orange & Stolorow, 1998; Renik, 1995, 1998a, 1999). Among these writers, moreover, the impression is often given that self-disclosure is curative in itself, simply because it creates a new relational experience, a unique kind of "constructive intimacy" whose value is "heralded more or less on its own" (Gerhardt, Sweetnam & Borton, 2003, p. 538; see also Bass, 2001a; Ehrenberg, 1992; Fiscalini, 2004; Renik, 1993).

Meissner attempted to describe this radical position explicitly. Referring to a 1995 paper by Renik, Meissner summarizes Renik's basic premise in this way: "If everything willy nilly, reveals (i.e., discloses) the analyst, the best policy with few if any exceptions, is to be disclosing and trust to the analytic process to weave whatever consequences into a golden thread" (Meissner, 2002, p. 853). The fact that Renik, in the same paper, explicitly states he is *not* advocating "willy-nilly spontaneous self-revelation by the analyst" (1995, p. 467) suggests the picture some analysts have formed of the radical relational perspective may be comprised somewhat more of impression than reality. Still, Meissner's description cannot be dismissed out of hand, since it at least captures the spirit of some of those theorists' exuberant defense of self-disclosure, if not the explicit content of their words. Similar confusions, for example, about the actual position radical relationalists hold toward self-disclosure have been noted elsewhere in the literature—see for example the exchange between Williams (2001) and Bass (2001a) about the implications of Bass' views in his paper, *It Takes One to Know One* (2001b).

Spontaneous and excessive self-disclosure used merely as a means of creating a new relational experience, in fact, seems to be a practice few advocate explicitly, but that many have criticized convincingly. Because those criticisms, however, are applicable only to the *excessive* use of disclosure, they have not dissuaded theorists, particularly those occupying the middle ground, who advocate its more moderate use at selected moments. Defending a more reasoned and principled use of elective disclosure, these theorists have attempted to reconcile its use as a technique with reconceptualized versions of the traditional principles of authority and neutrality. The result has been a mixed model that suggests that elective self-disclosure, when conducted under specific conditions, can help the patient work toward accomplishing therapeutic goals, whether they are framed in individual or relational terms. It was in this light that Bolognini and Séchaud listed the possible benefits of self-disclosure, which include:

> confirming the authenticity of the analyst and of his interest in the patient's progress; recognizing the other (when possible) as a person; providing direct emotional communication that reduces intellectualization; facilitating a reduction of idealization of the analyst when the situation allows for or requires it; introducing some elements of livable symmetry into the correct frame of the asymmetrical analytic setting; revealing some elements of the analyst's personal psychic situation. (2000, p. 164)

If elective self-disclosure has the potential to be beneficial under specific conditions, the task becomes one of specifying what those conditions are (S. Levine, 2007; Meissner, 2002; S. Pizer, 2006). In what follows I will review the theory that stimulated therapists' interest in this topic, with an eye toward developing specific criteria for determining when self-disclosure is warranted. To illustrate these points, I'll present an example from individual therapy that clarifies some of the fundamental questions about self-disclosure. A case from couple therapy will follow.

GERALD

For the first three years of twice-weekly treatment, my conversations with Gerald were chiefly about the emotional and physical abuse he experienced as a child, and were accompanied by frequent episodes of unrestrained self-devaluation that could trigger severe depressive episodes. By the fourth year, Gerald's self-attacks diminished, which allowed us to deepen our work with his transference and with his narcissistic and dissociated defenses against aggression. At first, his transference was framed symbolically (e.g., he worried about what his dentist thought of him because of his cavities) or in indirect and neutral terms. But as the year progressed, he became more overt and animated in stating that because he wasn't worth being cared about, he didn't understand how I could care about him. Gerald had great difficulty acknowledging the aggression underlying these self-devaluations. Most interpretations I made to illuminate it were ignored, or briefly considered, and then avoided. He clung to his belief that his depression was not caused by his own aggression, but by the "fact" that others couldn't love him.

We addressed the tension between Gerald's aggression and his need to deny it for the better part of a year, making painstaking progress, until the issue came to a head in an unusual session. When I greeted him in my waiting room, Gerald's expression, which seemed to me to say "you don't want to see me because you don't believe I'm worth it," triggered particularly strong emotions in me. I felt hurt and resentful that he continued to see me in this light, and I thought: "After all we've been through together and after all the time I've actually cared about him, he treats me like this."

I was puzzled. Given that I was familiar with the dynamics underlying Gerald's distrust of me, I wondered why I was experiencing these emotions at this particular time. Gerald began the session by speaking about his depression, and he raised an often-repeated association to his mother's sadistic treatment of him when he was ill. He then said of his older siblings that they "barely even offered to help." With this statement, and the way Gerald said it, I realized his anger seemed nearer to the surface than I had ever seen it.

This observation helped me understand my response to Gerald's expression in the waiting room, which I thought had contained the same aggression he now felt toward his family. The fact that his anger now seemed nearer to the surface led me to wonder if it was also more intense than usual when I greeted him, and if this stimulated my unusual emotional reaction. I reminded him of those moments before we entered my office, and suggested he might have wondered if I wanted to see him today. He said he wonders that every time he sees me. I said he seemed to be thinking I was like his family and I would barely want to help. He said that sounded right, adding that he thought I wouldn't want to help because he had not been making progress in therapy.

This last statement reflected three of Gerald's interrelated defenses: denial of aggression, displacement of anger with me onto himself and unconscious refusal to consider the possibility that his behavior had an impact on me. The latter seemed central at this moment, as it facilitated both his denial (how could he have been angry if I was unaffected?) and his displacement of aggression into himself in the form of self-deprecation (I was unaffected because he wasn't good enough to matter to me). These defenses allowed him to discharge aggression without having to think about its meaning and interpersonal consequences. I said, "You're trying to convince both of us I have good reason not to help, but I suspect you're angry about it." He became anxious and said, "I keep coming back because I know you're here to help." With this statement, I wondered if Gerald was attempting to repair me, which suggested he felt he injured me in some way. I then thought it was possible that he perceived, if only unconsciously, my emotional reaction. I decided to explore this possibility. I said he now seemed worried that his distrust had hurt or angered me. He said he didn't know how he could have hurt me: "All I was thinking about was that I don't deserve your help—I wasn't thinking about you at all."

With this admission, it seemed to dawn on Gerald that he *had* excluded me from his thoughts and he might actually have impacted and hurt me. The realization, I thought, arose with anxiety, but also with a trace of interest. To be able to hurt me meant he had standing in his relationship with me—something he hadn't let himself consider before. He asked, uncertainly and tentatively, "*Have* I hurt you?" I thought about my response for a moment, then nodded and said that yes, he had.

ELECTIVE SELF-DISCLOSURE: ERROR OR TECHNIQUE?

Would my self-disclosure with Gerald ultimately prove detrimental to our working relationship? Or was it a legitimate technique to help him integrate the denied elements of his psyche—particularly those pertaining to his place in interpersonal relationships? There are extreme positions on both sides of this debate, with classical analysts arguing against the use of self-disclosure altogether (Rothstein, 1997; Shill, 2004) and a few relational theorists at least appearing to advocate its spontaneous and unexamined use (Bass, 2001b; Ehrenberg, 1992; Renik, 1995, 1999). Meissner has argued that because the implementation, in clinical practice, of either of these extreme positions leaves the therapist "open to countertransference distortions that undermine the alliance and create unproductive misalliances" (2002, p. 845), disclosure cannot be judged *a priori* to be either helpful or detrimental, and must instead be evaluated according to a criterion of whether it fosters therapeutic progress. The decision whether and what to self-disclose, Meissner suggests, "should be guided by the analyst's perspective on neutrality, conceived as a mental stance in which the analyst assesses and decides what, at any given point, seems to contribute to the analytic process and the patient's therapeutic benefit" (p. 827).

Meissner's view, however, raises a pivotal question: What exactly counts as being to the patient's "therapeutic benefit"? This can be restated as a question about the goals of psychoanalysis. For many years, practitioners and theorists accepted the classical view, anchored in individualistic conceptualizations, that the central goal of analysis was to make the unconscious conscious (Freud, 1915, 1919) through the use of interpretation and insight (A. Freud, 1979; Tubert-Oklander, 2006a) for the analysis of transference and resistance (Freud, 1914b). Supporting this formulation was an assumption that the patient's ego would utilize insight to replace pathological internal structures with more adaptive compromise formations (Jacobs, 2001). Because middle ground theory, however, has acknowledged alternative conceptualizations of almost every element in this formulation (including, most centrally, the concepts of the unconscious and transference), it has also necessitated a reconsideration of the goals of analysis altogether.

TENTATIVE STATEMENT OF MIDDLE GROUND MODIFICATIONS TO THE GOALS OF PSYCHOANALYSIS

We've already seen how the middle ground approach has integrated one-person conceptualizations of such phenomena as transference, countertransference and the unconscious with two-person, relational conceptualizations of those same phenomena. The approach's acknowledgment of the relational dimension, however, both in theory and clinical application, has implied that the traditional goals of analysis—to make the *patient's* unconscious conscious through interpretation and insight into the *patient's* transference and resistance—are in need of expansion. Consequently, middle ground theorists have suggested reformulating these goals so they target the dual contributions of both the personal and the relational unconscious. While the development of the patient's insight into intrapsychic dimensions remains of primary importance, so too does the creation of what can be called *relational insight* into the unconscious aspects of their interactions with others (Cooper, 1998). And one of the techniques that can help the patient achieve relational insight is elective self-disclosure.

The development of relational insight through elective self-disclosure serves the patient's interest in two ways. First, it yields information that is directly applicable to helping the patient work through pathological *intrapsychic* conflicts and resistances. Bollas, for example, has said that through self-disclosure "the analyst is able to release certain countertransference states for elaboration and, in so doing, he makes certain split-off elements of the patient available for knowing and analyzing" (1987, p. 207), and Bass has suggested that disclosure establishes "something different from the patient's customary object relations . . . so as to make possible a way of being and relating that is not supported by the 'structures' already in place" (2001a, p. 720). Second, relational insight provides a unique dimension of self-understanding, specifically about the self-in-relationships, that is unavailable through insight into the intrapsychic unconscious. The Barangers, for example, who redefined insight as a "process of joint comprehension by analyst and patient of an unconscious aspect of the field," suggest that it "leads to a reduction in the pathology of the field, and the rescue of the respective parts involved" (Baranger & Baranger, 1966, p. 60). Frank adds that the process of developing relational insight generates "new experiences of mutuality, of constructive intimacy, and of self-awareness" (1997, p. 284).

An implied aspect of insight is that it not only fosters the patient's self-awareness, but also facilitates *containment* (Bion, 1963; Reisenberg-Malcom, 2001) of previously unconscious and unmoderated experience. Containment goes beyond self-awareness in that it entails the moderation of difficult experience so it may be integrated into a coherent, continuous sense of self. Containment is intimately related to affect regulation, mentalization and the capacity to make linkages both within the mind and in interpersonal interactions. In a subsequent section I will suggest that two forms of containment—of the intrapsychic unconscious and of the relational unconscious—are relevant to considerations of self-disclosure. Before I do so, however, it will be helpful to return to Gerald.

GERALD REVISITED

Gerald's response to my disclosure that his distrust hurt me was complex. He worried that he had now given me reason to reject him, but he was also curious about his having an impact on me. "What was it in what I did that hurt you?" he asked. I answered that it was the aggressive devaluation embedded in his distrust of me. "My distrust devalues you?" he asked. I said I knew it had been difficult for him to accept his anger, but his unflattering image of me as not wanting to help revealed his anger nonetheless. He wondered why he was angry with me and added he always assumed he was the "flawed one" in our relationship. I said his distrust indicated he felt I was flawed as well. He said this was the perplexing part of the entire sequence for him: "I've always thought that I thought," he said, "that you were here to help me."

Our discussion of these topics continued into subsequent sessions, in which Gerald began to feel more comfortable speaking of his anger. He was tentative at first, but in the following months he almost eagerly told me of disturbing, aggressive dreams that revealed how deeply enraged he was and had been. As he realized that his belief that he was disconnected from others had protected him (and them) from his rage and so excluded him from the rewards of real relationships, he began to grieve for what he had been missing. This triggered new rounds of anger at the family members he blamed for his losses, but his treatment was now on much more solid footing to understand and metabolize these emotions.

It is now some years after my exchange with Gerald and we are now planning for termination. He told me that my decision to reveal my hurt and anger was a turning point for him. It "pulled" him, he said, out of "complacency," and opened his eyes to "a world that had always been there right in front of me."

RELATIONAL CONTAINMENT

My intervention with Gerald is an example of the use of relational insight and relational containment in the service of developing a patient's awareness and integration of both intrapsychic and relational aspects of his experience. As I've described earlier (see chapters 1 and 2), containment (Bion, 1962b, 1963), or more specifically the relationship of the container-contained, refers to the ability of one participant in an interaction to receive projective identifications from the other, enter into a process of reflection, mentalization, contextualization and mitigation, and return a transmuted and moderated version of the original projections back to the sender (Bion, 1963, 1970; Grinberg, Sor & De Bianchedi, 1997).

As Billow (2003) points out, Bion emphasized the developmental and relational aspects of containment and claimed it to be an interactional source of learning and meaning-generation. Bion's original model of the container-contained was the mother-infant relationship:

> The infant, filled with painful lumps of faeces, guilt, fears of impending death, chunks of greed, meanness and urine, evacuates these bad objects into the breast that is not there. As it does so the good object turns the no-breast (mouth) into a breast, the faeces and urine into milk, the fears of impending death and anxiety into vitality and confidence, the greed and meanness into feelings of love and generosity, and the infant sucks its bad property, now translated into goodness, back again. (Bion, 1963, p. 31)

In this example, containment is interactive in the sense that metabolization and moderation of the infant's psychic material occurs within the context of its relationship with the mother. The content of that containment, however, is intrapsychic, since it originates within the infant's internal world.

Relational containment, in contrast, takes as its content the unformulated elements of the shared, relational unconscious and through reflection, mentalization and contextualization attempts to transform them into tolerable and comprehensible aspects of experience that can be integrated into the patient's sense of self in relationship with others. In my interaction with Gerald, I utilized both intrapsychic and relational containment. My intrapsychic containment targeted his split off aggression and consequent self-devaluations. My relational containment focused on his unconscious use of aggression in devaluing me, his inability to recognize his role in our relationship, and my own emotional responses that were in part linked to his aggression and devaluation.

My choice to augment intrapsychic containment with relational containment followed a certain logic. When Gerald asked if he hurt me, I certainly might have said something that maintained our focus on the intrapsychic—such as "It would surprise you if your aggression had injured me." I believed, however, that by saying this I would have revealed that his distrust *did* have an impact on me, I just would not have specified what it was. As I pictured myself saying those words, they seemed coy and mystifying, rather than authentic and helpful.

I also realized that by remaining quiet about my reaction I would have left unused a relational event that had the potential to move Gerald toward acknowledging his aggression, and away from the insulated position his denial of it had placed him in. Because my hurt and anger were indicators of the central role his aggression played in the relational field between us, I felt that if I could use my reactions to illuminate that role, I might be able to help him contain both the intrapsychic and the relational aspects of himself that he disavowed.

This example from my work with Gerald illustrates that the therapist's use of elective self-disclosure can foster relational insight and containment by calling the patient's attention to the realities of the interactions occurring within the therapeutic dyad. My disclosure, I believe, had its intended effect in large part because it was selective, meaning it was used at a specific moment when it had the potential to help break through Gerald's isolating defenses, and because it was a technique I used sparingly. In my view, more excessive use of self-disclosure with Gerald would have vitiated the impact of each intervention, no matter how much I attempted to link my disclosures back to his intrapsychic and relational experience. It would also have run the risk, as many commentators have observed, of reducing the therapeutic relationship to a personal relationship, thereby interrupting my capacity to listen with "free-floating responsiveness" (Sandler, 1976) to Gerald's transferences, diluting and disrupting our therapeutic alliance, and drawing us into a detrimental pattern in which my disclosures may have become an expected, and hence intrusive, part of our relationship which would have, in effect, forced Gerald into "the role of object" (Aron, 1991, p. 42; see also Gutheil & Gabbard, 1998; Hanly, 1998; Kantrowitz, 1999; Kernberg, 1997, 2007; Meissner, 2002; Shill, 2004).

LIMITATIONS ON THE ROLE OF ELECTIVE SELF-DISCLOSURE

The therapist's failure to protect the therapeutic relationship from the deleterious consequences of excessive self-disclosure reflects, in the extreme, the abrogation of two historically fundamental principles of psychoanalysis and psychoanalytic therapy. Those principles, of authority and neutrality, have been defined in varying ways over the history of psychoanalysis. The traditional perspective on authority, for example, assumed that analysts automatically possessed it on the basis of their superior knowledge of the underlying structures and contents of the patient's mind. One consequence of this perspective was that the analyst's interpretations were viewed as effectively pedagogical, in that they instructed the patient about aspects of themselves of which they presumably had no awareness. A less palatable consequence was that, because analysts' presumed their knowledge was based on objective, scientific fact, they felt justified in labeling their patient's disagreements with their interpretations as resistance (Maroda, 1991; McLaughlin, 1998). As Mitchell has ironically suggested, this viewpoint led to a commonly held assumption that "any patient in his right mind would cede . . . authority and knowledge to the analyst" (Mitchell, 1997, p. 215).

Middle ground theorists have long been uncomfortable with this conceptualization of the analyst's authority. They note that the indeterminate nature of the relational unconscious challenges the very notion of an "objective fact" on which the traditional view is founded. Further, they argue that the joint contributions made by therapist and patient to the relational unconscious should, at the very least, give pause to those theorists who want to defend the unquestioned legitimacy of an *asymmetrical* relationship in which the therapist claims expertise and authority over the patient. This is not to say that middle ground theorists are prepared to abandon the principle of authority altogether. Rather, while they realize that their knowledge, either of theory or of the patient, will never be absolute and will always evolve, they also know that for the good of their patients they must retain responsibility "for being in control and preserving the necessary limits and restrictions that constructively define the therapeutic relationship" (Maroda, 1991, p. 31).

The principle of authority has thus been "relativized" by middle ground theory so that it retains some, but not all of its traditional connotations. A similar transformation has occurred with the principle of neutrality. Traditionally, neutrality has been defined in behavioral terms, according to which analysts were deemed neutral if they committed no acts in the course of treatment that revealed either personal information or personal opinions about the patient. Recognizing the overly restrictive implications of this definition, particularly in the light of middle ground theorists' exposition of the potential therapeutic value of self-disclosure, Meissner has suggested that the concept is due for modernization. Neutrality, he suggests, "lies not in the action, but in the mental process determining whether the action is appropriate and purposeful" (2002, p. 854–855), and is better conceived as an aspect of the therapeutic alliance, in which the therapist evaluates the patient from a "relatively dispassionate, relatively objective, and self-decentered mental perspective" in order to "guide the analytic process in therapeutically beneficial directions" (p. 855).

The primary implication of these modernized versions of neutrality and authority is that neither automatically prohibits the therapist's use of self-disclosure; rather, they now constitute general guidelines for determining when and whether the therapist's self-disclosure may be warranted. Elective self-disclosure, these principles would suggest, may be considered when the therapist has determined (under the exercise of authority) that it has the potential to serve the patient's interests (the principle of neutrality) by leading to greater insight and containment (intrapsychic or relational), resolution of the patient's internal conflicts and resistances, expansion of their capacity for affect management and self-regulation in relationships, and appreciation of mutuality and a deepening of their concepts of both themselves and others.

The following questions, which can be seen as elaborations and specifications of the principles of authority and neutrality, are helpful in determining if a specific act of elective self-disclosure is appropriate, and should be asked by any therapist who is considering such a disclosure. Although the answers to these questions may not always be available to the therapist, the act of asking them will at least help to remind the therapist of the pitfalls of engaging in disclosure without forethought: (1) Does the self-disclosure represent an enactment of uncontained countertransference, or of other unanalyzed neurotic or characterological needs on the part of the therapist? (2) Is the purpose of the self-disclosure to illuminate an element of the patient's experience, whether in the intrapsychic or relational dimension, in order to help the patient achieve both awareness and containment of that element? (3) Is self-disclosure "intended to introduce or lead to interpretation" (Meissner, 2002, p. 837), or to other interventions that help to clarify and contain the patient's unconscious experience, and not act as a substitute for interpretation? (4) Is the patient in a position to hear the intent of the self-disclosure, to think it through, and not be overwhelmed by it? (5) Is the patient in a position, or at a stage of development in treatment, where he or she may be available for the insight and containment that may result from self-disclosure?

In the case of Gerald, my consideration of these questions led me to initially delay my disclosure, because I knew I needed to understand and contain my emotions before their revelation could be useful to him. In that interaction, I did not enact my countertransference, and my reaction did not explicitly appear in our conversation until I guided us toward it. In the following case from couple therapy, I played a more substantive role in a transference-countertransference enactment that was complicated by contributions from all three participants. The principles guiding my subsequent intervention, however, remained the same.

DAVID AND LAURIE

David and Laurie entered couple therapy in the fifth year of their marriage, after two years of escalating conflict and decreasing sexual passion and frequency. Both agreed the first three years of their marriage were happy (although they said their sexual relationship lacked the excitement each hoped for), and their conflicts intensified with Laurie's discovery, two years prior, that David had been in e-mail contact with an ex-girlfriend. David maintained his contact was innocent, but Laurie said he never fully explained his actions, and didn't convincingly express either remorse or empathy for the impact they had on her.

David, an only child, described his father as inflexible, silent, and intolerant of his son's opinions and desires, and his mother as an insecure and unhappy woman who turned to David for comfort, retained tight control over him, and was unable or unwilling to recognize his desire for independence from her. David's experience of these parental characteristics resulted in an internal object that was controlling and devaluing, especially of David's desires and needs for autonomy. When he projected his internal object into others, he expected to be punished and rejected, particularly if his desire was contrary to theirs. Consequently, he developed a cautious and passive manner in his expressions of desire, under which lay a deep-seated anger at the control he felt from others. Because his anger, though, was also suppressed, he substituted secret rebellions for the open expression of desire, which indirectly allowed him to discharge his anger in a passive-aggressive manner.

Laurie's personality complemented David's. The middle child of five, she described her father as a boorish, selfish man, who was frequently violent with her mother and whose least favorite child was Laurie herself. Her mother, who Laurie said was attentive in her early childhood, became increasingly depressed and disengaged as Laurie reached puberty. When Laurie was fourteen, her mother abandoned the family, leaving the children in the increasingly chaotic care of their father. Laurie ran away from home at the age of sixteen to live with friends and relatives. While she retained contact with her siblings, her father, she said, did not protest her absence and did not ask her to return home. At the time of treatment, Laurie had still not been able to locate her mother.

As a result of her neglect and abandonment, Laurie formed a powerful, shame-inducing object in regard to which she felt insecurity, anxiety, and hatred and which created expectations that others neither valued nor desired her, and that she would eventually be abandoned by them. In the first three years of her marriage to David, Laurie's insecurity was relatively mild. Once she discovered his communications with his ex-girlfriend, however, it intensified dramatically. Subsequently, Laurie vacillated between two stances with David: she was either actively enraged at him, or she removed herself into a self-protective detachment. Either position triggered David's fears of rejection and control, which stimulated his own defenses of passivity, avoidance, and secrecy. In a vicious circle, these actions by David further augmented Laurie's insecurities.

In a session early in the second year of treatment, the frustrations created by these interacting dynamics intensified and both partners decided they needed to try something different. Laurie began the session by returning to the topic of David's ex-girlfriend. Ever since the discovery, she said, she had not believed that David wanted her. David remonstrated he *did* want her, but was too afraid and too angry to express it because *she* was so angry and withdrawn. Laurie was unconvinced. Near the end of the session, she said, softly and tearfully, that she wanted David to do two things: "genuinely" apologize for contacting his ex-girlfriend, and tell her, Laurie, "in a way that would finally convince me," that she was the one he wanted. Laurie's tears impacted David. With some tenderness he said he "truly" wanted to give her these things. He then paused, looked away, and said, "But I'm not sure how to go about it. Let me take some time to think it through, and I promise I'll make this better." Laurie, visibly frustrated with David's deferral, turned away and looked out the window. I said to David, "I think as you were considering the possibility of expressing your remorse and desire to Laurie, you also became afraid, and maybe angry, at having to reveal yourself. So you retreated—and that helped to trigger Laurie's retreat." The session was over. As they left, David said to me, "I see what you mean, but I am going to do it."

David began the next session by announcing he had something to say to Laurie. He then spoke to her with a directness I had rarely seen from him. He apologized for his behavior with his ex-girlfriend and he concisely and empathetically summarized the injuries he caused Laurie. As she listened to him talk, Laurie's expression softened and she put her hand on David's knee—indications, I thought, of the same tenderness I'd seen between them in the prior session. David then, however, shifted to describe his love and desire for her. In stark contrast to the directness of his apology, his words now were so abstruse, intellectualized, and dry that Laurie, the purported object of his desire, was hardly discernible in them. Laurie now became upset and said this wasn't desire at all, but David's attempt to avoid the whole topic. My feelings were similar to Laurie's. Doesn't David understand, I thought to myself, that his abstruseness is the opposite of the straightforward expression of desire she wanted? I said to him that his abstractness was another attempt to protect himself from being criticized and overly controlled, but I realized as I spoke that my tone conveyed my frustration. David became defensive and silent, saying he had "tried to do what Laurie had wanted, but no one appreciates it." The session ended with those words.

As I thought about this session afterwards, I realized our final interaction was the result of contributions each of us made, from our own internal worlds. David's fear of being preempted or rejected by Laurie upon expressing his desire was the result, at least in part, of the projection of his controlling and devaluing internal object into her. And the intensity of Laurie's insecurity about David's inability to convince her of his desire for her originated, again in part, from the projection of her shame-inducing object into him, and from her own expectations of abandonment. My own contribution became clear to me later that evening, as I recollected an argument between my mother and father I witnessed when I was thirteen, which started because my father had unilaterally purchased a couch for the living room that my mother hated. I remembered how frustrated I was with him for angering my mother, whose bad moods could last for several days. This is one of my internal objects, I thought: a bungling husband and father who creates anxiety for me about the loss of my access to my mother.

It is possible to think of an internal object, not as a thing (although the word "object" carries that connotation), but as a narrative with a preferred plot line waiting to be told about events and people in the lived environment. In this session, the stories from our three internal objects became intertwined, or intertextualized, to create a new narrative, composed of elements of each, but so melded together that each reinforced the assumptions of the others. It was because of this intertextualization that we each participated in the anxieties and angers that marked our interaction.

David started the next session tentatively, saying he had little confidence in his relationship with Laurie, and no matter what he did, she would see him as a pathetic failure. His mood was depressed, resigned, and passive. I said, "Our interaction last time seems to have had quite an effect on you. I wonder if you're declaring your submission to me and Laurie because you've become more angry or more afraid of showing your desire for her." David responded, "I know that last time nobody said I'm lousy at describing my feelings, and I know what I'm feeling now is irrational, but trying to pursue this, trying to even show my interest in it, feels like I would look ridiculous. Laurie would just sneer at me." I said I thought he wasn't just thinking Laurie would sneer at him, but that I would too. Laurie said, "I wasn't sneering at you." David said, "I know, I know. I know this is all just in me."

This last statement typified David's characteristic defense, in that he attempted to resolve his anxieties about our interaction by retreating into confined and isolated space in his inner world. I said, "David, I'm sure you're anxious and angry about being sneered at by Laurie and me, but I think you're trying to avoid talking about it by claiming this is all just in you." He said, "Well, we've talked about how I can feel like Laurie acts like my mom and my dad, and how I can get scared of her like I was scared of them." I said, "Yes, but I think something more is happening here, having to do with your feeling that I was critical of you. We've attempted to talk about this a couple of times, but we've slipped off each time, as though it's a pretty forbidding topic."

Laurie said she noticed this also. David said, "I think I see what you're talking about. When I was talking last time I couldn't help but feel that you were being critical of me too. I guess I can feel my parents in both of you sometimes." David was making a valiant attempt, but his difficulty in thinking about the reality of our interaction again prevented him from acknowledging I actually had been critical of him. He and I were now facing a crucial moment—one that many therapists will recognize—when I knew my countertransference enactment in the prior session influenced David's self-experience, and that any interpretation I made that limited itself to just his transference would feel like an inauthentic distortion of the truth, and so a disservice to him. I realized, moreover, if I were to let him believe his reaction to me was merely about his, or his and Laurie's, transferences, I would be collaborating with his defense of managing our interaction by backing down from it.

I considered whether this was the time to press this issue and whether by doing so I could help David contain his fear of the interpersonal world and recognize how it led him to negate it and blind himself to it. I had a momentary feeling of relief that this conversation hadn't taken place in the prior session, when, I thought, I was too caught up in my countertransference to be able to speak about it clearly. I decided David was ready for me to be more direct. I said, "You're taking responsibility for elements of your parents that you may have located in me, but I suspect that by doing so you're forgetting that you actually did experience me criticizing you. By claiming it all as your projection, you pull into yourself and away from any confrontation with me. But what would happen if you thought of me as actually having been critical?" This immediately energized David, as though I released a desire to confront his accusers that was inside him all along. He said, "Well, were you being critical?"

Here was a moment of relational truth. I certainly could have attempted to remain neutral, in the behavioral sense, and reflect the question back to him, but that would have amounted to yet another sidestepping of the reality of our interaction. I said, after a pause, "Yes, I think I was." "Why?" he asked. Again I took a moment to think. I realized the details of my reasons for my frustration, rooted in my relationships with my parents, would neither be relevant nor helpful to David, and revealing them would run the risk of diverting our focus from the potential benefits we could gain from this moment. What *was* relevant was that I contributed my own frustration, which David had been at pains to deny, but now seemed willing to consider. I said, "I think it was complicated. I was caught up in the moment with Laurie's frustration with you; but I also added my own frustration, coming from my own history, with how your abstract speech had disconnected you from both of us." David thought about this for a moment and said, "It pisses me off, but I see what you mean. When I withdraw it means I'm giving up trying to work anything out." I nodded, and said, "You're trying to work this out with me right now, including the anger you feel at my criticism." He said, "It feels better not to be so afraid of talking with you honestly."

The conversation proceeded from this point. David talked about feeling scared and angry at my criticism and Laurie spoke about feeling supported in her anger at David by my tone. Both recognized the complex origins of these experiences—origins that were murky and intertwined, but capable of being thought about nonetheless. As therapy progressed, David became increasingly able to confront the situations he feared, which had the unexpected (for David) effect of increasing discussions with Laurie about problems, but decreasing the tensions around them.

CONCLUSION

My interactions with Laurie and David contained both a countertransference enactment and an act of elective self-disclosure. The first was communicated by my tone when I became frustrated with David. If left unaddressed, this enactment had the potential to create a barrier between us that would have compromised my therapeutic alliance with both members of the couple. The enactment, I felt, necessitated my self-disclosure, which occurred when I asked David to consider the real interaction between us. For this disclosure, I followed the principles of authority and neutrality (as modified by middle ground theory), and deliberately made the decision to disclose under the expectation it would facilitate relational insight and containment, which in turn would allow us to refocus on David and Laurie's internal worlds and the roles they played in their interpersonal interactions.

Elective self-disclosure is a double-edged sword. Its dangers are manifold and its undisciplined use can sabotage treatment. When used sparingly, however, under the exercise of the therapist's authority and neutrality, it can deepen the treatment and expose unconscious or disavowed aspects of the patient's experience that would be difficult to reach by any other means.

Chapter Five

The Narcissistic Couple

Disillusion and Shared Resistances

The problem of narcissism in couple relationships is a particularly thorny and difficult one for the couple therapist to manage. The "narcissistic couple" may present with a wide variety of symptoms that engage both partners in a series of compensatory, but pathological, maneuvers that attempt to address the narcissistic needs or fears of one or both partners. Often, even if only one partner is identified as narcissistic, the therapist will find that both partners have unconscious investments in the interactive patterns they have established around that partner's demands. In this chapter, I will first consider the core psychic structures associated with narcissism, since they determine the kinds of accommodations couples will make to narcissism in their relationship. I'll then illustrate how shared narcissistic defenses in a couple can lead to both disillusionment with the process of therapy and shared resistances against therapeutic progress.

CORE STRUCTURES IN NARCISSISM

When surveying the psychoanalytic literature on narcissism, one is surprised to find so many different conceptualizations of a disorder that at first glance appears to be both unitary and characterized by such easily recognizable features as grandiosity, fantasies of omnipotence or perfection, and disregard for the feelings and perspectives of others. It is disconcerting to discover that analytic writers have described many different kinds of narcissism—moral, positive, negative, healthy, pathological, primary, secondary, etc.—from the standpoint of seemingly widely divergent metapsychological assumptions.

One point of dispute between competing conceptualizations of narcissism has concerned the nature of the narcissist's relationship with objects. When Freud, for example, in his essay "On Narcissism" (1914a), differentiated between primary narcissism (the libidinal cathexis of the ego that occurs prior to cathexes of external objects) and secondary narcissism (the withdrawal of cathexes of objects back to the ego), he attempted to make the case that the narcissistic condition is the result of an object-less state in which the ego abandons both external and internal relationships with objects. This lack of relationship with objects explained two symptoms Freud assumed characterized narcissistic personalities: their inability to develop transference and their impenetrable resistance to treatment.

Although Freud's view of narcissism prevailed for some time, its inability to explain the full range of narcissistic phenomena was evident almost from the beginning. In 1924, for example, K. Abraham suggested that a key feature of narcissism is not the absence of objects, but the presence of exploitive relationships with objects that the narcissist is willing to destroy without hesitation (1924). Soon after, Federn (1928) linked narcissism to alienation from objects. With the rise, in the decades that followed, of object relations theory—which asserted that relationships with objects, both internal and external, "are operative from as far back as one can discern" (Segal, 1979, p. 64) and are central to the creation of both normal and pathological psychic structure (Fairbairn, 1952; Klein, 1957)—the view that narcissism derives from an object-less state became increasingly less defensible. Thus, in 1960 M. Balint reversed Freud's theory by equating primary narcissism with "primary object love" (1960, 1965); and in 1964 Rosenfeld suggested that "much confusion would be avoided if we were to recognize that the many clinically observable conditions which resemble Freud's description of primary narcissism are in fact primitive object relations" (1964, p. 332). From the 1970s onward, many writers, including Kohut (1971, 1977), Kernberg (1975), Bach (1985), Rosenfeld (1987), Grunberger (1989), Masterson (1993), Symington (1993) and Green (1999, 2002), have advanced theories of narcissism that have secured, seemingly permanently, the perspective that it arises from, and involves a variety of enactments of, internalized pathological object relationships.

The theory advanced by Kernberg in 1975 is illustrative of this object relational approach to narcissism. For Kernberg, in even the most severe form of narcissism, in which the narcissist establishes a pathological relationship between the "self identified with an object" and "an object identified with the self," "an object relation still exists" (1975, p. 324–25). Kernberg viewed any form of narcissism as originating in internalized representations of relationships in which the self is experienced as "hungry, enraged, empty" and "full of impotent anger at being frustrated, and fearful of a world which seems as hateful and revengeful as the patient himself" (1975, p. 233). To defend against such relationships, the narcissist merges images of the ideal (or idealized) object with the self, thereby creating the narcissist's characteristic inflated self-concept. This idealized self-image then becomes an impermeable internal sanctuary from which the narcissist can both deny his dependency on objects but still use them for either idealizing (to elicit the object's admiration) or devaluing (to evacuate psychic material that is inconsistent with the omnipotent, need-less self-image) projective identifications. In either case, the object is emptied of most content that would make it a *live* object, viz., a real person, and is instead transformed into a "shadowy," "lifeless" "marionette" that makes no claim on the narcissist, and hence poses no danger for him.

Kernberg's theory thus takes two related stands in regard to Freud's views about the narcissist's objectlessness. The first denies the basic premise of Freud's theory: the narcissist is not without objects, but is rather embedded within, and develops from, an unavoidable matrix of pathological object relationships. The second, though, constitutes a recognition that with his idea of objectlessness Freud had captured, if inaccurately, an important aspect of the clinical picture of narcissism: that the narcissist *strives* to avoid, minimize or eliminate object relationships in order to escape the dangers associated with them, even if such escape occurs only in fantasy.

Kernberg's theory also specifies a *method* by which the narcissist achieves his fantasized separateness from objects—through the creation of the ideal-object/ideal-self merger from which dependency on objects is denied, but through which objects are still used to regulate self-esteem. While this particular method is characteristic of the best-known type of narcissism—the grandiose type—it is not the only method of narcissistic retreat available. Two other methods are important for our purposes, because they, along with the core psychic structures on which they rely, are common determinants of interaction in narcissistic couples. They are: (1) the retreat to a fantasized "intrauterine state" (Bolognini, 2008, p. 106) in which the object is not even thought of as an object per se, but rather as a womb-like container in which the narcissist embeds himself and lives as close to a drive-less and need-less state as possible; and (2) the retreat to a state of self-denial in which the narcissist, to avoid dangerous objects, assumes he doesn't deserve contact with objects at all. The first option is best described by Grunberger's (1989) theory of the "monad"; the latter by Green's (1999, 2002) theory of "negative narcissism."

Grunberger's theory of narcissism centers on his hypothesis that in the womb the fetus experiences *prenatal coenesthesis*—a state of near-perfection marred by neither conflict, desire, nor need because the womb takes care of all metabolic, regulatory and protective needs before they arise. After birth, this coenesthetic experience "leaves sufficient traces for it to be fantasized as a state of *perfect bliss, absolute sovereignty* or *omnipotence*" (1989, p. 16). When the infant then has to face the conflicts of growth and development, all of which mobilize drive-related object relating, it may utilize these traces to create a fantasized "monad"—a "nonmaterial womb which functions as though it were material" (p. 3)—in which the illusion that the infant can function apart from object relationships predominates. If ongoing object relationships are too difficult to negotiate, the infant may over-invest in the monadic retreat, and thereby create a narcissistic cocoon in which the cohesiveness of the self is preserved through the fantasized elimination of both drives and objects—with the exception, of course, of the womb-object, which the infant, and the adult narcissist, uses for its containing function but nothing else.

In contrast, in Green's (1999, 2002) "negative narcissism," early failures in drive-related object relating lead to "a kind of rampant paranoia" (1999, p. 97), in which the object is felt to be "a deadly authority which wants neither life, nor development, nor creative capacities but the preservation of a parasitic, cold and rigid relation" (1999, p. 98). There follows a "struggle for territorial integrity" in which the narcissist, finding himself unable to escape his depriving internal object, adopts "a strategy of mutual asphyxiation" through which he hopes to suffocate the object by suffocating himself (1999, p. 98). That is, he *enacts* the depriving and anti-life attitudes of his internal persecutor under the paradoxical expectation that by enacting them—i.e., by embracing the object in relation to which he feels "worthy only of universal contempt" (2002, p. 645)—he can carve out his own separate domain in which *he* has willed his deprivation and thus has escaped the power held over him by his persecutor. Such escapes are only temporary and illusory, since the narcissist's embrace of the internal object implies that it will always be ascendant. As this strategy, though, is repeated and perpetuated, it leads the narcissist to a state of mere survival, punctuated by neither joy nor lively pain, but rather by sadness and deadness. The unconscious reward in the deadness, however, is that it has allowed the narcissist to escape relationships with dangerous objects.

Clearly, the three kinds of narcissistic retreat described by Kernberg, Grunberger and Green—viz., to the ideal-object/ideal-self enclave, to the womb-object of the monad, and to the depriving object in the paradoxical expectation of autonomy and freedom—are not just retreats *from* painful and dangerous relationships with objects. They are also retreats *to* a particular internal structure in which the narcissist finds some form of fantasized protection from those relationships. While these structures differ in content, they are each the result of internalizations of object-related experiences in the infant's early life. Thus, the ideal-object/ideal-self structure to which the grandiose narcissist retreats is the result of an internalized relationship between a loving object and a valued self; the womb-object/contained-self structure that forms the protective enclave of the monadic retreat arises from an internalized relationship between the protected infantile self and an object into whom a fantasized womb has been projected; and the persecutory-object/devalued-self structure to which the negative narcissist retreats results from an internalized relationship between a depriving and devaluing object and a powerless, shamed self. Each of these structures contain polarized material, pushed to the extremes of all-good or all-bad, because they are the result of the narcissist's splitting of the original external object into good and bad part-objects, which have thereafter been unavailable to the tempering influences that might have blended those part-objects into a single, whole object. Thus, the persecutory object remains frighteningly dangerous because the narcissist failed to achieve a position (the "depressive position"—Klein, 1935) from which he could experience the object as *both* good and bad and thereby feel that each side of the object is tempered by the other. With this object retaining its frightening characteristics, the "good" objects (the ideal object and the womb object) also remain polarized (in which their goodness is elevated to unrealistic heights) because only then do they offer the possibility of rescue from the narcissist's frightening bad objects.

In my clinical experience, I've found that, regardless of the kind of narcissism expressed, the typical narcissist's internal world contains all three of these polarized structures in repressed and split-off arenas of the unconscious. These structures, however, vary in terms of their strength, reliability and capacity to radiate their influence through the rest of the self—and it is this variability that influences whether the narcissistic defenses will be grandiose, monadic or negative. Consider, for example, the persecutory-object/devalued-self configuration. This structure is identified by nearly all object relational theories of narcissism (cf., Kernberg, 1975; Masterson, 1993; Robbins, 1982) as playing a powerful, central role in both the development and maintenance of the narcissistic personality, because its frightening persecutory object provides the primary motivation for the narcissist of any type to attempt to escape objects in the first place.

The centrality and power of this structure, however, does not necessarily mean that it is the destination of choice for narcissistic retreat; if this were the case, then most narcissistic patients would be negative narcissists. Rather, it is the relative strength among the three internal structures that determines which particular form of narcissistic retreat is used. If for example, the narcissist as an infant had sufficient experiences with loving objects (in addition to his experiences with persecuting objects) to allow him to internalize a stable ideal-object/ideal-self configuration, then he will be more likely to utilize that structure for his retreat from dangerous objects, thereby creating the grandiose type of narcissism. If he had less reliable experience with a loving object but was still able to evoke reliable fantasies of the womb-object, then he will utilize the monadic retreat. And if his early experiences were such that neither the ideal-object, nor the womb-object is a strong or reliable internal presence, then he will utilize the more desperate measures employed by the negative narcissist, in which the retreat is to the paradoxical embrace of the persecutory-object/devalued-self structure itself.

Although narcissistic patients typically utilize the form of retreat that is linked to their relatively strongest internal structure, there will be times, particularly in intensive clinical work, when traces of the other structures (however weak or ill-formed), as well as the retreats associated with them, will become visible. In some patients, these appearances will only be momentary, as when the negative narcissist wistfully expresses a wish to be loved, but other patients may exhibit a relatively facile capacity to move between each form of retreat. In either case, the ability of the narcissist to alternate between types of retreat implies that the narcissistic structure is not monolithic, but is rather a collection of defenses united by the common purpose of escaping relationships with persecuting objects. Because of the alternating patterns of retreat that some narcissistic patients may exhibit, the clinician is hard-pressed to track the regions of the internal world the patient is accessing at any particular time. The matter becomes even more complicated when the clinician is facing a narcissistic couple, in which cycles of projective and introjective identifications, all rotating around the exigencies of alternating narcissistic retreats, are shared by both partners.

NARCISSISM IN THE COUPLE

One of the underlying themes of both the object relations and the relational understanding of couples is that they *become* couples, in part, because the specific psychic configurations of one partner *fit* the configurations of the other partner in one form or another (Ruszcynski, 1992). This fit, moreover, not only draws couples together, but is also formed and reshaped by the partners, in ongoing ways, as their relationship progresses. The process of establishing the fit between partners is chiefly facilitated by cycles of projective and introjective identification.

In a narcissistic couple, the fit achieved between the two partners commonly appears to revolve around the narcissistic partner's defenses, although a closer look reveals that the internal worlds of both partners have played pivotal roles in determining the course of their relationship. Narcissism, in other words, is not simply the characteristic of one partner, but rather implicates both partners in patterns of behavior that meet the needs of both. Indeed, it is a commonly recognized clinical phenomenon that couple relationships—especially those that are long-lived—with a narcissistic partner develop a joint personality that, depending on the depth of each partner's defenses, is at risk of devolving into stereotyped, repetitive interactions that offer *satisfaction* to neither partner, but that do provide *safety* from internal conflicts for both.

Because narcissistic couples tend to develop joint personalities, it has been tempting for a number of writers to suggest that such couples may be classified into various types (Barnett, 1975; Lackhar, 1992; Slipp, 1984). In this spirit, Maltas (1991) has outlined three kinds of narcissistic relationship: (1) an autonomous-dependent type, in which the narcissistic partner withdraws into a cold, need-less detachment while the dependent partner finds emotional value and meaning in the pursuit of connection; (2) a superior-inferior type, in which one partner devalues the other to gain self-esteem, while the other accepts the devaluations in a masochistic scheme that rewards them for helping the other to be competent; and (3) a twinship type, in which both partners are oriented toward narcissistic gratification, both feel idealized by the other and both gain additional gratification from having a "grandiose object as a possession" (1991, p. 578). While I have sympathy for the endeavor of categorizing narcissistic couples—particularly for heuristic purposes—I'm cautious about it for two reasons. The first is that such categorizations tend to break down in the face of variations *within* types. Consider, for example, two couples who are categorized as autonomous-dependent, according to the schema above. In each couple, the "non-narcissistic" partner may participate in the deprivations entailed in the relationship out of a wide variety of motives, including, among others, altruistic, masochistic or narcissistic needs. These unavoidable differences in the motivations of the participating partners make such categorizations less helpful than they at first appear. The second reason is that, as I've already suggested, narcissistic partners do not always utilize just one form of narcissistic retreat. Consequently, within the course of any single relationship, the narcissistic partner may alternate, sometimes rapidly, between being disengaged and removed (as in the monadic retreat), idealizing, controlling or critical (the grandiose retreat), or depressed, cold and withdrawn (the negative retreat). With each variation, the other partner is given the challenge of unconsciously finding a way to match parts of his or her own personality to whatever form of retreat the narcissistic partner is currently using. In my experience, I've found that in relationships that have had, over the years, many opportunities to become familiar with the narcissistic partner's patterns of retreat, the two partners typically establish a more fluid kind of joint personality, in which each becomes quite facile in rapidly adapting not only their own psychic organization, but the shared unconscious organization of the couple, to the shifting strategies employed by the narcissistic partner. Such was the case in my treatment of Olive and Shawn, who I will now describe.

OLIVE AND SHAWN

Olive and Shawn were self-referred for couple therapy because Olive caught Shawn in an affair with one of his colleagues. The two attempted to manage the stresses associated with her discovery on their own, but found they could not. In our first session, they told me they were on the verge of breaking up and the only thing preventing them was their commitment to their six-year-old child. I noted the matter-of-fact way Shawn discussed his affair (it lasted for a year and a half), and the rational-sounding arguments he advanced to convince Olive there was little to be upset about. I also noted Olive listened to these arguments and seemed half-convinced.

As therapy progressed, Shawn's basic assumptions about the nature of his relationship with Olive became clearer. He treated her as though her primary role was simply to provide the conditions under which he could do anything he wanted, without contributing an equal share to the relationship on his own. Shawn was a moderately successful artist who rented a studio with other artists. By both partner's reports, he spent much of his day talking with friends, going to coffee shops, reading, and only intermittently painting, and he rarely devoted time to Olive or their child: he helped transport the child to school and other activities only one day a week, and he often scheduled meetings with friends and other artists during the evenings—the only time Olive was free. Olive, on the other hand, worked full-time, arranged most meals, did most of the cleanup around the house, and managed the largest proportion of the child's schedule. Although she complained about the lack of balance in their relationship, her complaints were weakly formed and never gained traction. In each instance she encountered an unalterable inability on Shawn's part to recognize there was any problem in the way the relationship was already structured.

Olive came from a strict and religious family that rarely spoke about emotions or emotional topics. She knew her mother loved her, she said, but she rarely heard any acknowledgment or saw any demonstration of it. Instead, her mother was exacting, obsessive, and rule-oriented. As long as Olive and her siblings stayed within the bounds of what was expected of them, they experienced a peaceful, if not particularly warm household. If they disappointed their mother by not living up to expectations, they were punished by anger and silence, but also by the cool and detached destruction of something (such as a toy) they liked. Olive said she learned never to challenge the dictates and decisions of her mother, because the consequences of such challenges were usually more injurious than the mother's original action. Her father, she said, provided a model for such acquiescence: from early in the marriage he steadfastly avoided conflict in the family by leaving significant decision-making to his wife.

As a result of these experiences, Olive internalized two separate representations of her mother. Under the most dominant representation, the mother was felt to be demanding, punitive, and the source of painful consequences if Olive wasn't obedient or compliant. In regard to this mother, Olive had at least three well-developed emotional positions—that of the bad (or guilty) child, the frightened child, and the angry child. These positions were not fully integrated within Olive's internal world and she moved between them without being able to come to a more moderated or contained stance—either toward her own anxieties or toward the urgency of the felt demands from her internal mother. Consequently, when she was in the bad or frightened child position, she felt compelled to demonstrate she was not raising protest and not making a scene. The angry child, on the other hand, made only rare appearances and typically was quickly drawn back into the unconscious by overwhelming feelings of guilt. Olive's other internal representation, of a loving and protective mother, was constructed in part by actual experiences with her mother, but also in part by fantasy. Although this internal mother was felt to be protective, such protection was only available contingently: Olive earned it only if she was particularly convincing in demonstrating her devotion. The structure of Olive's internal world, then, was analogous to that of a narcissist: she had an internal persecuting presence of which she was frightened, and which she attempted to escape in order to find her way to a good and loving mother.

Shawn was the fourth of five children, also raised in a religious family. His older sibling was only twelve months his senior, while his younger sibling arrived sixteen months after his birth. Shawn described his mother as almost always occupied with something else—usually his other siblings. Although at times his mother was warm, more often she conveyed how tired and harried she was, and how her nerves were frayed. Shawn said he often suspected his mother did not care for him and used her exhaustion as an excuse to avoid him. This thought, in turn, raised intense primitive anxiety for Shawn, which was augmented by his mother's pattern of periodically exploding in a near-paranoid rage, viciously berating everyone in the family. When these rages occurred, his mother retreated to her bedroom for several days.

Shawn described his relationship with his father tentatively, as though he was unsure of its real foundation. He said his father was a brilliant man, a highly respected attorney, whom Shawn admired and desperately wanted to please. There were times, he said, when he felt he pleased his father, and those times were described in blissful terms. But when Shawn felt he disappointed his father, then his intense and primitive anxiety emerged once again. In one session, for example, Shawn related how his father once promised to watch Shawn play an evening baseball game. Shawn waited all through the game for his father to appear, and even after the game stayed at the ballpark, hoping his father had been delayed by something out of his control. Finally, Shawn walked home alone, "crying and whimpering for what felt like hours."

From these experiences Shawn developed a richly endowed persecutory-object/devalued-self internal object relationship, in which he felt an intense, paranoid anxiety about criticism or failure. Because he projected this perse-cutory object into others, especially Olive, he felt, unconsciously, that deval-uation and judgment constituted the only expected outcome of relationships. In defense against these dangers (whether internal or projected), Shawn re-treated internal structures available to the narcissistic patient: the ideal-ob-ject/ideal self, and the persecutory object the womb-object/contained-self configurations devalued-self structure itself. By far, Shawn's most common retreat was to the womb-object/contained-self structure. From this internal position, he then projected the womb-object into those around him, leading him to expect them to play the role of a perfectly providing parent who was willing to give him everything he wanted without asking for anything in return. In addition, because of this projection, Shawn felt under no obligation to think about or be cognizant of the internal experiences of others. In fact, he seemed to assume they did not have internal worlds at all, especially internal worlds that could harm or devalue him—such was the extent of his monadic retreat. This was why Shawn was not bothered by Olive's complaints about their relationship: While at the core of his psychic structure he experienced her complaints as dangerous persecutions, in his monadic retreat he eliminat-ed his capacity to recognize her complaints mattered and instead saw her as the conflict-free gratifier of all of his needs and desires.

Although the monadic retreat was Shawn's preferred defense, he at times also utilized the grandiose or the negative narcissistic retreats. Of these two, the grandiose retreat, in which he attacked Olive for not doing enough for him under the self-aggrandizing assumption he deserved more from her than she already gave, was more common. He reverted to negative narcissism, in which he became depressed, lethargic, and self-debasing, only in times of high anxiety (such as prior to an exhibition of his work) when no other defenses succeeded in protecting him from his internal persecutions.

As I suggested earlier, couples in which one partner utilizes multiple narcissistic retreats tend to develop a fluid joint personality that rapidly adapts to whatever defenses that partner is relying on in the moment. In Olive and Shawn's relationship, that fluidity was achieved and was held in place by the fit between the dominant internal dramas of each partner. Where Shawn's internal drama was of a devalued, anxious, and frightened child who's pri-mary strategy for safety was to retreat from dangerous objects into grandiose and monadic enclaves, Olive's drama was of a frightened child who found safety by denying her own needs and becoming almost exclusively oriented toward the needs of her mother. The internal structures underlying these dramas complemented each other in multiple ways, thus creating the facility with which they could adapt to each other's shifting emotional positions. Thus, when Shawn projected his womb-object into Olive, to effect his monadic retreat, she identified with it because it matched the forbearance and tolerance her child self was required to show to her demanding internal object, which, in turn, she projected into Shawn; and when he projected a devalued object into her so he might regain his grandiose sense of value, she could also identify with that object because of its resonance with her bad or guilty self. The mutual projective and introjective identifications between the partners had, in fact, created a fairly stable, if pathological and sometimes painful, relationship in which neither partner seemed particularly motivated to change the basic foundations of their interactions. In a moment, I'll describe a session in which these resistances, anchored in the joint personality they constructed, became a specific focus of treatment. Before I do, however, it will be helpful to review the foundations of disillusion in a narcissistic couple.

DISILLUSION AND RESISTANCE IN THE NARCISSISTIC COUPLE

Because the separateness from dangerous objects that the narcissistic patient seeks is necessarily an *illusion* (because it cannot occur in actuality), he is particularly prone to experiences of disillusionment. These occur when (1) the patient brings into a relationship, whether with a spouse or therapist, transferential expectations that the other person will perform the functions (e.g., containment, protection, admiration, identification with devaluing projections, etc.) dictated by the particular internal structure to which the narcissist has retreated, and (2) that person somehow violates those expectations. The most common way this disillusionment occurs in couple therapy is when the less narcissistic partner, perhaps with the encouragement of the therapist, refuses to conform to the outlines of the narcissist's projections, and instead asks that the validity of his or her experience be recognized. To the narcissist, this refusal is tantamount to the intrusion of an alien object whose dissimilarity from his projections makes it unpredictable and full of potential danger. This, in turn, triggers the narcissist's paranoid anxieties, which then re-energize his efforts to re-establish the couple's narcissistic regime.

The narcissistic patient's attempts to re-establish the characteristic patterns of the couple's shared narcissistic patterns create a natural source of resistance to the progress of therapy. While this resistance may remain located solely in the narcissistic partner, in which case it will create a triangulating obstacle to treatment, it is equally possible that it will spread into the shared experience of both partners. For example, the emotional investment the narcissist pours into re-asserting his narcissistic defenses will often act as a siren call to the other partner, asking him or her to pitch in to help the narcissistic partner escape his fear. If the other partner has already been participating in a joint personality organized around the narcissistic partner's defenses, then that partner will find it difficult to refuse the narcissistic partner's requests for help—particularly since those requests speak to the same valencies that had led to the creation of the joint personality in the first place. Consequently, the two partners may band together in the creation of a *shared* or *intersubjective resistance* (S. Gerson, 1996), which effectively becomes a shared transference in which they join together in refusing the therapist's help in transforming the narcissistic patterns in their relationship. These shared resistances reflect the couple's fear of change and their attempt to halt or at least titrate its pace (Bromberg, 1995), but they can also lead to the co-creation of a "confusion of tongues" (Wolstein, 1992), in which therapist and patients are suddenly working toward diametrically opposing goals.

SHARED RESISTANCE IN OLIVE AND SHAWN

I'd like now to describe a sequence of sessions that illustrates an instance of disillusionment and shared resistance in my work with Olive and Shawn, and that also illustrates the unexpected ways such resistance can embroil the therapist in countertransference reactions that, unless examined, have the potential to further the cause of the couple's resistance, rather than abate it. This sequence occurred at the beginning of our second year of treatment. We'd worked enough with Shawn's defenses that he could discuss, at least to some extent, his anxiety about criticism and the extent to which he tried to protect himself against it. In the session, for example, just prior to the sequence I will describe, Shawn told us about waiting for his father at the baseball game. Because Shawn seemed quite moved in that session, I think it gave all of us a sense that something had softened in the rigid patterns between him and Olive, and it seemed to give Olive a feeling that she had license to reveal some of her complaints about him. Consequently, in the following session she suggested, with a surprising forcefulness, that Shawn was self-centered and didn't fully appreciate all she did to maintain their relationship. At first Shawn listened to Olive, but he soon became enraged, and brutally criticized her for never doing enough for him. That was the main reason he had the affair, he said—because Olive was so inattentive to him and his needs.

    This response signaled Shawn's shift from the monadic retreat, which he most often utilized and which Olive had just criticized, to the grandiose retreat, from which he then utilized two additional defenses: first, he projected the "badness" or failure away from himself and into Olive, so that he then deceived himself into believing she was the only person who deserved criticism; and second, he then elevated himself into someone who "deserved more," which effectively communicated to Olive that she should idealize him in the same way he idealized himself. The brutality with which he attacked Olive was itself a measure of just how terrified he was of the persecutory aspects of his internal object. The session ended in a standoff: Olive held to her criticism and insisted she thought their relationship was unbalanced; and Shawn held fast to his anger.

When they entered my office for the next session, it was immediately apparent Olive and Shawn's moods had shifted substantially. Shawn was back in his blissful monadic state, in which he conveyed everything was going perfectly and there were no problems between him and Olive. He did not refer, for example, to our prior session, nor did he express any interest in what had transpired for Olive since then. Instead, he told both of us how excited he was to spend time with a famous artist from San Francisco, and how he then sat in a café discussing that artist's work with friends until past the dinner hour. The purpose of these reports did not so much seem to be to convey information as to evoke within himself a reminder of the privileged and protected state he convinced himself, in his monadic retreat, was the primary nature of his life.

As Shawn exhibited this attempt to retrieve and re-assert his preferred narcissistic defense, I watched Olive's response. She seemed to be in a complex and, perhaps, oscillating state. On the one hand, she looked angry and frustrated with Shawn's domination of the conversation—a feeling, I thought, that had some continuity with her complaints from the prior session. On the other hand, she looked defeated, as though she conceded the fight and now meekly accepted Shawn's directions. This mood, of course, reminded me of Olive's acquiescence to her mother and I was aware I felt a desire to rally to her defense and encourage her to continue to challenge Shawn's narcissism. As I reflected on these feelings, I also knew I harbored some anger at Shawn. I wanted him to realize this was not an appropriate way to treat a partner.

The session continued and the conversation shifted to other topics, but still neither partner mentioned the conflict from the prior session. It was at this point I suspected a collusive resistance, one rooted in a shared transference, had arisen to prevent revisiting that conflict. I suspected that Olive, feeling the intensity of Shawn's anxiety from the prior session, had unconsciously decided to join Shawn in his attempt to reassert his monadic retreat and, therefore, reassume her role of his uncomplaining provider and protector. As I considered these possibilities, I decided something needed to be said about what the couple refused to address. At an appropriate point I asked what became of their disagreement from the prior session. Their answers surprised me. Olive asked, "What disagreement?" and Shawn said, "Oh, that wasn't really a disagreement. We were just fine afterward." These responses convinced me I was indeed facing a mutually constructed resistance, according to which both partners treated the couple as though it was an unblemished container in which no conflicts occurred, and me as though I was an irrelevant provider of containment in which their unconflicted relationship could proceed (viz., I had become a womb-object for both partners!). In other words, both partners resolved Shawn's disillusionment, after Olive's complaint, by returning to and enacting, with energetic and almost perverse single-mindedness, his predominant narcissistic defenses.

Although I felt I understood, at least to some degree, what was happening in this session, I was also aware I now felt frustrated with both Shawn and Olive. Consciously, my frustration centered on my realization that by suspending the discussion of their conflicts, they were undermining their chances to create meaningful change. I wondered, however, whether my frustration also constituted a countertransference resonance with something else that happened in the couple. As I explored my frustration, I realized a thought was emerging on the horizon of my awareness: Olive was a "coward" and Shawn was a "jerk." Was this *my* thought, I wondered, of *theirs*? I listened further to Olive and realized that although she was acting defeated, she also seemed to carry traces, hidden but not perfectly so, of anger—and it seemed her anger might be both with herself (did she think of herself as a coward?) and with Shawn, for coercing her to submit to him. As I thought of the session's interactions in this light, I then realized Shawn's breezy dismissal of the conflict from last week might also be a dismissal of the conflict in this very moment. It then made sense to me to think that perhaps he realized Olive was angry with him and saw him as a jerk, and he was utilizing his standard narcissistic defenses because he was frightened of her anger and didn't trust he could manage it in any other way.

Armed with these possibilities, I decided to push further into the dynamics of the moment. I said that perhaps a hidden or unconscious agreement not to approach the difficult topic from the last session had occurred between them. I added this seemed to indicate the topic was frightening for both, possibly for different reasons. At first they responded with silence, as though they hadn't understood me. Then three things started to happen at once. First, Olive doubled down on her refusal to revisit the conflict by saying she was resolved about any issues she had raised. Second, Shawn's anxiety about conflict and disillusionment started to rise again, especially as I continued to remind them of the details of the prior session. And third, *I* came to be seen as the one who was injecting disharmony into their relationship by perversely raising an issue that, in their minds, was resolved. In a word, I now occupied Olive's position from the prior session, but now not only was I the target of Shawn's anxiety and anger, but I was also the object of her abandonment and perhaps anger as well.

I had inadvertently become implicated in a three-sided transference-countertransference entanglement. I immediately wondered how I got there. Although it was difficult to think through at the time, in subsequent discussions the following became clear: Shawn and Olive had indeed come into this session with a mutual resistance (mobilized by both partner's fear of Shawn's disillusionment) to further exploration of the real foundations of their relationship. In this resistance, they each denied their relationship contained any conflicts, although in reality both revealed, in this session, substantial conflicts that motivated the mutual construction of their resistance. Olive, for example, was torn between wanting to stand up to Shawn and feeling guilty for that desire, which then led her to feel obligated not to do so. And Shawn was conflicted because although he attempted to regain his blissful state, he still felt, unconsciously, that there was danger present in his relationship with Olive, primarily in the form of her criticism. These conflicting elements, repressed and unconscious as they were, were then split off by each party and projected in my direction. For my part, I obligingly resonated with those projections (beginning with the moment when I realized I was thinking of her as a coward and him as a jerk) and felt frustrated and critical in my countertransference. When I made my intervention, although I believed I contained my countertransference, I have no doubt, in a subtle way, my communication came across as judgmental—especially to two individuals who were already operating in the presence of internal, if repressed, persecutory objects. In response, both partners unconsciously and automatically sealed the meaning of the event: I was the one who was the source of conflict and, hence, the appropriate target of anger and exclusion.

The enactment of our entanglement took place over perhaps a ten-minute period, but it was to this period that we returned repeatedly in subsequent sessions. Through our analysis, Shawn was ultimately able to accept his history had created in him an intense anxiety that led him to experience even the subtlest or well-meaning criticisms as terrifying, and to defend himself he either denied the criticism altogether (the monadic retreat), or attacked its validity and elevated himself above it (the grandiose retreat). (Shawn's negative narcissistic retreat did not make an appearance during this sequence.) Olive, on the other hand, acknowledged her tendency to submit to Shawn—in part because she was afraid of his terror and anger, and in part because this was how she had soothed her mother. These realizations helped the couple to recognize the joint personality their complementary defenses created, and from that they were able to negotiate conflicts somewhat more effectively. Because the couple ended treatment prematurely to relocate to another city, however, we were not able to complete our work. When I last saw them, Shawn's narcissistic retreats were alive and well, if moderated by the insight and containment we engendered, especially through our analysis of the couple's shared resistance. Olive's fear of her internal mother also could still haunt her at inopportune times, although throughout treatment she steadily gained in her capacity to tolerate her fear of refusing to be coerced into compliance.

CONCLUSION

Working with a narcissistic couple tests the therapist's ability to balance the treatment's focus between the individual or intrapsychic configurations in each partner and the relational elements that emerge in the mutual interactions between them. When, in particular, the treatment reaches the point of disillusionment for the narcissistic partner (which it necessarily will if the structures of that partner's retreats are to be opened for analysis), and in response the couple develops a mutual resistance to the process of treatment itself, the therapist must utilize restraint and self-analysis in order to avoid being drawn into the seductive call of the patients' mutual projections, all of which may be focused on bringing therapeutic progress to a halt.

Chapter Six

Crypts, Phantoms, and Desire

Intergenerational Trauma in a Marital Relationship

A child of a traumatized parent lives in a divided state in which her self is not entirely her own, but is occupied by the ramifications of the parent's trauma, and the parent's inability to express, work through or even know its content. The child is haunted by the parent's failure to metabolize their traumatic experience, and thereafter is spurred by the haunting to try to rescue the parent, to solve the riddle in the gap of their self-understanding. This rescuing occurs in registers of the child's mind that are not only unconscious, but that are also alien to her identity; because fragments of the parent's unthought and unspoken experience are lodged in her own stream of experience, she enacts, without knowing why, dramas that were the parent's, not her own. And because these dramas were mute in the parent, their presence in the child creates psychic dead zones that suppress inherent liveliness and desire.

In this chapter I will explore the effect these internalized fragments of a parent's trauma, which Abraham and Torok (1994) called *phantoms*, have on both the individual and the couple. We will discover that when a phantom becomes lodged in an internal object, that object has a radically different character than other objects because the phantom's muteness renders it virtually impenetrable. Because of this impenetrability, the phantom functions in the couple like an inscrutable third party that, in order to be understood and exorcised, requires the therapist to investigate not only the patient's traumas, but the traumas of the parent as well. The phantom thus introduces into the individual and the couple a different kind of relational experience—one that

redraws the boundaries of psychopathology and extends the realm of possibilities for its cure by suggesting the existence within an individual of a collective
psychology comprised of several generations, so that the analyst must listen
for the voices of one generation in the unconscious of another. (Rand, 1994, p.
166)

CINDY AND BOB

Both in their mid-forties, Cindy and Bob entered treatment because their
relationship lacked emotional and physical passion. They were like acquain-
tances, they said, who happened to live together. They were sexually intimate
on only rare occasions and when they were, Cindy felt no desire and found
sex tedious, and Bob performed perfunctorily with no attempt to establish an
emotional connection. They were considering discontinuing their sexual relationship, but both felt this indicated something was amiss in their broader
relationship.

Cindy and Bob were polite with one another, but underneath their poli-
tesse seemed to be an anxiety about what could be unleashed if they became
fully engaged. Bob's deepest fear, for example, was of triggering Cindy's
anger, which was sometimes sharp, he said, but mostly was expressed
through her dull and deadened retreats. To protect himself from this anger, he
utilized a strategy of passivity and non-responsiveness that was designed
both to instigate as few conflicts as possible and to soothe Cindy when she
was upset. Cindy, on the other hand, seemed committed to live her life
following a strict injunction: Do not call attention to yourself; do not have
any needs or desires. In obedience to this injunction, she pursued no hobbies
or enduring interests, developed few friendships, and was undistinguished in
her career. Even her voice seemed to embody her abandonment of desire: she
spoke so softly I strained to hear her in many of our sessions. Moreover, in
most instances, with some notable exceptions, Cindy steadfastly *collapsed*
upon any initial display of spontaneity, desire, or energetic engagement. By
"collapse" I mean the rapid withdrawal of energy and a replacement of the
spontaneous moment with a restrained and somber passivity.

One of the exceptions to this pattern occurred during the fifth month of
treatment, when the couple had an argument at home about a dress Cindy
wanted to buy. Ordinarily an issue like this would have generated no conflict,
because Cindy would have had little desire one way or the other. When Bob,
however, balked at the price of the dress, she became uncharacteristically
insistent. Regressing to the point of "behaving like a child," she loudly and
repeatedly insisted she wanted the dress and deserved to have it. She then
angrily accused Bob of being "mean" and of not wanting her to "look pretty."
The conflict lasted through the evening and ended with Cindy's retreat to the
guest room. Neither spoke again about the dress or the argument.

The collusion of silence between Cindy and Bob extended to their treatment. For four sessions, they didn't report the incident, even though it was an unusual occurrence and related to the issues that brought them to treatment. It finally came to light when Bob, in an attempt at humor, reminded Cindy of how "crazy" she got over the dress. As he said this, Cindy gave Bob a furious look, but said nothing. The atmosphere in the room then shifted and both partners became reticent and pensive. When I noted the change in mood, they described the incident, although their reports were hampered by obvious anxiety. As we explored that anxiety, it emerged that both were afraid to rekindle the argument, which they seemed to regard as toxic and dangerous.

Their fears were enacted only a few moments later. As I attempted to gather information about the argument, I asked what I thought was a simple clarifying question. I said, "The dress was beyond your budget?" Cindy responded immediately. "You don't have to rub it in," she said, "Bob already has."—as though I just accused her of something shameful. I said she seemed to feel I was being critical of her, and she said, angrily, "I don't know what you were trying to do." "But you feel I was shaming you," I said. Her response now was only a nod and a firm set to her jaw. For the rest of the session, she remained passive and sullen and responded to my attempts to engage her with either silence or brief answers. Just before the session ended, however, she announced she had something she wanted to say. "This whole thing," she said, sweeping her arm to include both Bob and me, "reminds me of my mother, who all my life punished me for having any desires at all."

As we were to discover, many layers of internal and interactive dynamics were at work in shaping this session. These layers didn't emerge easily and it took many sessions for us to formulate them and to understand their specific contributions. Initially, we focused on the couple's most obvious transferences. The first, a transference-countertransference entanglement, co-constructed and enacted by both partners, had led them to delay telling me about their argument and to be frightened of the consequences when they did. The second was Cindy's individual transference toward me, in which she became certain I shamed her and she had done something for which she "should" (although she was conflicted about this) feel shame. These transferences, we discovered, were rooted in aspects of each partner's internal worlds that were linked by thematic similarities.

Cindy reported she was raised by a "cruel" and "shaming" mother who regularly disparaged her when she expressed need, pleasure or, especially, desire. "There were times," she said, "when I felt my mother wished I hadn't been born at all." Her mother's cruelty particularly targeted erotic matters. When anyone told Cindy she was pretty, for example, her mother ridiculed her for being pleased by the comment, and when Cindy expressed interest in a boy, her mother told her not to be "idiotic" for believing in love. In response to her mother's criticisms and attacks, Cindy, early on, realized safety lay in being "half-dead"—that is, in withdrawing and suppressing her desire and spontaneity so she presented as small a target as possible. As a result, she internalized a critical and shaming maternal object in whose presence she felt frightened, paralyzed, and ashamed, but about whom she also felt a hidden rage that clearly emerged in the above session.

Bob said he was raised in an intact family with a loving but passive mother, who created a "safe haven" to which he turned, if he could, when he became afraid or anxious. The chief source of anxiety for Bob was his domineering father, who was prone to frequent and irrational rages full of caustic attacks on whomever had frustrated him. Bob felt he was a target of these attacks more frequently than his other siblings and in response he learned to "go numb" and wait until his father's irrationalities subsided.

Each partner thus entered the marriage with similarly frightening internal objects and similar defenses of submission and self-suppression. Their mutual projections of these objects into each other, as well as Cindy's periodic expressions of anger, created the transference-countertransference entanglement in which each felt reinforced to see the other as emotionally dangerous and to use their customary defenses against them. This entanglement was the reason their relationship had become passionless and it also explained why they were afraid to mention their argument to me: in effect, they worried that even describing it in retrospect courted new danger. Cindy's individual transference toward me was founded on similar mechanisms. Her projection of her internalized attacking mother into me resulted in her certainty that I shamed her, against which she then felt compelled to defend herself, first through anger, then through withdrawal and passivity.

This was the first picture we formulated of Cindy and Bob's internal worlds and of the interactions between them. Even as we developed this picture, however, material emerged that led me to suspect other factors were involved. The first indications of these additional factors were in Cindy's associations, made from time to time, which didn't fit with the story we were telling. In one session, for example, as we discussed her habit of rarely purchasing anything for herself (she hadn't purchased the dress), she said, matter of factly, that she really didn't want anything. When I said, thinking of the dress, "You don't want the dress anymore?" she responded: "Bob would kill himself if I wanted anything that badly." Later in the same session, she said, "My wanting that dress cut him to the quick."

These associations, and others like them, suggested an alternate internalized structure in Cindy—one from which she viewed herself, not as fearful and ashamed, but as dangerous and toxic; and from which others were seen not as attacking and shaming, but as suffering from the dangers she posed them. At first I thought this structure referred to Cindy's anger, and that this was what she felt was toxic to others. But it soon became apparent that, in her eyes, the most dangerous aspects of her personality were her desire and liveliness.

In another session, Cindy described how her liveliness was the source of her mother's pain. "My mother's moods," she said, "dominated the household. When she was upset, everything had to stop so we could talk her off the edge." She paused, then said, "My mother was always on the edge. She was mean to all of us, but she also needed so much from us. I remember her fear. It was always there just before she blew up. I never forgot how much she suffered from it." Cindy's tone, especially in the last sentence, carried a tenderness that starkly contrasted with the fear and shame she expressed on other occasions. As I thought about this tenderness, I felt I had just heard a mother describe her concern for an injured child, not vice versa. I said, "You understood your mother deeply, and in many ways became her caretaker." Cindy got tears in her eyes and said, "She needed a lot of protection." I asked, "And making everything stop was a way of protecting her?" Cindy said yes, then added, "What my mother really needed protection from was me—especially if I was excited about anything—like if I found a ladybug or if I liked the way I'd done my hair, or if I'd seen a new toy I wanted—it was all so painful for her."

The image of Cindy's mother conveyed in this sequence was entirely different than the shaming, attacking mother we had considered. This new image was of a mother who suffered from Cindy's liveliness and who, because of her suffering, elicited Cindy's empathy and desire to offer protection through deadening herself. This alternate image thus revealed a second internal object relationship—a suffering-mother/protective-child configuration—that we would discover was as powerful as the first in terms of its capacity to influence the course of Cindy's experience and behavior.

The interactions among the three of us about the dress were an example of the dual influence of Cindy's two internal object relationships. When Cindy insisted, in her child-like way, she wanted and deserved the dress, she allowed herself to engage in a rebellious act of desire that threatened not only to draw the attacking mother's criticisms, but also to cause the suffering mother pain. When the energy in Cindy's rebellion subsided, her internal configurations became re-energized, leading her to project both objects into Bob, and subsequently me. Thus, from one perspective she experienced each of us as attacking and shaming, but from the other she saw us as suffering from her desire. In this light, the "collapse" of her desire for the dress and her refusal to participate in subsequent discussions about it could be seen as addressing the two unconscious goals of protecting herself from attack, and protecting us from the suffering her desire caused us.

Cindy's dual internal object relationships, then, contained two forms of pain or trauma: the first pain was Cindy's own; but the second resided in her internal representation of her mother. As we attempted to explore these two forms of pain, we discovered there were radical differences in the way they were held in her internal world. When Cindy spoke about her own pain, related to attacks by her mother, her associations came rapidly, and were filled with many emotions, among which despair, shame, and anger were predominant. These associations, moreover, were multi-faceted, energized, and attached to memories in which her trauma was a real component that could be described in detail. This pain, in other words, was "empirical," in the sense it was grounded in memories of real experiences in Cindy's life.

In contrast, when she spoke of her mother's pain, which she projected into Bob and me, she could offer little or no explanation for it, and could provide no details that explained its origin. Although she had many memories that referred to it, in the form of her mother's suffering, none of them contained elaborations of the pain's meaning or topography, and none could describe any specific experiences of her mother's that originally gave rise to it. It was as though this pain was an *a priori* assumption for which Cindy had no evidence but which she never questioned. When I asked her, for example, how her desire caused Bob and me to suffer, she said, "I don't really know. I just know that it does." When I asked how her desire caused her mother's suffering, she said, "I don't know that either. I just know that it was always there and that anything I did that showed I was having fun or that I wanted or needed anything caused it."

The contrast between these two forms of pain was striking. Cindy knew all the nooks and crannies of her own pain, but when it came to her mother's pain, she had nothing to say. Instead, her mother's pain was held in her mind like a monolithic entity that not only was impenetrable, but never even aroused her curiosity about its inner workings. This hadn't stopped Cindy from developing an internal object relationship around this pain and the object (her suffering mother) that contained it. Indeed, Cindy exhibited many emotions (concern, empathy, tenderness), motivations (to soothe, calm and protect), and behaviors that were specifically directed at that object. But because she had no understanding of the original reasons and motivations for these behaviors, they were conducted automatically, mechanically, and without real conviction in their expressed intent and purpose. It was as though, as Abraham and Torok described, she was possessed, or haunted, by a remnant of her mother's mind that her mother never elaborated, but had nonetheless organized many aspects of Cindy's life.

THE CRYPT AND THE PHANTOM

Garland defines trauma as an event that "overwhelms existing defences against anxiety in a form which also provides confirmation of those deepest universal anxieties" (1998, p. 11). To this, Tarantelli adds that trauma is a breakdown of the established ways of going about life, "an utter absence, a radical break in being, an instant in which nothing exists" (2003, p. 916). When trauma overwhelms our defenses and exposes us to radical breaks in being, it creates fragments of experience that remain lodged in the mind and body, but that are disconnected from the rest of the self because to think about, symbolize or remember them is tantamount to re-triggering the trauma. Being undigested and perhaps indigestible, these disruptive experiential fragments are banished to isolated psychic regions that remain unpenetrated by the moderating influences of the self's symbolizing capacities.

Abraham and Torok use the term "crypt" to refer to these sealed-off places to which fragments of traumatic experience are consigned. A crypt is comparable "to the formation of a cocoon around the chrysalis" (1975, p. 141), in that it creates a blind or mute zone around the reality of the trauma that shifts the entire psyche away from its contents. This doesn't mean that the denied content of the crypt doesn't exert influence over the remainder of the self. Rather, the rest of the self becomes organized around attempts to solve, neutralize or eject the trauma, even though the contents of the crypt remain unknown. This tendency of the individual's behavior to be drawn into orbit around the crypt, in order to solve a problem to which the self remains blind, is one of the origins of the many symptoms traumatized individuals may exhibit (Yassa, 2002).

A brief example: A male patient, who as a young adolescent was sexually assaulted by an older man in the bathroom of an abandoned building with a filthy floor, sought treatment, not because of his trauma—which he didn't remember—but because of phobic and compulsive symptoms about dirt on his shoes that forced him to sterilize them before he entered his home. This patient's symptoms could be understood as having originated in an encrypted trauma whose gravitational mass within the self could bend behavior and symbolization in its direction, while at the same time keeping its essential topography concealed.

A person with an encrypted trauma enacts the distortions—of thought, behavior, emotion, etc.—imposed by that trauma in nearly every part of life. To an observer, the meanings of these distortions are as inaccessible as they are to the sufferer, and they remain inconceivable until the trauma is unearthed and examined. If the traumatized person becomes a parent, the child too will find the parent's blind and mute zones impossible to penetrate, although the child will still feel the parent's suffering through the medium of the parent's distorted behavior. Because these two aspects of the parent's internal life—the crypt and the distortions imposed by the crypt—are unavoidably infused into interactions with his or her child, the child internalizes them as two dimensions of her own internal life. That is, she internalizes the gap or absence in the parent's self-understanding, and in this way establishes "a direct empathy with the unconscious or the rejected psychic matter" of the parent (Torok, 1975, p. 181); and she identifies with the parent's efforts to solve the unspeakable problem, and takes on the same, or complementary, behaviors the parent turned to for safety or soothing. These two dimensions thus begin a process in the child, which may last a lifetime, to attempt to solve, by similar means as the parent's, the incomprehensible problem of the parent's trauma.

Abraham and Torok term this process, in which the child brings into her self the impenetrable crypt and the parent's attempt to solve its riddle, the *haunting of the phantom*. When a phantom takes residence in a child's mind, it creates an irresolvable internal conflict because it imposes two contradictory expectations: the child must at the same time maintain her ignorance of the parent's secret (because it, like Medusa, is too terrifying to behold) *and* attempt to "eliminate the state of secrecy" in order to alleviate the parent's suffering (N. Abraham, 1975, p. 188). This contradiction is rendered even more complex by the fact that the child's internalization of the parental crypt is *truly empty*—that is, as long as the trauma is held in a split-off portion of the parent's mind that conceals its meaning, the only part of it available for the child's internalization is the impenetrable vessel that holds it. Because of this impenetrability, the child's subsequent attempts to expose and solve the trauma in the internalized parental crypt are both meaningless and doomed to failure.

The meaninglessness of the child's efforts in regard to the phantom imposes a particular quality on them. Because they revolve around an empty center in the child's mind, they are enacted in a dream-like state, in which the child functions less as the source of her own motivations and more as a puppet doing the bidding of the phantom. "What haunts," according to Abraham, "are not the dead, but the gaps left within us by the secrets of others" (N. Abraham, 1975, p. 171)—secrets that, in the form of the phantom, work "like a ventriloquist, like a stranger within the subject's own mental topography" (p. 173).

Ultimately, these characteristics differentiate the phantom from other internal object relationships. Whereas most such configurations are created by dynamic repression, through which the child's own fantasy, aggression or erotic impulses are bound in unconscious representations of both self and object, the phantom, as the representation of the parent's unspoken trauma, has "nothing to do with fantasy strictly speaking" and instead is "gratuitous in relation to the subject" (N. Abraham, 1975, p. 173)—in the sense that it contains nothing of the child's self, but only of the parent's unconscious. For this reason, the phantom's activity in the self cannot be counted as an instance of the return of the repressed. Instead, it is the signal of a "bizarre foreign body," unrelated to repressed aspects of self, that only bears witness to the fact that the child is "possessed not by his own unconscious but by someone else's" (p. 173).

THE PHANTOM IN THE COUPLE

Before I describe the effects of Cindy's phantom on the couple's relationship, I'd like to briefly note how I will use the term. Because Abraham and
Torok's writing styles are literary and filled with rich, associative metaphor,
they are very helpful in giving the reader the feel of their topic, but they also
impede the reader's ability to determine exactly what their theoretical position is. Because of this, I have found it useful to merge their thoughts about
the phantom with object relations theory. Thus, the phantom, as I conceptualize it, refers neither to the internal object (in Cindy's case the suffering-
mother), nor the object relationship that develops around it. Instead, the
phantom refers only to the unspoken, unsymbolized trauma that is embedded
within the internal object, since this is the only part of the internal object
relationship that has "nothing to do" with the child's fantasy, and that has the
potential to take over parts of the child's mind like an alien presence.

There were three indicators that suggested the pain embedded in Cindy's
internal object was related to trauma her mother underwent but was unable to
think about or metabolize. The first was the impenetrability of the object's
pain, which I've described above. The second were the repetitive behaviors
Cindy developed around that pain. These behaviors, which centered on her
need to rescue others from the suffering her desire caused them, were essentially "meaningless" for Cindy, in the sense that she couldn't describe or
explain the pain they were expected to solve. Their meaninglessness, in turn,
illustrated the two contradictory expectations Abraham and Torok described
as characteristic of the phantom. On the one hand, Cindy unconsciously
devoted herself to saving her suffering-mother, whether internal or projected,
from pain. But Cindy also followed an unconscious rule against inquiring too
closely into the meaning of that pain: as described above, she accepted it, and
what she felt she had to do about it, as an *a priori* aspect of her world. This
rule was never explicitly given to Cindy, but it dominated her unconscious,
nonetheless, because of her mother's inability to put her trauma into words.
Thus, Cindy was caught in a repetitive set of behaviors that were not only
meaningless, but were designed to *fail* to reach their target. That is, they were
never intended to truly solve the trauma that set them in motion.

The third indicator of Cindy's phantom was her identification with her
mother's pain, on which her empathy for her mother was founded. This
identification, as I came to understand it, was anchored in Cindy's original
primary identification (Fairbairn, 1941; Glover, 1947) with her mother. Arising out of the natural merger between mother and infant, in which dependency needs and fantasies of oneness dominate the infant's internal landscape,
Cindy developed an intuitive, intimate connection with her mother's internal
states. As her relationship with her mother grew and incorporated the developing emotional and motivational capacities of the child, her original pri-

mary identification evolved into a capacity both to intuit the onset of her mother's pain, and to feel the same pain. That is, even though she didn't understand its origins, her mother's pain pained her as well, as was evident when Cindy described her mother's fear with surprising tenderness. Cindy's empathy, then, was built upon this deeper foundation of an identificatory merger with her mother. On the basis of such a merger, her attempts to protect her mother could be seen not only as acts of devotion, intended to rescue her mother, but also as attempts to unconsciously re-establish the original intimate connection between the two.

These were the dynamics Cindy introduced, through the medium of the phantom, into her relationship with Bob. We saw earlier that Bob's angry-father/frightened-child internal object relationship complemented Cindy's attacking-mother/frightened child configuration, thereby creating a transference-countertransference entanglement in which each saw the other as dangerous. But Bob's internal structure also resonated with Cindy's suffering-mother/protective-child configuration, in which the phantom resided. Because Bob's primary sense of himself was of a frightened child, he easily identified with the role of the pained and suffering mother when Cindy projected it into him. In fact, when Cindy projected this image and subsequently protected Bob from her desire, her was unconsciously reminded of his own mother, who had created the safe haven of his childhood. As a result, a second transference-countertransference entanglement developed between the two, in which Bob identified with Cindy's projected suffering object and looked to Cindy for maternal protection, while Cindy assumed the role of her empathetic self and looked to Bob as someone in need of rescue. Although the content of this entanglement differed from the first, in the couple's actual interactions the two entanglements rarely appeared separately. Rather, they blended into and reinforced each other, so that the couple's patterns were multiply determined and relied on primitive and infantile motivations in both parties.

I'll describe one other joint transference that arose on the basis of Cindy's phantom. This was revealed in a conversation about the couple's infrequent sexual activity. At a certain point in the discussion, Bob, without prompting and with an eagerness that struck me as premature (and perhaps dissociated from other parts of himself), said, "I know Cindy gets anxious about sex. I'll do anything I can to help her with it. If it means not asking for anything from her, if it means not asking for sex, I'm happy to do it. It doesn't matter that much to me." With this statement, it seemed to me, Bob merged his own defense of going numb (in the face of his father's anger) with Cindy's strategy of suppressing desire, thereby blending psychic material from both partners into a jointly coordinated effort to suppress desire wherever it appeared in their relationship. Earlier I suggested the couple's entanglement around Cindy's attacking– mother/frightened-self configuration contributed to the lack of passion in their relationship. Here we discovered a shared transference, organized instead around the suppression of desire as an act of protection and rescue, could do so as well.

WHAT TO DO ABOUT A PHANTOM?

The hallmark of the phantom is it is an alien presence, lodged within a patient's internal objects, whose meaning lies *outside* of the patient, in the details of the parent's trauma, not the patient's. Because this trauma can neither be understood, nor contained by reference to any part of the patient's unconscious, the traditional tools of psychoanalytic treatment, which rely exclusively on material gathered from the *patient's* associations, transferences, dreams, etc., are of little help in working through the phantom's influence. Consequently, if the therapist is to help a patient with phantom-related difficulties, it is necessary to go beyond traditional technique and create a collaborative relationship in which the parent's trauma becomes a deliberate topic of investigation. Only in this way will the patient be able to discover the original meaning that underlies their apparently meaningless behaviors, and thereby begin the process of separating themselves from the phantom's demands.

The kind of collaborative relationship I'm referring to evolved, in my work with Cindy and Bob, out of our mutual curiosity about Cindy's inability to answer the question I had posed to her—How had her desire caused her mother's suffering? Because Cindy could find no answer to this question, we began to discuss how she could discover more about her mother's life. Although Cindy's mother, Beverly, had died twenty years earlier, some of Cindy's relatives, who knew about Beverly's upbringing, were still alive. Consequently, by mutual agreement among the three of us, Cindy and Bob started to interview those relatives. In what follows, I'll briefly describe what they discovered.

Cindy's mother, Beverly, was born to two teenage parents who were forced to marry because of their pregnancy with her. Her mother (i.e., Cindy's grandmother) was, by all accounts, a narcissistic and hateful woman who deeply resented having had to marry and bear a child. Unable to contain these resentments, she was abusive and harshly critical of Beverly, and, in particular, punished her, often severely, for expressions of joy or desire— perhaps because they reminded the mother of the pleasures she had lost. As Beverly grew into an adult, she became depressed, rigid, frightened and, unsurprisingly, devoted to her mother. She avoided marriage for many years, preferring to live with her mother in an isolated asexual lifestyle that recapitulated her childhood. Beverly finally married at age thirty-six, three years after her mother died, to a quiet, religious man she met at the local church. The couple had two children in quick succession, the first one being Cindy.

As Cindy gradually filled in the story of her mother's early life, she began to realize that her mother's trauma was similar to Cindy's own, particularly in terms of the punishments her mother had received for expressions of desire and pleasure. Cindy's discovery of this parallel, in turn, began a slow process through which nearly every aspect of her experience of herself, and of the way she conducted her relationships, was transformed. This transformation centered on a core realization: that her need to protect her mother from her desire had *not* been internalized because her desire itself was dangerous. Rather, the danger lay in her mother's trauma, which Cindy now understood was rooted in her mother's experiences with *her* mother. That is, Cindy realized that she had spent much of her life trying to protect her mother from a trauma that had already occurred and that could not be reversed, but for which she had, because of her internalization of the phantom, taken full responsibility.

These realizations, in turn, effected incremental shifts in the relationship between Cindy and Bob. The first shift we noted had to do with their joining together, in ways they had not been able to do before, in mourning the losses Cindy's mother's trauma had caused—not only for their own relationship, but for Cindy's mother as well. This mourning took many forms—anger at Cindy's grandmother, pity for Cindy's mother, and sorrow and regret for the patterns of disengagement that had burdened their own relationship—but its net effect was to help the couple begin to separate themselves from the demands of Cindy's phantom. The transformation of the phantom, with its nameless pain, into a filled-out picture of a mother who had been traumatized in her own childhood decades earlier, allowed both partners to begin to distance themselves from the "meaningless" behaviors through which they had been trying to cure that pain.

Additionally, Cindy's growing recognition that her need to protect others from her desire was rooted in pain she had not caused allowed her to begin to experiment with expressions of desire and pleasure. For example, during this phase of our treatment, the frequency of the couple's sexual activity increased, as Cindy began, in tentative ways, to tell Bob when and how she wanted to be intimate. Bob's initial response to this was an increase in anxiety, because he had grown accustomed to a relationship without desire, and because he expected Cindy to return to old patterns. As we analyzed his anxiety, however, particularly in the context of our understanding of the changes Cindy was undergoing, he was able to find more enjoyment in the sexual relationship as well.

Working through the phantom, then, allowed Cindy and Bob to introduce dimensions of spontaneity, desire and pleasure into their relationship that they had heretofore been unable to tolerate. While these improvements in their functioning persisted, they had not solved every difficulty the couple faced, because the phantom was not the only source of their problems. The exorcising of the phantom had, in effect, lifted a fog that allowed the couple to gain more clarity, not only about their own desires, but about the deeper motivations that had contributed to the dysfunction in their relationship as well. With this clarity, we also recognized that other internal and interactive structures remained active within the couple that required additional analysis. I will not describe this additional phase of the treatment; instead, I would like to end this chapter by considering the factors that must be present in a parent-child relationship for a phantom to form in the child's unconscious. These factors, I believe, are related to the child's capacity to internalize a belief in and a feeling of the legitimacy of desire.

THE ORIGIN OF DESIRE'S LEGITIMACY

Imagine an infant reaching for the breast, its first object. Imagine also that this act of reaching occurs on the basis of an unconscious wish-impulse, the rudimentary precursor of desire. Imagine further that when the infant reaches, the breast presents itself, ready and willing to provide whatever the wish-impulse is aiming for (nurturance, attachment, physical touch, auto-erotic gratification, containment, need responsiveness, etc.), and unwilling to punish or retaliate, or refuse to be used by the infant.

What does this "tell" the infant? First, that its wish or desire for the breast is matched by the environment's readiness to provide it, which means, for the infant, that the object (and the satisfaction it provides) is intimately tied up in the act of desiring, and that it appears *because* of the desire. "The mother," states Winnicott, "at the beginning, by an almost 100 per cent adaptation affords the infant the opportunity for the *illusion* that her breast is part of the infant. It is, as it were, under magical control" (1953, p. 94). Second, it tells the infant, if only in rudimentary form, that the object (or the world in general) will receive its desire, will not reject it, and will treat it as legitimate. *Your desire*, the gratifying object says, *is accepted in the world. Your satisfaction is the proof of its legitimacy.*

Imagine now that the mother, who at first allows the infant's omnipotent illusions to prevail, gradually begins, as the infant's capacity to tolerate frustration grows, to withdraw from her "100 per cent adaptation" to the infant's desires, and instead provides the infant with intermittent experiences of disillusion and dissatisfaction. What happens now? If the mother is able to titrate her withdrawal so that it is gradual and non-traumatic for the infant, it instigates processes of internalization that lead to the formation of psychic structures that help the infant cope with the demands of the increasingly real and separate world.

What does the infant internalize? As Abraham and Torok point out, Ferenczi's theory of introjection offers an intriguing answer, one directly related to the role these early internalizations play in the development of the adult's feelings of the legitimacy of desire. Ferenczi defined introjection as the attachment of wish-impulses to an object, which is then identified with and drawn back into the ego in order to "mitigate the poignancy of free-floating, unsatisfied, and unsatisfiable, unconscious wish-impulses" (1909, p. 47). The content drawn back into the ego, however, does not just include the object, but instead all of the emotions, wishes, and desires that had already been projected into it. Introjection in Ferenczi's view becomes a mechanism of enriching the ego, by introducing into it previously unconscious (free-floating and unsatisfied) emotions and desires that have now become mediated and focused by their contact with the object. Introjection thus "transforms instinctual promptings into desires and fantasies of desire, making them fit to receive a name and the right to exist and to unfold in the objectal sphere" (Torok, 1968, p. 113).

The object's responses to the infant's wish-impulses are pivotal in determining whether the infant can introject a feeling of the legitimacy of those impulses and the desires they eventually become. If the mother accepts and is responsive to those wish impulses, the infant introjects both her responsiveness and the impulses themselves, with the result that legitimized desire is created within the infant. "The function of the object," says Yassa,

> is to assist the child in the naming of desire, in all its different aspects. . . . This means that the caretaker returns to the child its emotions and wishes, which, with the object's mediation have been legitimized by the verbal code of the outer world, thereby gaining the right of residence in the child, as the *child's* love, pleasure, etc. (2002, p. 86)

As the child grows and this introjective process continues, and as the mother transforms her own role from sole object of the child's wishes to facilitator of its desire for other objects, the original introjected object-and-desire recedes into the unconscious and becomes increasingly forgotten and diffuse. That is, the original object *as a specific object* takes a place in the unconscious background, leaving its acceptance and responsiveness embedded within the child's desire as a feeling of its legitimacy. The accumulation of these traces of legitimacy within the child's growing consciousness then forms a "halo effect" around its desire, which in later life is experienced as a non-illusory optimism about the possibilities of finding what one wants, and of forging the world according to one's own vision of it.

What happens, however, if the mother is *not* able to accept the child's desires, and instead punishes the child for expressing them? The child's introjection will be blocked, with the result that it is unable to own desire as a part of the self. The child then has no choice but to remain focused on the mother as the source of gratification, since it is only through the mother that the child can find safety from further punishment. Thus, instead of introjecting the legitimacy of desire, the child learns to find pleasure only secondarily, through pleasing the mother and thereby mollifying her in her anger. The child becomes stuck and suspended midway through the introjective process, as its innate desire is dissociated and relegated to disavowed regions in the unconscious, its fluidities frozen, and its free-ranging exuberances clamped and hobbled. The primary punitive object becomes the central internal and external figure the child is devoted to pleasing, and its narcissistic needs are treated as the child's own. As the child matures, and as the object is perhaps lost, these internal structures remain. The child retains a flattened form of desire that expresses itself only in terms of pleasing the internal object. No other desires can be counted as legitimate.

The acts of self-denial and self-negation necessary to deflect the mother's punishments do not come without a cost. The child, of course, is frustrated and angry with the mother who is unavailable for its needs. With this rage, however, the child faces a dilemma: to express its anger directly is the equivalent of *expressing desire* (since its anger arises from the frustration of desire and need), which of course is expressly prohibited. The child then is forced to utilize a number of methods to manage this dilemma, most of which entail the displacement of anger—either onto other external objects or, more detrimentally, onto the self. While the displacement of anger onto the self has several benefits (including providing the means for the child to both hate the mother without notice and to portray a semblance of unity with her through identification with her punitive attacks), still it represents a masochistic turning against the self, a self-betrayal in which the child creates one more reason (in addition to its need to please the mother) to collapse its desire. The child caught in such a dilemma is thus a victim of multiple forces within its own self, all related to its vulnerability and need to preserve its attachment with the mother in any way it can, and all focused on suppressing its liveliness and independence, and turning it instead into a faded mirror of the mother's narcissistic needs.

THE ORIGIN OF THE PHANTOM

The phantom takes up occupancy in a child's mind because of the child's internalization of unsymbolized and disavowed parental trauma. Why, however, would a child internalize this trauma? What conditions would have to be present for the phantom to take hold, and take control over, the child's mind? In my view, three conditions, all related to the processes I've just described, pave the way for the phantom: first, the child has to deny its own desire; second, the child has to make the parent's needs primary, at the expense of its own; and third, the child has to be able to rely on an ongoing mechanism by which it suppresses its desire. In Cindy's case, each of these conditions was met.

Cindy's mother was a frightened and angry woman who, in a profound act of dissociation and displacement, had transferred the traumas of her early life into a tenacious pattern of attacking the desires of those around her. Because Cindy was the primary recipient of these attacks, she had been unable to introject—in Ferenczi's sense—her own desire, and consequently had been unable to believe in or feel its legitimacy. Instead, she had been required to orient herself toward her mother's needs, and to use those to guide her emotions and behavior.

Cindy's absorption in her mother's needs meant that, from an early age, she'd had to effect an internal split in how she approached the very topic of desire. On the one hand, she had repressed her own desires; but she had also elevated a single paradoxical desire—to please her mother through having no desire of her own—to a dominant position within her psyche, from which it demanded her constant obedience. This desire was at the root of the self-negating injunction I mentioned earlier, by which Cindy had tried to conduct most of her life.

These self-sacrifices had not been executed without anger. Cindy *was* angry—intensely so, even as a young child—but she turned this anger onto herself, and used it as a means to suppress her energy and liveliness. In this way she ensured she remained in the half-dead, non-desiring state her mother wanted.

Each of these three conditions, then, were present in Cindy's life, almost from the beginning. Together, they created the fertile ground in which the phantom took root. If any one of these conditions had not been present, if, especially, Cindy had been able to learn, through her earliest introjections, that her desire was legitimate, the phantom would have had no purchase in her mind.

The intergenerational transmission of trauma, in the form of the phantom, is not an isolated psychological phenomenon, capable of arising in the absence of other significant pathology. Rather it requires failures in the early treatment of the infant, so that no room is left for the development of the child into a desiring, self-possessed and independent subject. In Cindy's case, because early experiences taught her that her desire was illegitimate, all she had to motivate her were her mother's needs and her one thin desire of pleasing that mother. Because she was given little else on which to ground her life, the incorporation of the phantom was a natural and comprehensible strategy through which she found at least a modicum of safety.

Chapter Seven

Violence and Sacrifice in a Marital Relationship

"One of the most curious features of the social manifestation of hostility is that it is always rationalized."

—Fine, 1978, p. 16

Couple therapists are familiar with the type of couple who seem devoted to creating a cycle of accusations and retaliations that, if unchecked, can lead to the destruction of the therapy and, potentially, the couple. The partners in this kind of couple are usually intelligent and perceptive, and their uncanny ability to unearth each other's fragile vulnerabilities provides the ammunition for emotionally violent and hurtful attacks. Violence within these couples is not necessarily physical, although that possibility is never absent. More often, their violence is emotional or psychological, in that each partner's value, honesty, intentions, etc., are subjected to persistent and unmerciful denigrations. Violence, however, constitutes only the first phase of the typical pattern within these couples. The second phase occurs when each partner uses the violence they perpetrate for the regulation of their own inner turmoil—i.e., for their own fantasized salvation. These two phases comprise a form of interpersonal sacrifice that is often fatal to relationships, but that can also create a cycle of violence and sacrifice to which both partners become addicted.

The term "sacrifice" does not often appear in psychoanalytic literature, although for these couples its use is justified. In his seminal work, *Violence and the Sacred* (1977), René Girard describes the hidden purposes behind acts of sacrifice, which begin in a *sacrificial crisis*. The crisis may consist of escalating violence between two groups, or a catastrophe (such as a plague or natural disaster) visited upon a single group. In either case, the solution to the crisis depends on the creation of an *illusion* that one individual, the scapegoat, is its cause. This illusion allows the groups to deceive themselves into believing the crisis has been averted and their communities saved by the sacrificial destruction of the scapegoat.

Girard focused his analysis of sacrifice at the level of social phenomena, i.e., within or between large groups in both primitive and advanced civilizations. In doing so, he ignored, and in fact dismissed, psychological dynamics at the intrapsychic and interpersonal levels. I believe this was an unfortunate omission in Girard's theory, and that acts of violence and sacrifice at those levels can be viewed as foundational models for acts of sacrifice in any context. On the intrapsychic level, I'll argue that an individual who sacrifices him or herself first commits the violence of *erasure* against the "offensive" parts of self that do not conform to the dictates of an aggressively judgmental internal object. Because this erasure occurs under the illusory hope that a crisis of threatened punishment can be avoided and safety and innocence (for the remainder of the self) restored, the erased parts of the self comprise his or her intrapsychic scapegoats, and their elimination thereby constitutes an act of sacrifice. When this process moves to the arena of couple interactions, an additional, related mechanism becomes available. Instead of sacrificing oneself to the demands of a harsh internal object, one partner may sacrifice the other by first projecting that object into them. This projection requires that the sacrificer commit the violence of erasing his or her awareness of the other as a real and whole person, and then denying and even assaulting the victim's innocence in the service of making the projection convincing. Once the sacrificer then adds the illusion that by projecting the harsh object goodness can be regained, the victim of violence becomes the scapegoat, whose erasure thus attains the status of a sacrifice. When both partners of a couple engage in similar acts of sacrifice, the result is an escalating cycle of violence and sacrifice that seems to have no end.

In what follows, I will explore the intrapsychic and interpersonal realms in which cycles of violence and sacrifice within a couple operate. To examine these dynamics, I will describe the case of Carl and Sarah, who presented an enduring pattern of exaggerated devaluations of each other in order to achieve a sense of superiority, triumph, and moral goodness. Because I saw Carl individually for eight years before working with the couple, I'll begin by describing his internal world. I'll then present material from couple therapy that portrays the mutual benefits and losses that accrue to a couple who has entered into what Girard termed the "collective self-mystification" (1977, p. 83) of the cycle of violence and sacrifice.

CARL

Carl, the youngest child of college-educated parents, described his mother as a severely paranoid woman whose delusions and inability to acknowledge their debilitating impact on the family could be both frightening and enraging. Her paranoia was so preoccupying that she was only meagerly available as an object of attachment or source of security, and Carl remembered she was largely unable to respond to her children's emotional distress without in some way blaming them for it. Carl described his father as self-absorbed and selfish, capable of offering companionship when Carl was willing to take part in activities his father liked (such as riding motorcycles), but distant and uninvolved in activities Carl preferred. Moreover, his father was compulsive about order and cleanliness, and insisted everyone in the home follow his rules. If Carl inadvertently broke something in his father's shop or left a tool dirty, his father flew into a rage that lasted only a few minutes, but during which Carl was subjected to devastating criticism.

The fragile narcissism and paranoid anxieties of Carl's parents were a toxic combination for his psychological development. In response to both parents, he felt despair and rage, but because these emotions were prohibited by the rules of the home, and he had no means by which to metabolize or contain them, he split them off and projected them, most commonly into his parents. The resulting aggregation, however, of his parents' real aggression and Carl's projected aggression created images of his parents that were frighteningly more hostile and punitive than they actually had been. These images contributed to the creation of a harshly aggressive internal object in relation to which Carl felt irredeemably bad and unworthy of being loved, protected or even acknowledged.

To defend against the sheer intensity and harshness of Carl's internal object, he utilized projective identification to locate it in others. As a result, he often felt he faced an excruciatingly critical judge of his value, in whose presence he had few options for finding comfort. At times he attempted to soothe his judges by placating them, which commonly entailed identifying the part of himself that displeased them, and then sacrificing it—that is, hiding, distorting, or eliminating it so he could gain a semblance of safety.

Carl, though, did not always placate his judges. Intermittently, he became angry at the people he believed were aggressive or judgmental toward him and had, therefore, demanded his sacrifice, and he launched into diatribes against them. One aspect of these diatribes stood out above the rest: he believed, with absolute certainty, his perceptions of others as demanding his sacrifice were accurate. This certainty was a clue that later helped unfold, in a moment of rage toward me, the dynamics of his willingness to sacrifice *both* himself and others to maintain emotional equilibrium.

SACRIFICE IN THE TRANSFERENCE

"My wife really pisses me off," Carl fumed. I waited for him to go on and he explained, with sarcasm in his voice, that she had once again neglected to pay the phone bill, which meant they would get a "double charge" on the next bill. I asked about the double charge and he said it wasn't really an extra charge—the bill would just have charges for two months rather than one. "But still . . . ," he said plaintively, indicating in his fantasy a severe consequence had to be paid for his wife's mistake. I had seen a pattern like this many times before, when Carl escalated a minor offense into a major injury. After a few more exchanges, I reminded him that because of his expectations of harsh judgment he could misperceive the gravity of other people's mistakes. Carl nodded, said I was right, and he went on to other topics.

After several minutes, though, I began to feel our interaction had shifted moods. When Carl began the session, his manner seemed to convey he believed I would be eager to hear of his wife's transgressions. Now he was still, with eyes averted, and our conversation halted. When I noted the change, he said he didn't notice anything. When I said *something* seemed to have changed, he didn't respond. I let the silence deepen. After two or three minutes, during which he stared at his hands, he started to speak, softly at first, but with rapidly growing power and emotion. He said when I told him he exaggerated other people's mistakes, I "certainly" put him in his place. I always did that, he said, I always told him about himself as though my pronouncements couldn't be challenged. He said my authoritarian way of treating him scared him and, for a long time, he was too frightened to challenge me. He was scared now, he said, but now he just didn't care. He knew I would disagree with him and he knew he was supposed to just take what I said and not contradict me. If he did contradict me, he said, I would keep pushing him and I wouldn't stop. But he didn't care because he discovered something about me. He discovered I was wrong. I could shame him all I wanted, but he still knew I was the one who didn't know what I was talking about. I was the one who was "full of shit."

Carl was yelling by the time he finished. His tone, especially at the end, seemed triumphant, as though he was certain he had cracked the code of my game, discovered the essence of my failings, and thus achieved a victory over me. His victory, in essence, consisted in turning the tables on me: he was now the good person and I the bad and, consequently, he felt justified, even morally righteous, in his anger.

I said simply, "You're angry at me," at which Carl continued, but as he did the power in his voice and his assuredness rapidly diminished. He explained that when he agreed with me, earlier in the session, he did it just to keep me happy, because he thought if he didn't keep me happy I would "destroy" him and there wouldn't be anything left of him. Afterward, he said, when he had a chance to think about it and realize what had happened, he got so angry he wanted to explode. He didn't want to explode now, he said with embarrassment, but he did at the time. Then he paused and said, "I don't know what comes over me." We continued our conversation and for the rest of the session he remained timid and cautious.

This interaction illustrates the basic alternating pattern in Carl's psychic states. On the one hand, he could feel like a terrified child who had neither power, nor legitimacy to stand up to the threatening other when they demanded sacrifice. On the other, by discovering how bad his persecutors "really" were, he could regain strength and legitimacy and, thereby, feel righteously victorious over them.

These two positions each depended on the way he managed his relationship with the aggression that was bound up in his harsh and demanding internal object. In the first position, when he was timid and self-negating, Carl could not acknowledge his own aggression and had to project it into me, leading him to discover both aggression and judgment, intensified by his projection, in me. The anxieties he felt upon this discovery motivated him to attempt to soothe me out of my annihilating aggression. These were the dynamics that underlay his initial acquiescence to my statement that he misperceived the gravity of others' mistakes.

The second position was more complex. In it, Carl was able to own and acknowledge his aggression, and in addition feel victorious or triumphal in his certainty that I was the bad person in the room, not him. His aggression in this position seemed to derive from his appropriation of and reunion with (since much of it was his own) the hostility that was located in his disapproving internal object, which he then used to attack me after I injured him. His feelings of triumph and moral justification, alternatively, did not seem to be related to internal aggression, but to an approving and even admiring presence that was active at the moment he achieved his reunion with the lost portions of himself.

The appearance of an approving presence in Carl at the same moment he was aiming aggression at me indicated he could access a second internal object, one that offered him love and acceptance, at those moments when he escaped his harsh object by achieving a reunion with his own aggression. These two objects were thus related to the alternating positions Carl took in the session: when his harsh object was ascendant, he was frightened and prone to self-sacrifice; when he could neutralize the harsh object by taking over its aggression, his loving object appeared, and he felt powerful, good, and triumphant. In what follows, I will analyze these two phases of Carl's presentation, both of which underscore the multifaceted and sometimes fragmented aspects of the violent patient's internal dynamics.

PHASE I: VIOLENCE AND THE PROJECTION OF THE SUPEREGO

Carl's movement among fear, shame, aggression, and triumph in this session was the result of his varying relationships with the diverse objects, both punishing and admiring, that comprise the multiple aspects of the superego. These objects, which are loosely organized around the common purpose of monitoring and controlling behavior, are nevertheless heterogeneous, and their heterogeneity guarantees their availability for multiple roles within and outside of the self, some of which set one aspect of the superego in conflict with another. The theory of a heterogeneous and dispersible superego developed in response to the perceived inadequacies in Freud's treatment of the topic. Freud described the superego in detail (1914a, 1922, 1923, 1926, 1933), but it remained for him a relatively unitary structure focused primarily on proscribing behavior; he left largely undeveloped those aspects of the superego, such as the ego ideal, that constitute a more positive presence within the psyche (Laplanche & Pontalis, 1973). It was only when later theorists, such as Klein (1935, 1948, 1963a) and Fairbairn (1943, 1944), reinvestigated the concept of the superego that its heterogeneity was fully recognized.

The Kleinian superego, for instance, is inherently syncretic, and is composed of both "good" (approving) and "bad" (disapproving) aspects, which can appear in both primitive and mature forms. The approving superego, in its primitive form, is the source of protection, love and admiration, while in its mature form it provides self-pride and feelings of moral goodness or justification. The disapproving superego, on the other hand, is cruel, aggressive, condemning and persecutory in its primitive manifestation, and morally judgmental and the source of guilt and remorse in its mature form (Klein, 1948, 1963a). For Klein, each manifestation of the superego is the result of a history of both instinctual experience and internalization that together construct internal objects that take on superego-related roles. For example, the primitive approving superego is constructed out of interactions with a loving mother, from whom traces of aggression, disapproval or frustration have been erased, and who is therefore preserved as a source of unambiguous admiration and approval.

Klein's theory of a multifaceted superego is helpful for understanding Carl's participation in acts of both violence and sacrifice. His experience of me as persecutory, aggressive and judgmental after I told him he misperceived others' mistakes suggests that he had projected both the primitive and mature portions of a *disapproving* superego into me, while his celebratory claim of goodness, superiority and moral justification when in his triumphal position suggests that he had regained access to primitive and mature aspects of his *approving* superego. In the next section, I'll describe the essential role the approving superego plays in transforming Carl's acts of emotional violence into acts of sacrifice. For now, though, we only need to note that his acts of violence rested upon the completeness with which he projected his disapproving superego into me.

In essence, Carl's emotional violence toward me consisted in perceiving me to be judgmental and aggressive *without* creating space in his mind to consider that I might be different than his projections made me appear. This erasure of my reality in favor of his projections, which is similar to Green's foreclosure (1999) or Morgan and Freedman's perverse denial (2009), was so complete (at times) that he could see no trace of me behind them, and hence felt free to indulge, if only momentarily, in the certainty and violence of his unquestioned accusations against me.

The fact that Carl's erasure of me amounted to the same act of erasure and sacrifice that he felt was required of him when faced with others' aggressions pointed, incidentally, to an irony at the heart of his participation in sacrificial dynamics. The irony lay in the fact that *his own act* of violent erasure against me, by which I was transformed into an aggressive and persecutory judge, created the very conditions under which he then felt he had to commit the same violence of erasure against himself.

Carl's perpetration of this violence, though, is only the beginning of the sacrificial cycle. In the second, triumphal phase, we discover how and to what extent his resurrection of the approving superego sets the stage for his sacrifice of both himself and others.

PHASE II: TRIUMPH AND THE SUBVERSION OF SUPEREGO FUNCTIONING

The triumph and victory Carl exhibited in our session was made up of three emotional and moral components: First, he aggressively condemned me (e.g., when he said I didn't know what I was talking about); then he justified his condemnations on the basis of my intolerable behavior (e.g., I would have continued to push him and wouldn't have stopped); and finally, he felt the flush of victory, which he celebrated as the triumph of his cleverness and moral superiority. Supporting each of these components was his underlying belief that he enjoyed, at least in the moment, moral immunity and thus had license to behave as he wanted without fear of attack or critique. This expectation of immunity implied he effectively liberated himself from the dictates of his harsh internal object, which would ordinarily have monitored his aggression and leveled judgments against it. It also reflected, however, the awakening of the loving and admiring aspect of the superego that Klein referred to when she spoke of the child turning to her "good object" for "internal riches and stability" (1952c, p. 58). This loving object appeared in Carl in both primitive and mature forms. In its primitive form, it functioned as a felt internal presence that provided him with something akin to an accepting, approving and idealizing mother; in its mature form, it gave him the feeling of being morally justified, and it said to him, in the name of an external code of morality (as in Lacan's Name-of-the-Father), that he had rational reasons for behaving as he did.

Because Carl had already projected into me the condemnations aimed at him from his harsh internal object, he was in a more commanding position to retrieve an intimate relationship with the approving and loving object that remained. This retrieval culminated in the attainment of a state of ideality, that is, of being an ideal self under the gaze of a loving mother. Such a state, which is more common than might be assumed, was humorously illustrated in a *Seinfeld* episode called "The Café." In this episode, Jerry gives advice to a restaurant owner, Babu, that he is certain will lead to Babu's success. As Babu expresses his gratitude, we hear Jerry's internal voice cooing to him that his mother was right: he *is* a wonderful, special guy who will go to any trouble to help a friend in need (David et al., 1991). Here Jerry is reveling in the smug superiority that results from communing with an internal object that has taken on both idealized and idealizing properties. The fact that the episode ends badly for Babu, who loses his restaurant and is imprisoned and deported, is a telling reminder of the dangers of listening too closely to our internal idealizing mothers.

By projecting his harsh internal object into me Carl removed the obstacle separating him from his idealizing object, and, with this object's approval, was then able to reclaim the aggression he long felt unable to own because it was prohibited under his parents' rules. This expelled aggression, now sanctioned by his loving object, was welcomed back to the self as an act of healing unification and regained authenticity, and his exhilaration at this reunion found its first external expression in his certainty that he was morally justified in aiming it at me.

Carl's triumphal position depended, then, upon the execution of three procedures: his projection of aggression and judgment into me; his retrieval of his own long dissociated anger; and his reconnection with an approving object that affirmed the goodness and authenticity of his anger. There is still, however, one additional twist in this drama, having to do with Carl's condemnation of me for my aggression and judgment, while at the same time failing to recognize (and condemn) the same offenses in himself. This maneuver suggests that even though he projected his harsh and judgmental object into me, he still was able to use its power of condemnation for his own purposes, which in turn suggests that he had split it into two parts, both retaining the power of condemnation, but each with different trajectories. One part—the part that continued to condemn *him*—was projected into me. But Carl succeeded in reversing the aim of the other part, so that it no longer condemned him, but instead could be used in judgment against *me*. More specifically (and this is the irony of the mechanism), Carl used the *second* part of his condemning object—the part whose aim he reversed—against the *first* part of that same object, which he projected into me. It was as though his projections accomplished what he could never achieve from the inside. They not only gave him breathing room and helped to strengthen him against his harsh object, but they also allowed him to divide that object, to project part of it and to commandeer the rest for use in attacking me. He thus exacted the ultimate revenge against a harsh master. He subverted its own judgmental power to use against itself and, thereby, empowered his illusion that he was free from its attacks.

All of the procedures and maneuvers Carl undertook within the confines of one session constituted the playing out of a fundamental internal drama dominated by a central narrative. In it, Carl played the role of an unfairly criticized child who felt the demand to sacrifice himself. In both retaliation and hope, he transformed his internal structure and triumphed in his victorious reunification with his aggression—and he attempted to keep all of this in place through the condemnation of the part of himself he had ejected, hoping that such condemnation would keep it at bay. That it didn't stay away reveals the limit of his defenses. At some point, he lost the energy in his rebellion and re-absorbed his harsh self-judgment. This forced him to return to the position of the frightened and self-negating child, but it also set the stage for his next act of rebellion. He was like the phoenix that grows to full plumage only to be consumed by a fire of his own making.

Nevertheless, for Carl the experienced benefits of seeking his position of triumph were substantial. The only act he had to commit to receive these benefits was the violence of erasure against me, since by erasing me he evacuated his harsh object and regained access to internal admiration. His retrieval of internal love was the crucial factor that transformed his act of violence against me into an act of sacrifice, since it momentarily guaranteed the illusion that he was now innocent, loved and safe from persecutions and condemnations. Little wonder he was willing to commit this sacrifice if it could script a new ending to his internal drama.

We now have a more complete understanding of Carl's internal and interpersonal dynamics and how they contribute to acts of violence and sacrifice. The characteristic intensity of a *cycle* of violence and sacrifice, however, occurs when *two* individuals with interlocking psychic structures participate. It is then that we see a repeating cycle of violence, sacrifice and, paradoxically, repair (because each partner is dependent on the other to remain a viable screen for projection), that is inherently toxic to healthy couple functioning.

CARL AND SARAH

Carl, Sarah, and I began couple treatment two years after Carl terminated his individual treatment with me. I hadn't assumed, when he ended individual therapy, that he had completely worked through his internal conflicts, but I supported his termination because he had made significant gains and because he wanted a break from therapy. When he asked if I would consider working with the couple, I interviewed each party and decided it was appropriate to proceed.

It will surprise no one who has studied the dynamics of object choice in marriages that Carl's wife shared many characteristics of his internal objects. While Sarah was a likeable, professional woman, raised in a respected family by two professional parents, the most common attitude she displayed in her relationship with Carl was one of almost serene faultlessness. In most inter-actions, Sarah seemed to assume the role of Carl's advisor—whose mission was to help him improve himself—rather than his partner who was equally implicated in the difficulties the couple faced. In sessions, this assumption led Sarah to attempt to become my co-therapist, coolly and dispassionately considering the foundations of Carl's problems. Intermittently, however, she would abandon her disengaged demeanor and criticize Carl in a sarcastic and arrogant manner.

Sarah initially described her upbringing in positive terms. Her parents, she said, were "wonderful" and she described her attitude toward them, since childhood, as loving and tolerant of the minor flaws in their personalities. As treatment progressed, though, a more complicated picture evolved. Her father, who she described as "mostly" even-tempered, could also be aggres-sively critical of those who didn't live up to his standards. This aggression was usually masked by a neutral mien, but because she knew her father well, Sarah felt she could often, *though not always*, discern when his equanimity was feigned. Sarah described her mother as pleasant and always in the back-ground doing chores, but not particularly available for a close relationship.

In my formulation of Sarah's internal dynamics, I came to believe her father's judgment, whether real or imagined, frightened her more than she was able to acknowledge. In particular, the possibility that he could be angry or disappointed in her, while she was unaware of it, created in her a powerful insecurity—linked to suspicions that she was more deficient than she knew—that she was unable to resolve. To protect herself from her suspected inade-quacies (which included fears that she wasn't smart, committed, or exacting enough), she split them off and disavowed them, and retreated to a protected internal space in which she believed she had no significant flaws. Because she hadn't acknowledged her insecurities, she was prone to projecting them into others.

From these descriptions we can discern some of the unconscious founda-tions of Carl and Sarah's relationship. Because of her suspected inadequa-cies, Sarah unconsciously looked for a partner who was also insecure, so he would be a receptive container for her projections. By locating her inadequa-cies in Carl, she convinced herself he was the source of the problems in their marriage, which then sustained her belief in her faultlessness and further fueled her criticisms of him. Internally, this suggested Sarah subverted her superego functioning in the same way Carl had. Unlike Carl, though, she had not projected the judgmental, disapproving parts of herself, but only those characteristics that didn't live up to her idealized standards. In this way, Sarah established contact, as did Carl, with an admiring and loving internal object, in whose presence she felt authorized to act as his advisor and my co-therapist.

Sarah and Carl's defenses complemented each other closely. Where Sarah needed to project inadequacy in order to become a faultless, judging author-ity, Carl needed to project his aggression and condemnation in order to gain safety—either through placating others or reuniting with his triumphal ag-gression. Each partner, then, found in the other's personality a receptive screen on which their projections stuck, which in turn allowed each to dis-cover internally their innocence and goodness. In other words, each partner found in the other a fitting and willing victim for their acts of sacrifice.

The following conversation occurred in a session late in the first year of treatment. Sarah began by describing an argument she and Carl had the previous night, about a promotion Carl said he intended to apply for, but hadn't yet. As she described the argument to me, Sarah said, "I was only trying to suggest what he could do to get the application in, but he got angry." Carl replied that he had become angry because her suggestions wer-en't really suggestions—they were more like "dictations"—and besides she was treating him like a child. Sarah said she didn't see anything wrong with trying to give Carl advice, at which Carl answered that he didn't need her advice, he needed her understanding, because the whole process of applying for the promotion made him anxious. In an innocent tone, as though she hadn't heard Carl's request for emotional understanding, Sarah then said, "I still don't think there's anything wrong with giving you advice. I just don't understand why you'd get angry about it."

The attitude of detachment Sarah took in these initial few minutes of our session had become familiar to me over the past year. In it, she seemed to make several assumptions: that Carl's anger was irrational, unrelated to any-thing she had done, and indicative of his own impairments; and her own behavior was well-intended, positive, and helpful. In other words, Sarah's attitude revealed she had projected her own vulnerabilities and faults in order to absolve herself of any role in Carl's distress.

Sarah's last statement, though, rekindled Carl's animosity. "You don't understand?" he said. "You don't understand why I would get angry because you never listen to me?" He then turned to me to say, "She acts like she has nothing to do with what's wrong in our relationship, as though I could cause it all by myself." He went on in the same irritated tone, describing how Sarah's detachment was always an issue and how he bore the "total responsibility" for trying to keep their marriage afloat.

While Carl spoke, Sarah turned to me with a complex expression of anger, amusement, and satisfaction—as if his anger was a victory for her. When Carl was done, she said, with an equally mixed tone of bewilderment, concern, and sarcasm: "I guess I really didn't understand what this all meant for Carl." Still angry, Carl responded immediately: "That's exactly what I'm talking about," he said. "You haven't understood what our relationship has been like for me. You've only seen it as my problem, not *ours*." He then turned to me. "You see it, don't you?" he said. "You see how she pretends she's some sort of goddess who has nothing to do with anything?"

This exchange highlights several issues central to Sarah and Carl's difficulties. The first had to do with a pair of distortions that were similar for each partner: while each could accurately identify the offenses the other committed, each also exaggerated those offenses through their own projections. Thus, Carl was correct in identifying Sarah's detachment and judgment, but he also experienced her as being more aggressive and damaging than she'd actually been; and Sarah was right that *some* of Carl's anger had nothing to do with her, but she also saw him as more angry and dysfunctional, and herself as less involved, than was actually the case.

Second, the reader may have noticed a rhythm to Sarah and Carl's offenses and projections: Sarah committed the first offense, at which Carl took umbrage, which allowed Sarah to take umbrage at Carl, which set the stage for him to feel further offended by her. This back-and-forth quality of their interactions is an example of a joint personality (Dicks, 1967) created by each partner's unconscious agreement to serve as the victim of the other's sacrificial violence—i.e., to receive their partner's projections so the partner could enjoy the internal gains that follow from evacuating disturbing parts of the self. Because each partner depended on the other to play the role of victim, they had developed a joint personality in which an alternating cycle of sacrifice—first one and then the other—became their primary mode of interaction.

The final issue concerns the transferences Sarah and Carl enacted toward me in this session, which were also similar. Each wanted to enlist me not only in seeing their partner as they did, but in condemning that partner as well. These transferences were the result of each partner's core defenses: if each could convince me the other was as bad as their projections made them appear, they would feel reassured that their view of the other, but more importantly their view of themselves, was accurate and acceptable.

Because Carl just made his transference toward me explicit by asking me to agree Sarah was pretending she was "some sort of goddess," I chose to focus on that. I said I understood he was trying to identify something real in Sarah's behavior, having to do with her detachment and belief in her fault-lessness. "But," I continued, "the intensity of your anger suggests that you've taken a similar position—that *she's* the one with all the flaws, not you. And, I think you'd like me to agree with you and condemn her."

This interpretation echoed my interventions with Carl when I worked with him individually. Because he worked through many (though not all) of the conflicts that had given rise to this pattern, I knew he was capable of containing his emotions and beginning the process of withdrawing his projections. He became quiet and thoughtful, then turned to Sarah and said in a calmer voice, "He's right. I know I get angry at you and blame you, and I know that I've contributed to our problems. It has a lot to do with how frightened I get when I feel that someone is criticizing me. . . . But it's important to me that you also realize how you treat me. You treat me like you're above me and all you do is look down on me." Carl was now getting angry again. "But the truth is, Sarah, you have some real problems yourself."

At this last sentence, Sarah stiffened. "Well," she said, "what do you think I should do? It's your opinion that I have problems. But I know I don't have the same problems you do." Given that Carl had just made a moderately successful attempt to contain his projections and think about what was happening in the couple, this resurgence of Sarah's need to sacrifice him was puzzling. I took it to mean either she was retaliating against him for having said she had problems, or she was taking another opportunity, now that Carl had at least attempted to disengage from attacking her, to use him for sacrifice. This latter possibility bears upon the idea of revival. My impression of Sarah and Carl was that their projections felt less effective when either seemed overly damaged—perhaps when the cycle of sacrifice went on too long. Consequently, they periodically broke out of the cycle and replaced it with more caring interactions. I thought of these periodic reprieves as serving two purposes: they indicated genuine affection and concern for each other; and they served to prepare each partner to be strong enough and available for the next acts of sacrifice. In this exchange, I suspected Sarah leaped to projection because Carl had shown himself to be a revived and revitalized target.

The conversation between Sarah and Carl continued along these lines for several more minutes. In an indication that Sarah's defenses were not impenetrable, at a certain point she seemed to "get" what Carl was talking about—that by assuming she was flawless, she not only helped create the relationship's dysfunction, but she also injured him. With a gesture of helplessness and remorse, she said if that was what she was doing, she was sorry. "I don't want to hurt you," she said to Carl, "that's never been what I've wanted to do. Maybe I do it because I get scared too." Although her remorse was tentative, it also seemed genuine, and I thought it indicated that she, like Carl earlier, had momentarily withdrawn her projections and realized she wasn't as innocent as she portrayed.

The session was almost over. I said, "It seems we've discovered that you both get frightened, and when you do, you turn each other into the cause of everything wrong in your relationship." Sarah then looked at Carl and said, "We're quite a pair, aren't we?" and they both laughed gently. Because her words were said lovingly, Carl responded accordingly. I thought their laughter represented an exit from the sacrificial cycle and an entry into healthier functioning. But I also wondered if it served as another act of revival: by being loving, in the context of repeated acts of sacrifice, the two kept each other close, committed, and available for the coming rounds.

THE RELATIONAL FOUNDATIONS OF VIOLENCE AND SACRIFICE

The dynamics of sacrifice between two people trade upon two complementary illusions. Sacrificers deceive themselves into believing that by projecting unwanted parts of self into the other, and then condemning or controlling them, innocence can be restored, inadequacies healed, and the love of internal parents regained. Victims, on the other hand, convince themselves that through sacrifice there can be made, as Reik observed, a "precautionary offering which is intended to ward off a threatening evil or an expected punishment, to assuage the anger of the gods" (1930, p. 269). For both Sarah and Carl, the "threatening evil" was similar: In each, a *loss*—of value or security or love due to attacks from a disapproving internal object—was averted not only through their sacrifice of the other, but also through their submission to the entire cycle of violence and sacrifice.

Sarah and Carl's shared fears of loss and judgment were the primary motivators for the original creation of their cycle, and of the joint personality that perpetuated it. In fact, an analysis of the details of their moment-to-moment interactions reveals how coordinated their defenses became around those fears. Sarah, for example, began the session by projecting her insecurities into Carl, which required that she foreclose upon the realities of his mind, in order to find goodness in the eyes of her loving object and gain a safe distance from her fear. As Carl absorbed her projection, he also absorbed two additional, but more hidden, elements: the fear that motivated it and the violence of erasure on which it rested. These projected elements then resonated with and augmented his own fears of criticism. In order to escape his now escalated fear, he then foreclosed upon the reality of Sarah's mind, projected his aggression into her and triumphed in his identification of her as the one who had failed. Just as with Sarah's projection, however, Carl's projection also contained the now aggregated fear of disapproval that both partners shared, as well as the retaliatory violence of erasure. When Sarah then absorbed these projected elements, they augmented *her* inner fears, and she was even further motivated to escalate her defenses, which she did when she said, condescendingly, that she didn't have the same kinds of problems as Carl.

Sarah and Carl's shared fear was thus the engine that perpetuated the continuation of their cycle, and on its foundation the two had traded projections, introjections, erasures and sacrifices in order for each to secure internal salvation. Their fear intensified as the cycle continued, driving both to invest increasing amounts of energy in their defenses. Ultimately it became an oppressive presence, a third entity, rooted in their mutually formed relational unconscious, that was larger than both and so intertwined with each partner's projections that they seemed to be trapped in it, unable to resist its calls to repeat the cycle of violence and sacrifice again and again.

The image of Sarah and Carl being driven by their shared fear—functioning like a third presence, driving them to intensify their denials of fault and claims to innocence—is reminiscent of accounts of romantic obsession or possession, in which each participant is pushed by something larger than themselves to pursue their disastrous course. Philosophy and literature are replete with such accounts, from the excruciating cycles of indictment and forgiveness in Maugham's *Of Human Bondage* (1915) to Deleuze and Guattari's (1987) esoteric concept of the aggregate machine ("There are no individual statements, only statement-producing machinic assemblages," p. 36). But the most vivid image that captures the essence of the cycle of violence between Sarah and Carl is that of the Furies in Aeschylus' *Oresteia* (1975). The Furies appear in the final play of the trilogy in the role of instigators of blood vengeance against Orestes for killing his mother Clytemnestra (who had in turn slain his father in retaliation for having sacrificed his sister), but the chorus describes them long before they actually take the stage. "Ancient Violence longs to breed," says the chorus in the first play, "new Violence comes/ when its fatal hour comes, the demon comes/ to take her toll—no war, no force, no prayer/ can hinder the midnight Fury stamped/ with parent Fury moving through the house." (p. 131)

The Furies, as supra-human entities, do not merely represent one individual's thirst for revenge, but rather the supra-individual pressure for violence that feeds on itself once the cycle has begun. As the Furies goad each individual to retaliatory violence, they are indifferent to the cycle of violence that may be instigated. The Furies don't fear the revelation of their own hypocrisy because they represent the same defenses used by Sarah and Carl—projection, denial, and self-justification (according to Hughes's translation of the *Oresteia*, when the Furies first appear they justify their thirst for revenge by saying it is not their fault and that other gods are to blame—1999). They represent the dynamics, in other words, that are the heart and soul of cycles of violence and sacrifice.

Girard emphasized sacrifice occurs only within the context of violent cycles characterized by denial and refusal of the real moral meanings of one's own acts. In his view, sacrifice in groups occurs as an attempt to avoid the noxious consequences of reciprocal violence or natural disasters whose real causes are either denied or misunderstood. In the dyadic interpersonal cycle, acts of sacrifice may be consciously intended to halt the cycle of violence, but their effect is the perpetuation of that very cycle and all of the pain and suffering associated with it.

Chapter Eight

The Cultural Third

Integrating Cultural Issues in Couple Therapy

The relationship between the individual mind and its cultural environment has been the object of study, for many years, of a number of disciplines, beginning with anthropology (social, cultural and structural) and extending to the more recent sub-disciplines of psychology, including cultural, cross-cultural, ecological, and ethnic minority psychology. Each of these disciplines has taken its own specific perspective on culture, i.e., on what culture means, its influence on the individual, and the individual's role in its creation, with the result that theories about culture and the mind have proliferated into a veritable Tower of Babel. These theories, moreover, had tended to organize around seemingly irresolvable dichotomies, such as universalism versus relativism, essentialism versus deconstructionism, culture as meaning versus culture as information, and personal identity versus social identity (Aviram, 2009; Cohen, 2009; Goldberger & Veroff, 1995; White, 2004). In each of these dichotomies, selected aspects of the culture-mind relationship are elevated to the status of central explanatory construct, in terms of which other phenomena are interpreted and explained. Universalists, for example, suggest that underneath apparent cultural differences is a universal human nature, while relativists argue that culture so profoundly impacts the structure of the psyche that cultural meanings and practices are effectively incomprehensible to members of other cultures (Cohen, 2009; Norenzayan & Heine, 2005).

In recent years, however, a different kind of cultural theory has appeared, one that bypasses dichotomies in order to emphasize that psyche and culture, instead of standing in opposition to each other, are mutually interdependent and "mutually constitutive" (White, 2004, p. 658). Theories of this type are of particular importance to the practice of psychoanalysis and psychotherapy because they focus the therapist's attention on the fact that cultural influences are continuous, inescapable, and immediate within the here-and-now moments of therapeutic interactions (Altman, 1995; Bodnar, 2004; Walls, 2004; White 2004). One example of this new form of theory is Shweder's cultural psychology, which he defines as the study of "the ways subject and object, self and other, psyche and culture, person and context, figure and ground, practitioner and practice, live together, require each other, and dynamically, dialectically, and jointly make each other up" (Shweder, 1990, p. 41). Similarly, Dalal has suggested "the social and the psychological are two aspects of the same process" (2006, p. 144), and Tubert-Oklander has said the "dialectic confluence of the personal and the impersonal, the individual and the collective, the conscious and the unconscious, is the essence and the subject matter of all psychoanalytic inquiry" (2006c, p. 149).

Underlying each of these theories is a central premise: none of the identifiable dimensions of experience and behavior—whether individual, interactive or cultural—is foundational, and none can be elevated above the rest to a position of explanatory centrality. Instead, these theories accord equal value to all dimensions and assume they interrelate dialectically, in such a way that each is mutually transformed and transforming of the rest. Many factors contribute to the rise of these inclusive, dialectical theories—including the injection of postmodern thinking into both cultural studies and psychoanalytic theory (Elliott & Spezzano, 1996; Dalal, 2006; Layton, 2000), the increasingly multicultural characteristics of psychotherapists and their patients (Bodnar, 2004; Leary, 1997), and diversity and liberation movements, which call attention to the underlying racial, gendered, and ethnic biases in society in general as well as in analytic theory and practice (Benjamin, 1988; Fogel, et al., 1996; Herron, 1995; Walls, 2004)—but these theories are also a natural outgrowth of relational theory and the middle ground approach in psychoanalysis. Because the middle ground perspective is committed to exploring the interface between the individual and the relational, it has of necessity included considerations of broader cultural factors, since culture lies, at least in part, in the meaning attributions that occur between individuals in interaction (S. Gerson, 1998; Javier & Rendon, 1995; Kadyrov, 2002; Tubert-Oklander, 2006c; Zeddies, 2000).

In this chapter, I would like to make a small contribution to these discussions about the role culture plays in the formation and shaping of both the individual mind and of minds in interaction. I'll do so by describing specific forms of culture-based transferences and transference-countertransference entanglements the therapist may encounter when working with couples in which the partners come from different social and political backgrounds.

Through my analysis of these transferences, I will attempt to expand upon the concept of the *cultural third*, first suggested by S. Gerson (2004, 2006, 2009).

INDIVIDUAL UNCONSCIOUS, RELATIONAL UNCONSCIOUS, CULTURAL THIRD

The foundational premise of the middle ground perspective is that the individual, intrapsychic unconscious is not a structure that exists in and of its own, independent of the transforming influences of other minds (Aron, 1996; Benjamin, 1995; Mitchell, 1988; Stolorow & Atwood, 1992). Instead, it is a participant in a near-continuous process of interplay with other minds, in such a way that its contents become interpenetrated with those of other unconsciouses. This interpenetration, in turn, has the capacity to create a supraindividual dimension of experience for all participants, which goes "beyond the singular dynamics of patient and analyst and is a unique quality of their interaction" (S. Gerson, 2006, p. 219). As noted elsewhere, the term most often used to describe this dimension is the *relational unconscious*, although it has also been described as the *analytic third*—in reference to the idea that it is tantamount to a third subjectivity operating between two partners in interaction (Ogden, 1994b, 2004).

Gerson (2004, 2006) has suggested that the metaphor of the third can be utilized to emphasize that, in addition to the individual and relational dimensions of experience, there is a third dimension, one that encompasses the broad array of social and cultural influences, in which individual psyches and their interrelationships are also shaped (see also Billow, 2003; Davidson, 1988; Tubert-Oklander, 2006c). Gerson termed this dimension the "cultural third" and suggested that it "serves as a point in a triangular structure that includes as well as organizes the intersubjective relation of the dyad" (2004, p. 78). In order to flesh out Gerson's important contribution, I would suggest that the concept of the cultural third rests on two primary assumptions. First, through identification and internalization of the values, beliefs, practices, etc. inherent in collective, cultural environments, individuals develop culture-based transferences and countertransferences that introduce the same kinds of limitations on experience—perceptual biases, unvarying emotional patterns, restrictions on behavioral repertoires, etc.—as transferences based on more personal material. Second, these cultural transferences and countertransferences enter into the same kinds of reciprocally modifying transactions as occur in the relational unconscious; in the cultural third, however, the psychic material that resonates between partners is derived from their histories and current affiliations with the cultural systems in which they have been embedded. While the cultural third is similar to Herron's (1995) cultural unconscious in that it refers to the historical identifications an individual has with "a particular group of people who have sufficient characteristics in common to give themselves a categorical name" (p. 525), it also emphasizes that interactions always take place within an immediate cultural context, and participants' cultural histories and affiliations can substantially influence their moment-to-moment exchanges.

ALAN AND RACHEL

To illustrate the interpenetration of the dimensions of the individual unconscious, the relational unconscious, and the cultural third, I would like to introduce the case of Alan and Rachel, who were self-referred for couple therapy because of conflict around finances and sex. Alan, a small-statured man, said he came from a family in which his father was distant and often absent, while his mother was intrusive and controlling in areas that concerned her, but neglectful and depriving in areas that didn't. The family environment was rigid and rule-oriented, with little communication about emotional matters and, as a result, the insecurities with which Alan struggled, because of both family dynamics and his size (he was "even smaller," he said, than his younger brothers), were left unrecognized and unmetabolized. These conflicts, in turn, contributed to the development of a punitive internal object, in relation to which Alan felt unacceptable and incapable. In defense against this object's devaluations, Alan utilized a dissociative defense—a kind of internal blindness to the full meanings of his emotions or actions. With Rachel, this defense appeared in his tendency to discount her opinions and undermine joint decisions, particularly in regard to their children, without recognizing what he had done or the meaning of his actions for Rachel.

Rachel, an only child, described her mother as distant and self-absorbed and her father as dismissing and critical. She remembered her childhood as lonely and filled with anxieties about how she would manage, on her own, whatever problems arose. When her parents divorced when she was fifteen, she attempted to forge individual relationships with each parent, only to discover both seemed to lack enthusiasm for contact. Her mother, who quickly remarried, was preoccupied with her new relationship, while her father believed she had contributed to the divorce by criticizing him to her mother. Rachel left home to attend college at eighteen, at a "low point," she said, of her relationships with her parents, and didn't see them again for several years. Because of how distant her relationships with them had become, Rachel chose to neither return home, nor to tell them that she was raped during her first year of college. As a result of these experiences, she internalized an uncaring, neglectful, and critical object, in relation to which she felt illegitimate, ill prepared, and subject to an unpredictable and unprotecting environment. In defense, she was overcautious and prone to exaggerate dangers and used hyper-competence, interpersonal control, and intellectualization to manage her anxieties.

During the second year of treatment, Alan and Rachel reported a vicious fight that began as a political discussion. As the discussion became increasingly heated, Alan said venomously: "You goddamned liberals with all your goddamned money. You think you're so fucking smart I could just puke." I asked how the conversation had taken on such intensity, noting as well that they exhibited a similar intensity in the session. Rachel said it erupted with no warning. Alan said he felt in control, but "something snapped" and he became enraged.

I pursued the themes in his statement: Rachel was smart, had more money and it made him sick. Alan had not worked for a year, due to a layoff, and Rachel, an attorney with a moderate income, supported the family. With probing and encouragement, Alan revealed one precursor of his anger: throughout his elementary and junior high school years, he was bullied by other kids, not only for being small, but also for being "stupid" and "dumb" (I suspected this wasn't because of low intellectual capacities, but rather because of his inability to read interpersonal situations). On the basis of this information, I suggested Rachel's willingness to support the family had indicated to Alan her superiority and, although he appreciated her help, he also hated it because it aroused the same feelings of inferiority he'd experienced as a child. I pointed out that she then became the target of the same fear and rage he'd felt toward the other children who bullied him. In response to my interpretations, Alan tearfully reported memories of being afraid to go to school and not knowing what to do or who to talk to. He apologized to Rachel, with what seemed like genuine recognition of the injury he caused her.

Rachel responded to Alan's memories with cool detachment and critical impatience, saying without empathy, "I think I understand better why you've never been able to adequately provide for your family." Alan's response, not unexpectedly, was to become angry again, and to criticize her for her lack of concern and compassion. I intervened at this moment to call attention to Rachel's detachment and, after some discussion, suggested she experienced Alan as a perpetuation of her parents' failures to provide an environment that felt protective to her, for which she was deeply resentful. In response, I said, she relied on her old defenses: emotional distance, control, and reminding Alan that only her superior competence kept the family afloat. She considered these interpretations, but also persevered in seeing Alan as the main source of their problems.

Chapter 8

THE RELATIONAL UNCONSCIOUS

To this point, I've described primarily the individual transferences that Alan and Rachel exhibited toward each other. Two further dimensions—the relational unconscious and the cultural third—also contributed to the interaction. We'll consider the relational dimension first. As I suggested in chapter 2, in couple interactions individual transferences rarely remain individual and, instead, become embroiled in joint transferences, i.e., shared transferences or transference-countertransference entanglements that are more indicative of the relational, rather than the individual, dimension of experience. In Alan and Rachel's case, each partner possessed valencies for the projective identifications underlying the other's transferences, with the result that, on both sides, introjective identifications and subsequent countertransference responses were elicited. The consequence of this interplay of psychic material from both partners was that the couple created a joint personality that followed the merged narrative of the more frightening aspects of each partner's individual unconscious.

For example, when Alan attacked Rachel's liberal views, he gave voice to anger and anxiety linked to childhood experiences, but he also evoked anger and anxiety in Rachel through two mechanisms. The first was projective identification, in which the fear and helplessness he felt as a child, but which he split off from his self-experience, was projected into Rachel. The second was by concretely giving her a frightening experience in which she felt both misunderstood and threatened. For her part, Rachel was prone to receive Alan's projections, because they resonated with her history of anxiety about being unprotected and neglected. Her defenses against this anxiety—detachment, criticism and assertions of superiority—implied she too split her anxiety off from her self-concept and projected it into Alan, thereby evoking in him his familiar anxieties and inferiorities, and setting off a new round of his anger, now intensified by the addition of her projected material. In the above exchange, this is where the couple's cyclical pattern stopped, but I had seen the pattern before and knew if it continued their anxieties and subsequent attacks would escalate, as each partner faced a devaluing, neglectful, and dangerous object made increasingly frightening by the mutually additive processes of projective and introjective identification.

The cyclical augmentation of transference- and countertransference-based emotions is characteristic of the dimension of interactive experience in which the relational unconscious is at work. In the relational unconscious, both partners' immersion in the blended psychic material originating from each individual unconscious creates a unified emotional theme that begins to function as though it has a life of its own, or has become something like the third subject described above (Barranger, 1993; Gabbard, 1997; Ogden, 1996). In Alan and Rachel's case, their relational unconscious in essence created a shared object (see chapter 3) whose primary characteristics were neglect and devaluation. As each partner received this object via projections from the other, they added their own anxiety, insecurity, and anger, so when they projected it back, it was with an enhanced sense of danger, which each partner was then doubly motivated to avoid via another round of projection. In the relational unconscious, each partner's "individual" experience becomes more and more the product of a complex mixture from both partner's internal worlds.

CULTURAL FACTORS IN PSYCHOTHERAPY

While the relational unconscious goes a long way toward explaining Alan and Rachel's interactions, the cultural third was also palpably present in the session. Although the influence of culture is all-too-often overlooked in reports of analytic treatment, particularly when patients are not members of an identifiable minority, no interpersonal interaction occurs outside of such factors as the cultural background of patients and therapist, the here-and-now cultural context in which therapy takes place, and the affiliations each party claims with various groups whose systems of thought and value may have some bearing on the enterprise (Altman, 1995; Bodnar, 2004; Javier & Herron, 2002; Kakar, 1985; Leary, 1997; Sue & Zane, 1987; Walls, 2004; White, 2004). The influence each of these factors has on patients and therapist is immediate and intimately relevant to the emotional, attitudinal, verbal and valuational exchanges between them (Comas-Diaz & Jacobsen, 1991; Zeddies, 2000).

What, however, do we mean by culture, and how can we chart its multiple influences over interpersonal interactions? While culture is a difficult and notoriously slippery concept, for our purposes it is sufficient to recognize that it as follows: (1) emerges in adaptive interactions between humans and their environments; (2) consists of socially constructed and shared constellations of such things as "practices, competencies, ideas, schemas, symbols, values, norms, institutions, goals, constitutive rules, artifacts, and modifications of the physical environment" (Fiske, 2002, p. 85), and (3) is transmitted across time periods and generations (Triandis, 2007). Culture, moreover, is not limited to racial or national identities. Every large-scale culture contains multiple sub-cultures, organized around parameters such as skin color, socioeconomic status, religion, musical preference or political party affiliations. Each of these sub-cultures is a true culture, although they may vary in the specific ways they function within the broader cultural environment (Cohen, 2009).

Cultures and cultural factors exert influence over their members from the moment of birth onward, and are particularly influential over interpersonal interactions. Such influences may be attributable to at least three major sources: the *developmental*, the *environmental* and the *interpersonal*.

The Developmental Aspect of Cultural Influence

Identifications and internalizations of the multifarious aspects of one's cultural environment can have both expanding and restricting effects on the development of the individual psyche. For example, cultural mechanisms facilitate the emergence of many of the qualities, talents, values, etc. that make up the self, and even may facilitate the creation of the self, itself, as an internal construct. Robertson, for example, argues that if the self is defined as a cognitive construct, "then it is necessarily a cultural construct. . . . Culture, in this sense, consists of all the ways of knowing, interpreting and doing that proliferate within a given society" (2010, p. 185; see also Cushman, 1990). On the other hand, a culture can also limit the options—of self, identity and personal characteristics—that are available to its members. Cultural factors, for example, are not only involved in determining racial, gender and class identities (Dalal, 2006; Layton, 2000; Walls, 2004), but also exert selective pressure on the expression or suppression of such personality traits as independence, empathy, resilience, rebelliousness and sense of agency. Snibbe and Markus (2005), for example, have shown that members of upper classes value control and agency, while those from lower classes forfeit those characteristics in favor of flexibility, integrity and resilience; and Kusserow (1999) has found that even though all white children in New York City are taught to be individualistic, the kind of individualism they exhibit varies with the kind of neighborhood they are raised in. These findings suggest there is some validity to Cushman's statement that "there is no universal, transhistorical self, only local selves" (1990, p. 599).

Cultural influences over the development of character, however, are not restricted to one's history of identifications. As individuals grow up in a culture with multiple sub-cultures, they are continuously faced with conflicts among the various sub-cultures' values, beliefs and practices. Each individual's negotiation of these conflicts is a uniquely complex process in which they identify with elements of some sub-cultures, but disidentify with others, in an attempt to integrate them into a more or less cohesive self-identity (Berry, 1997; Cohen, 2009; Herron, 1995; Mehta, 1998). The conflicts involved in these identifications and disidentifications are all the more heightened when the individual is attempting to assimilate into a different culture than the culture in which they were raised (Akhtar, 1995; Garza-Guerrero, 1974; Tummala-Narra, 2004). Regardless of the origins or breadth of assimilative conflicts, however, in any interaction each individual's history of identifications, disidentifications and attempts at integration will play a role in determining not only its course, but also the meanings attributed to interactive events, the emotions elicited by them, the values placed upon them, and the actions to be followed in response. This will be no less the case in therapeutic interactions than in any other kind of interpersonal exchange.

The Environmental Aspect of Cultural Influence

Bollas has said the external objects in our world are used for the expression of our personal idioms (1992, 2000), meaning objects contain "projectively identified self experience" and when we use or interact with them "something of that self state" stored in them will arise (1992, p. 21). Additionally, Bollas has suggested our method of planning and building our lived environments, including our work environments, "reflects unconscious forms of thinking"; and he wonders if there might be an "architectural unconscious" that directs the creation of a building and its internal environments, "finding its own vision out of the constituent elements" (2000, p. 28).

These considerations are directly relevant to the environmental aspect of cultural influence over therapeutic interactions. As therapist and patients interact, they are continuously confronted with the idiomatic expressions of each other's culture that are infused into the objects they bring to the meeting. A couple entering a therapist's waiting room, for example, may encounter Bach playing in the background, *People* and *Time* magazines, and chairs made by Scandinavian companies. In the consulting room, the patient might find colors by Ralph Lauren, an Eames chair for the therapist, art by local or international artists, psychotherapy books written by Caucasian authors, and knickknacks from the therapist's travels. Similarly, the therapist will encounter patients whose dress, jewelry, perfume, body decoration (e.g., hair style, makeup, tattoos, piercings, etc.) and accompanying objects (i.e., handbags, wallets, phones, keys or drinks) function as unconscious markers for their cultural identifications and disidentifications. Each of these markers, for therapist and patients, represent real-time cultural obstacles all parties must negotiate. Even if the patients and therapist are from the "same" culture, it is still helpful to think of these markers as obstacles, since they will have a tendency to limit the kinds of interaction that are possible between them.

Additionally, I would suggest tbat all participants' immediate interpersonal environment—i.e., the environment they "leave" as they enter the therapeutic hour—should be included under this category. A patient, for example, who has just been listening to hip hop music on an iPod, or who has just spoken to a parent whose culture doesn't approve of therapy, will be primed for an exchange with their partner or the therapist based on the still active traces of these interactions with their cultural environment. Similarly, a therapist who has just consulted with a colleague, or spoken with an insurance company, will have activated lingering traces of their own cultural environment. These reminders of each participant's cultural affiliations remain unconsciously present throughout the therapeutic interaction, serving to elicit internal identifications, and blending with other material already occupying each party's unconscious.

The Interpersonal Aspect of Cultural Influence: The Cultural Third

We are now at a point where the concept of the cultural third may be more fully explained. In this form of influence, the two cultural aspects just described—(1) the history of cultural identifications, disidentifications and attempts at integration and (2) the current cultural environments of each individual—enter into an interactive exchange similar to those that occur in the relational unconscious, and become the elements that modify—via *cultural transferences* and *countertransferences*—each partner's experience. To illustrate the cultural third's influence, let's return to Alan and Rachel.

We saw earlier that, in the argument between Alan and Rachel, each partner's history had created personal transferences that constructed the other as being identical to their hurtful and frightening internal objects. In defense against the anxieties those objects generated, each partner utilized projective identification, which only functioned to evoke similar anxieties in the other, leading to a transference-countertransference entanglement that escalated the conflict. The couple's interactions, however, also exhibited cultural transferences and countertransferences that, as we will see, resonated in powerful ways with their personal transferences. Alan came from—and at the time of this session still had strong ties to—a rigid, conservative, and religious family who emphasized the virtues of individual responsibility. He and his family subscribed to radical conservative policies and Alan identified himself as a defender of "common sense" against liberals' elitism and arrogance—an old-style libertarian who opposed any government role in social safety nets, health care programs, or Wall Street bailouts. In identification with the more angry voices in his subculture, and in disidentification with the more moderate conservative perspectives, he was contemptuous and dismissing of the liberal worldview.

Rachel, in contrast, was raised in a liberal environment and encouraged to make her own decisions about religion and political affiliations. In her adult years, she identified with the Democratic Party's platforms, especially their emphasis on social responsibility, and rejected the Republican Party's advocacy of individual responsibility as a cover-up for selfishness. Her identifications with the parts of liberal subculture that were hostile to Republicans, and her disidentifications with the conservative trends both in her family and her broader culture, led her to view conservatives as greedy, unthinking, and deserving contempt.

On the basis of experiences with their particular subcultures, then, Alan and Rachel had developed identifications and disidentifications that gave form to the cultural transferences each brought to the relationship. As happened with their personal transferences, Alan and Rachel's cultural transferences not only distorted their perception and treatment of the other, but also mobilized cycles of defense, projective identification, and anger that were similar in form to the entanglements (centered on more personal psychic material) I described earlier. Alan's contempt for Rachel's elitism, for example, allowed him to feel, in the moment he expressed it, both powerful and superior, because it proved his identification with his conservative subculture. Hidden behind his superiority, however, was anxiety about inferiority—a feeling that, I think a case can be made, is shared by both ends of the political spectrum in today's contentious climate. This inferiority, though, represented another split-off portion of Alan's psyche that he attempted to project into Rachel by devaluing her. Rachel was usually a willing recipient of these projections, because of her own feelings of inferiority, and in defense she tried to reproject those feelings back into Rob via her criticisms of his blindness—criticisms which represented her own comforting identifications with her liberal subculture. The end result was a culture-based transference-countertransference entanglement in which each partner's projections mobilized in the other an intensification of the emotions they already felt. This entanglement might be called the "pure" form of the cultural third, because it seemed to be based almost exclusively on Alan and Rachel's political identifications and disidentifications.

The real heart of the cultural third, though, lay in its participation in a dialectical confluence of both cultural and personal aspects of interactive experience. This confluence, which illustrates the full dynamic range of the cultural third's influence, is best illustrated by a brief exchange that occurred later in the session in which Alan and Rachel reported their fight. Just prior to this exchange, Rachel had defended her liberal perspective. Alan then turned to her and said, with frustration and aggression in his voice, "I just don't understand how you could believe those kinds of things. It's like you think you know what's best for everybody and you're going to give it to them whether they need it or not. Maybe I don't know what I'm talking about, but I think that's pretty arrogant." Rachel's response was rapid and equally energized. In a lecturing and sarcastic tone, she said, "It's not arrogant, Alan, it's just knowing the right thing to do—and I'm sorry to say but you just don't seem to understand that." Alan, with now escalated aggression, said, "Oh, that's just stupid and idiotic. Don't tell me I don't understand. I know a lot more about these things than you think I do."

Alan's initial statement in this exchange was defined by transferences derived from both the cultural and the personal realms: his complaint that Rachel was arrogant, referred both to his experiences of being bullied *and* to his conservative criticism of liberals. Rachel's response—that she knows the right thing to do but Alan doesn't—similarly reflected both her cultural transferences (e.g., conservatives are blind and ignorant) and her personal transferences (e.g., no one is going to know what I need). For each partner, the presence of transferences and transference-countertransference entanglements from both realms served to magnify and render even more intolerable their feelings of insecurity, anxiety, and inferiority—emotions they felt but denied, and try to split off and project. Once these amplified emotions entered the interaction, both partners felt an increasing urgency to project them—an urgency that led to their rapid escalation in hostility. The emotional patterns that were already occurring within the couple's relational unconscious had thus become compounded by the cultural third, with the result that the couple now seemed consigned to repeat, once again, their familiar pattern of conflict.

In this chapter, I have focused on the transferences and transference-countertransference entanglements—cultural and personal—that were exhibited by Alan and Rachel in a single session in couple therapy. While I haven't described the transferences each partner directed toward me, suffice it to say they were present and, at times, powerful. Consider, if only briefly, the position a therapist is in when two patients wrestle with each other for a political victory. Both Alan and Rachel assumed I am of the liberal persuasion, even though I spoke nothing explicitly of my own subculture affiliations, and this assumption created obstacles to my work with both of them: with Alan because he expected I would assert superiority over him; and with Rachel because she expected I would side with her to criticize Alan. Working through these transferences, which were also based in both cultural and personal aspects of each partner's internal world, became a significant part of my work with them. Adding to the complexity of their transferences and countertransferences, Alan and Rachel also differed in terms of how they viewed therapy. For Rachel, therapy was a culturally accepted and even encouraged endeavor, and she settled into it with comfort and a sense of easy familiarity. Because of his conservative, individualistic perspective, however, Alan felt his participation in treatment represented something of a disloyalty. He told me regularly he didn't want to blame anyone else—especially his mother—for his problems.

TREATMENT AND THE CULTURAL THIRD

In conclusion, I would like to review some of the principles of treatment for working with cases like Alan and Rachel's, in which personal and cultural transferences, individually and in combination, create patterns of interaction that are entrenched in potent and primitive emotions and are resistant to intervention. I would suggest that, first, the treatment of cultural transference material should follow the same principles of treatment of any other kind of transference. That is, therapists must prepare themselves to discover cultural transferences in the actual relationships in therapy (whether between partners or between therapist and the couple) and they must help patients recognize, accept, and contain the emotional foundations of those transferences. Second, therapists need to be capable of following transferences into either their personal or cultural sources (or both), and work with at least two levels of interaction: (1) between personal and cultural transferences in the individual; and (2) between the relational unconscious and the cultural third in interactions between individuals. This requirement can be particularly daunting, since in couple therapy there are many kinds of transference (individual, joint, personal, cultural) and many targets of transference (the other partner, the couple itself, the therapist, or the process of therapy), and the therapist must focus on those transferences that have the best chance of advancing the treatment. Finally, therapists must recognize cultural transferences are always present and always exert influence over the therapeutic process. In cases where the patient is clearly from a different ethnic group, the possibilities of cultural transferences should be obvious (although ethnic minorities commonly report frustration with having to "teach" their therapists about their culture, creating a possible source of mismatch and resistance to therapeutic progress). Even in cases, however, where the therapist and patient appear to share the same subculture identifications, cultural transferences still operate in ways that can create resistances, negative therapeutic reactions, and impasses that bring therapeutic progress to a halt. Therapists who pay attention to cultural contributions add a rich dimension and fuller understanding to the therapeutic process; those who neglect them do so at their peril.

In my work with Alan and Rachel, once I recognized cultural transferences accounted for nearly as much of their conflict as their personal transferences, I began to speak directly about them. I described how each partner treated the other as something akin to a stereotype, in which the full meaning of the other's experiences and actions was lost behind a limiting and diminishing picture of them. I pointed out how the sources of these pictures seemed to include past personal events, past political affiliations, and current identifications based on political ideology. My interpretations along these lines prompted both Alan and Rachel to explore the emotional foundations of their personal and cultural transferences (Rachel, for example, revealed that in college, liberalism was her only haven from what felt like a cold campus environment—an environment that replicated her earlier family experience). By exploring the foundations of both kinds of transferences, the couple began to approach, and find ways to contain, the histories of anxiety, insecurity, and anger that each brought, in high intensity and without understanding, to their relationship.

Chapter Nine

Who's Afraid of Virginia Woolf?

Postmodern Lessons in Truth, Illusion, and the Couple

"I'm a liar and I've run out of people to lie to." These were the first words Doug said to me as he, his wife Carol, and I began our initial meeting. He didn't fit my image of a liar. Well-dressed in a business suit and tie, he spoke in a confessional tone, suggesting honesty and remorse. He described some of the lies he told. None were extreme, but the lying was chronic. He'd lied to Carol about when he was going to pick up the kids, whom he talked to at church, when the roast would finish cooking, how much he spent at the store. These aren't the lies that usually bring couples to therapy, which are often about affairs or addictions or crimes, but their cumulative effect on Carol was discouraging and alienating. Their relationship suffered because of it and now they sat in front of me.

We spent the next several months talking about these lies: about their origin; the couple's response to them; their children's thoughts about them. Doug continued to seem open with me, willingly delving into his personal history to create a narrative about the genesis of his lying. His mother and father were more interested in his conformity to the image they wanted him to be than they were in the truth about his opinions, emotions, and desires. Intemperately and for their own convenience, they rewarded the falsehoods Doug promoted and punished his truths.

Carol, as we came to understand, was not uninvolved in the patterns leading to Doug's lying. A stay-at-home mother devoted to maintaining the status quo, her reactions to many of Doug's truths were similar to his parents. She was frightened by some of them, such as that he wasn't interested in continuing to attend church services with her, or that he spent $50 on a videogame for his son, of which she didn't approve, and worried about the impression they projected to their neighbors and friends. Consequently, Carol gave Doug contradictory messages: tell me the truth, but not too much, and don't scare me with it.

As therapy progressed, we explored motivations, interactive sequences, and intrapsychic conflicts that might help us understand Doug's habitual lying. When these explanations arose, they seemed to capture something real and truthful about Doug. But these "truths" soon gave way to other "truths"—ones that may or may not have been related to the prior truth. Each truth, moreover, was either presented or greeted (if I or Carol suggested it) by Doug as the new correct view with which he completely agreed—as though he was repeating his acts of compliance with his parents. When we discussed his anger at his father, for example, and its relation to his holding secrets about himself from him, he said, "That has to be it. *That's* why I lied to him." He said something quite similar when Carol suggested he was angry with her and when I suggested he was frightened of internal judgment and was trying to keep secrets even from himself. An image that recurred to me during this phase of therapy was of a stage with many curtains, one behind another. Each time we reached a new truth, a curtain lifted and the stage reconfigured. But there was always the feeling that more truths and more curtains would be discovered.

These successive truths were never totally false. They pointed to real aspects of Doug's personality, but they were also partial and provisional, as though in the act of revealing them, Doug also concealed other truths. More complete, multifaceted truths that better explained his behavior and the relationship he established with Carol never appeared, so we had to make do with his successive revisions. Even after his Big Lie was revealed, two years into therapy, we only found partial truths. Ultimately, though, the accumulation of those partial truths, and more particularly, the development of a communicative *method*, between Doug and Carol, for seeking out partial truths, had a positive effect and their relationship began to improve.

Doug and Carol's struggles with truth and illusion, and my feeling that our therapy was occurring on a stage with an infinite number of curtains, was reminiscent for me of the famous couple, George and Martha, in Edward Albee's play *Who's Afraid of Virginia Woolf?* As I re-read the play with Doug and Carol in mind, I began to discern, in the play's characters and action and in Albee's treatment of those characters and the audience, a deep and moving relevance to the dilemmas a therapist grapples with when facing a couple with an uncertain relationship to the truth. In this chapter, I will first review current thinking in analytic theory about the nature and value of truth. I'll then turn to an analysis of the play in order to illuminate its deliciously counterpoising treatments of truth and the possible roles it may play in the art of healing. Finally, I'll return to Doug and Carol, to show how the revelation of Doug's Big Lie spurred a process of reorientation toward the many truths in their relationship.

TRUE LIES: THE NATURE OF TRUTH IN A POSTMODERN WORLD

As described throughout this book, in the past thirty or so years we have witnessed a "sea change" in some of the foundational ideas of psychoanalysis. This conceptual shift has been instigated by theories of relationality and intersubjectivity (Aron, 1996; Mitchell, 1988, 2000; Stolorow & Atwood, 1992), which in turn have been influenced by such philosophical perspectives as postmodernism (Fairfield, 2001; Fairfield, Layton, & Stack, 2002; Frie, 2003), hermeneutics (Spence, 1993; Zeddies, 2002a, 2002b), deconstructionism (Stolorow, 1995) and social constructivism (Hoffman, 2002; Stern, 1985). One of the specific consequences of the infusion of these perspectives into psychoanalysis is the rekindling of questions about the validity of the concept of truth, its value in psychological healing, and the nature of the patient's and therapist's access to it. Influenced by these perspectives, many psychoanalysts have targeted the views of Freud in particular, because his incorporation of the precepts of early twentieth-century positivism and scientific materialism led him, they believe, to a relatively naïve view of psychological truth. His assertions, for example, that psychic truths lay lodged unchanging in the unconscious, ready to be unearthed by the analyst via a psychological version of archeological excavation (Freud, 1919; Heaton, 2000); that even unconscious truths are empirically verifiable and can become the raw material for scientific laws; and that the therapist can receive communications from the patient's unconscious that are undistorted by the therapist's own "receptive organ" (Freud, 1912, p. 115) are now viewed with skepticism.

This skepticism has been fueled, in large measure, by analytic theorists—particularly those who endorse the middle ground approach—who recognize that two realms of *otherness* are intimately involved in, and exert significant influence over, the creation of any truths we are capable of discovering. These two realms, the intrapsychic, individual unconscious and the relational unconscious, are thought to introduce such uncertainties and indeterminacies into the construction of even our most foundational perceptions that their influence not only *isn't* known in the moment, but *cannot* be known. The intrapsychic unconscious, for example, even under its most traditional conceptualization, is the realm of unknown aspects of the self that exert sometimes dramatic influence over experience and that can only be intuited via *indirect* means, such as free association, transference enactment and dreams

or "waking dream thoughts" (Bion 1962b; Ferro 2002). As such, the unconscious already bears the mark of alterity: to the experiencing self, its influence feels like it comes from *without* (this otherness is reflected, for example,
in Freud's original German term for the *id*: "das Es," meaning the "it"). More
recent elaborations of the unconscious have only served to increase its indeterminacy by suffusing it, far more comprehensively than Freud, with characteristics of the relational unconscious.

The relational unconscious represents the other pervasive locus of influence from the Other (S. Gerson, 2004, 2006; Scharff & Scharff, 2011; Tubert-Oklander, 2006b; Zeddies, 2000). This form of the unconscious refers to
a dimension of interactive experience in which the mental processes of each
participant are continuously and reciprocally transformed by similar processes in the other. In the view of middle ground theorists, the relational unconscious is conceived as an immanent determinant of all interactive experience—to the extent that every event that occurs in an interaction, even if it
appears to pertain to just one of the participants, must at least be considered
as having been constructed by both (Barranger & Barranger, 1966; Ferro,
2007; S. Gerson, 2004; Hoffman, 1991; Stern, 1991). Thus, because the
relational unconscious brings the full meaning-making potential of another
mind to bear on one's own mind, it too carries the decentering trace of
alterity.

The relationship between the intrapsychic and the relational unconscious
is notoriously difficult to describe or explain, and requires delving deep into
philosophic issues that are beyond the scope of this chapter. Perhaps the most
common explanation, though, particularly among middle ground theorists, is
that the two forms of the unconscious stand in a dialectical relationship. In
this dialectic, each form of the unconscious interpenetrates the other, meaning the blended experiences created by the relational unconscious are also
reblended with each participant's intrapsychic unconscious, and vice versa,
so that both dimensions of unconscious experience are in a continual state of
mutual transformation (Aron, 1996; Ogden, 1994a, 1994b).

The dialectic between the intrapsychic and the relational unconscious
implies, of course, that both forms of otherness play a central role in creating
the conscious and unconscious contents of all participants in any interaction
(Lyons-Ruth, 1999). The implications of this view for concepts of psychological truth, especially in a therapeutic context, are substantial. First, if any
characteristic that is perceived (by either the patient, therapist or both) to
belong to the patient is constructed by both the intrapsychic and relational
unconsciouses of the two participants, then its status as a "fact," or as the
"truth" about the patient, is immediately called into question. Since the therapist's contribution cannot be completely differentiated from the patient's in
the construction of this perception, its truth-value must remain, at least to
some extent, indeterminate (S. Gerson, 2006). Second, because of the contin-

ual interplay between the intrapsychic and the relational unconscious, any "truths" revealed about a patient in interaction with one therapist may differ from those revealed in interactions with a different therapist, because the revealing of each truth depends upon, and waits for, the gathering of forces within the particular dialectic from which it arises. (It is important to note that the extent to which a patient may differ in interactions with different therapists has been hotly debated, with the more radical relational theorists arguing that the patient will exhibit little or no continuity between the varying interactions.)

The concept of the dialectic between the intrapsychic and the relational unconscious has thus reinforced a new conception of the unconscious altogether. From this perspective, the patient's intrapsychic unconscious can no longer be considered a mere "receptacle of repressed material." Instead, it is a participant in a fluid and dynamic *process*—whose contents "await birth at a receptive moment in the contingencies of evolving experience" (S. Gerson, 2004, p. 69)—that is in constant transformation because of its openness to the alterity of the intersubjective other (Baranger, 1993; Ferro, 2007). In therapy, the processional nature of the unconscious implies, again, that the "truths" established by therapist and patient will always be marked by uncertainty (Ferro, 2006b), and must therefore always be regarded as tentative, since they will always leave "potential areas of knowing unexplored" (S. Gerson, 2004, p. 90). These observations have led more than one commentator to suggest the "text" of analysis or therapy—i.e., the patient/therapist interaction—is always "in the making" (Ferro, 2006b), and hence the therapy is never fully completed because the patient is never fully revealed (Ferro, 2007; Smith, 1997).

Freud's turn-of-the-century optimism about the ultimate determinability of psychic truths and realities and their potential place in forming scientific laws has thus been replaced by a cautiousness about truth that heralds from the recognition that the two Others exert a systematic influence over whatever truths can be discovered. Does this then mean Freud was wrong to emphasize the role of truth in psychological healing? In his essay *Mourning and Melancholia* (1917), for example, Freud asserted that a patient's capacity to recognize and accept the reality of a loss will determine whether he or she will respond to the loss with melancholia or healthy mourning. Was Freud misguided, or naïve, in believing this? Although some theorists—those who follow postmodernist logic to its extremes and argue that there are *no* truths worth committing to—will answer this question in the affirmative, most respond with a qualified no.

Analytic writers of all theoretical stripes (Billow, 2010; Chessick, 1996; Eagle, 2003; Faimberg, 1997; Spence, 1989; Stern, 1985) have recognized that as human beings we hunger for truth, even if the truth at times can be difficult both to find and to bear. Bion, for example, said truth serves to harmonize the thinking mind with sensory and affective data about the self, while its absence "induces a mental state of debility in the patient as if starvation of truth was somehow analogous to alimentary starvation" (Bion, 1962a, p. 310). Similarly, Stern suggests the patient/therapist pair's "acceptance of impermanence (since their truths may change) and imperfection of their work makes no less satisfying to them their discovery of words that fit experience closely" (Stern, 1985, p. 206). These theorists, and many others who have assumed a "mixed" model (Fairfield, 2001) in regard to truth— viz., of both respecting it but also recognizing its limitations—haven't so much abandoned truth as they have decided to trust it slightly less and to hold in mind that whatever truths are discovered, no matter how helpful, won't be permanent, but instead will require continuous scrutiny and intermittent revision. They take an attitude toward psychological truth similar to that assumed by the physicist Richard Feynman: "In physics the truth is rarely perfectly clear, and that is certainly universally the case in human affairs. Hence, what is not surrounded by uncertainty cannot be the truth" (Feynman, 2005, p. 301).

The decentering and destabilizing influence the two Others exert over our access to psychological truth has also necessitated, for middle ground theorists, a concomitant reformulation of the aims and goals of psychotherapy (for more detail on this point, see chapter 4). The middle ground theorist may still hold as valid Freud's famous formulation—that the aim of psychoanalysis is to make the unconscious conscious through insight (1915, 1919), but only after reformulating the "unconscious" as including both the intrapsychic and the relational unconscious, and "insight" as an ongoing process that does not, and cannot, reach finality. The perpetual motion injected into the unconscious by the dialectic between the intrapsychic and the relational renders it essentially a realm of infinite possibilities (Bion, 1965) rather than enduring realities. Consequently, insight—*if* its achievement is accompanied by expectations that it need only occur on a finite basis, limited to a few moments of clarity that will have lasting effects—is no longer sufficient as a model of therapeutic transformation. Instead, the procedures of attaining insight need to be ongoing, matching the always-transforming, kaleidoscopic nature of experience that is perpetually subjected to the influence of the two Others.

In the long run, our patients are helped less by particular moments of insight than by learning to use a *method* of being with themselves, of opening the boundaries between the conscious mind and the two Others, so a continuous stream of information about the foundations of the self, uncertain and indeterminate though they may be, is available to them. Faimberg, for example, suggests we help a patient most by ensuring "that he can become able to listen to himself" (1997, p. 442). A therapist infers the psychic reality of the patient, Faimberg says, by "listening to listening," by determining the "distance between what the analyst thinks he has interpreted and what the patient actually heard" and then assigning new meaning "retroactively (*nachträglich*) to the interpretation" (p. 442). She thus describes a process of successive approximation to psychic reality through inherently intersubjective mechanisms. By learning this same process, the patient begins to practice *responsibility* toward his unconscious:

> After all, when a patient is unable to acknowledge his psychic reality, he cannot acknowledge his psychic responsibility towards his unconscious. Psychic responsibility begins when the patient succeeds in seeing himself as the subject of his psychic functioning. . . . This recognition implies that psychic reality has real consequences in the intrapsychic and intersubjective links discovered by the patient in his analysis. (1997, p. 444)

The aim of therapy in the age of the two Others is not primarily to discover insight, though insight still plays an important role, but to "develop the capacity or *function* for self-awareness" (Holmes, 2001, p. 45) that will allow the patients to continue the unending work of listening to themselves and of thereby being available for the revelations of their transitory, but still transformative, truths. The unending work of therapy is tantamount to the unending work of living well. As Bion has said, we cannot live our lives satisfactorily without seeking the truth, even if the ultimate truth about ourselves is unreachable (Ferro, 2007, p. 5).

TRUTH AND ILLUSION IN *WHO'S AFRAID OF VIRGINIA WOOLF?*

Edward Albee's famous and controversial play *Who's Afraid of Virginia Woolf?* (1962) is superficially about the contentious and sometimes sadistic relationship between its two main protagonists, George and Martha. Seen in this light, the play has often been taken as little more than a *tour de force* depiction of the depravities to which a marital relationship can sink. A deeper reading of the play, however, illuminates a central theme of truth v. illusion, and reveals an author who asks both his characters and his audiences whether truth is essential to living a good life. In posing these questions, Albee the author also functions as something like a therapist to George and Martha, in that he guides them through the conscious and unconscious minefields they must negotiate to decide whether they can face their losses and give up the illusions they have erected against them, or whether they can live well enough by clinging to those illusions. In a style that is both intimate and destabilizing, Albee breaks down the boundaries between the audience and his characters, so the audience becomes embroiled in the same dramas around truth as George and Martha.

Throughout the play, Albee pits one fundamental ideology—truth is an enduring reality to which we must adjust—against another: truth is indeterminate and every apparent truth also contains illusion. What is most telling about Albee is he *never* decides between the two and he refuses to allow his characters or his audiences to decide as well. Thus, he assumes an essentially "mixed" model toward the truth: on the one hand, he presents George and Martha as though essential truths about them are in the process of being born as the play runs its course; on the other, he undermines those truths with a continuous stream of uncertainties, indeterminacies and contradictory revisions. Albee's *attitude* toward the truth is what ultimately illustrates, in vivid detail and form, the stance required of a modern therapist who recognizes the determining influence of the two Others. The therapist, just like a viewer of *Who's Afraid of Virginia Woolf?*, must find a way to comfortably keep a foot in two worlds, to "tread the fence," as it were (as a patient once said to me), between truth and fiction.

SYNOPSIS OF THE PLAY

Set in three acts ("Fun and Games," "Walpurgisnacht," and "The Exorcism"), *Who's Afraid of Virginia Woolf?* revolves around the relationship between George, a college professor, and Martha, the daughter of the college president. The play begins at 2:00 a.m. on a Sunday morning as the couple returns from a faculty social. Martha announces she invited Nick, a good-looking, young professor, and his "mousey" wife Honey over for drinks. Even before Nick and Honey arrive, George and Martha launch into one of many loud and drunken tirades in which they try to hurt each other with venomous attacks. Just before their company arrives, George warns Martha not to mention their child, "the kid," to them.

As soon as Nick and Honey enter, they become embroiled in the brutal battles between George and Martha. Martha flirts shamelessly with Nick and George sadistically tries to best Nick in verbal argument. When Honey reveals that Martha told her about their son, George escalates his attacks on Martha and she retaliates, criticizing George for his physical condition, his cowardice, etc.

The conversation turns more and more to the boy and George taunts Martha about bringing the topic up. Martha says George is unsure whether the boy is his and they argue about the color of the boy's eyes. George threatens to expose "the truth" about the boy. Martha accuses George of being a failure in his life and work, calling him a "flop" and a "bog." George starts to sing "Who's afraid of Virginia Woolf . . . so early in the morning." Nick and Honey join in drunkenly, until Honey runs off stage sick from alcohol. Martha and Nick follow her.

When Nick returns alone, he tells George he married Honey partly for her family's money and partly because she erroneously believed she was pregnant, and George tells Nick a story about a childhood friend who accidentally killed his mother and father. When Martha and Honey return, the conversation wends back to the boy. George says the son used to run away from home because Martha "cornered him." Martha says: "I NEVER CORNERED THE SON OF A BITCH IN MY LIFE!" Nick and Martha dance together suggestively. Martha reveals George wrote a novel about a boy who kills his parents and "pretends it's all an accident," that the novel's story is true and is about George himself, and George didn't published it because her father wouldn't allow it. Furious, George tries to strangle Martha until Nick pulls him away.

George announces he will now play a new game called Get the Guests. He tells them about his "second novel," which is a contemptuous retelling of the story of Nick and Honey's courtship and marriage. Honey realizes Nick told George about her hysterical pregnancy and leaves the room, ill again, with Nick following. During the interval, George and Martha declare "total war" against each other. When Nick returns, Martha seduces him in earnest. They embrace and kiss each other. George declares he's going to read a book while Martha "entertains" her guests. Martha hesitates, not wanting to believe George wants her to take Nick upstairs. They fight again and Martha leaves. Honey re-enters and reveals to George she is afraid of the pain of childbirth. George then announces, both laughing and crying, he received a telegram with bad news—his and Martha's son is dead.

Martha returns to the stage, joined shortly by Nick. Neither George, nor Honey is present. Martha reveals Nick was impotent, a "flop" like George, but she then talks endearingly about "George who is good to me and whom I revile." George enters with flowers. George and Martha debate whether there is a moon or no moon that evening, and George mentions sailing past Majorca as a graduation gift from his parents. Nick asks if that was after George killed his parents; George answers "Maybe," and Martha adds "Yeah; maybe not, too." George says to Nick: "Truth and illusion. Who knows the difference, eh, toots? Eh?" Martha then says to George, in an allusion to his belief she's had sex with Nick, "Truth and illusion, George; you don't know the difference." George answers, "No; but we must carry on as though we did."

George raises the topic of the boy and Martha launches into an extended description of his childhood. He was "so beautiful; so wise," she says, and George responds, "All truth being relative." They argue about whether the son respected or disowned his father, and to whom he wrote the most letters, until George announces the boy died in an automobile accident. Martha, devastated, argues that George "can't do this," he can't "decide these things." She pleads, "he is *not* dead; he is not *dead*," but George insists he is. Nick finally realizes George and Martha never had a child and "the boy" was their invention. Martha is bowed by great sadness and loss. Nick and Honey depart, leaving George and Martha talking softly to each other as day breaks. George says, "It will be better." Martha answers, "I don't . . . know." George says, "It will be . . . maybe," then sings "Who's afraid of Virginia Woolf?" soothingly. The play ends as Martha answers, "I . . . am . . . George . . . I . . . am . . . "

TRUTH V. ILLUSION

In a 1965 interview in the *Paris Review*, Albee said he found the question "Who's afraid of Virginia Woolf?" written in soap on the bathroom mirror of a saloon in New York City. Although he called the phrase a "rather typical, university intellectual joke," it "cropped up" in his mind again when he started to write the play a decade later. "And of course," he added, "who's afraid of Virginia Woolf means who's afraid of the big *bad* wolf . . . who's afraid of living life without false illusions" (Flanagan, 1988, p. 52). Virginia Woolf, the author and advocate of penetrating self-analysis and the eradication of illusions, is a fitting image to be evoked in Albee's play. Not because the play particularly advocates eradicating illusions (the play takes a significantly more complex perspective than that), but because Virginia Woolf's stance toward them serves as one side of a two-sided debate, about the relative values of truth and illusion, that Albee was most interested in exploring.

Because he was interested in illuminating both sides of the debate, Albee did not clarify his own position toward these questions within the confines of the play itself. This did not stop critical reviewers from assuming he *must* have taken a side. Several early commentators, for example, suggested Albee simply inverted the argument, in a "naïve" or "sophomoric" way, from Eugene O'Neill's play *The Iceman Cometh*, which portrayed illusions as necessities that shield us from painful realities. Albee's statement that *Virginia Woolf* was indeed a response to O'Neill (Gussow, 1999, p. 153), and his assertion in 1982 that he was "very concerned with the fact that so many people turn off because it is easier; they don't stay fully aware during the course of their lives . . . I find that anything less than absolutely full, dangerous participation is an absolute waste of some rather valuable time" (quoted in Roudané, 1990, p. 45), certainly helped to reinforce the perception that *Virginia Woolf* advocates a moralistic position that everyone should learn to live in the full light of reality.

But *Virginia Woolf* does not, in fact, take a side in this issue. Instead, it provides many examples in which competing views are advocated without resolution—so much so that Albee's "true" position becomes impossible to determine. George's line, "Truth and illusion. Who knows the difference, eh, toots?" is but one of many that equivocates in granting truth epistemic, pragmatic, or moral primacy over fiction. The exchange between George and Martha at the end of the third act, after George has "killed" the son-illusion from which they both gained comfort, also raises the question of the relative value of truth v. illusion, but refuses to provide an answer. George asks Martha, "Are you all right?" She answers with a contradiction: "Yes. No." George then sings to her "Who's afraid of Virginia Woolf," to which she answers, "I . . . am . . . George . . . I . . . am . . . " Moreover, throughout the play the audience is rarely granted the pleasure of uncorrupted access to anything resembling truth. It is never clear, for example, whether George was in fact the youth who shot his mother and killed his father in an automobile accident. Such refusals to grant epistemological license to the audience, to find comfort in certainties, requires an approach to interpreting the play that takes the multiplicity of positions taken by the characters into full account.

A similar argument can be made against those commentators who claim Albee is merely a nihilist who used his linguistic skill to indulge in a destructive rampage with no apparent redemption. Debusscher, for example, claims "Albee's work contains no positive philosophical or social message. His theatre belongs in the pessimistic, defeatist or nihilistic current which characterizes the entire contemporary theatrical scene" (1967, p. 83). And Harold Bloom, far from finding psychological growth or reconciliation in the final scene between George and Martha, thinks instead they are reduced to "blathering fools" (quoted in Roudané, 1990, p. 23). In order to make these claims, however, these reviewers must discount the obvious references to redemption—born out of truth and love—that can be found throughout the play. The clearest reference to truth's redemptive power lies in the symbol of dawn, which rises as George performs the "exorcism" of the illusion that hampered both his and Martha's emotional growth. And the salvational power of George and Martha's love for each other is alluded to in multiple places, even in the midst of the hatred they so cuttingly aim at each other. Martha makes the least ambiguous statement of this at the beginning of Act Three:

> George who is good to me, and whom I revile; who understands me, and whom I push off; who can make me laugh, and I choke it back in my throat; who can hold me, at night, so that it's warm, and whom I will bite so there's blood; . . . who can make me happy and I do not wish to be happy, and yes I do wish to be happy. George and Martha: sad, sad, sad.

The multiplicity of positions, whether dramatic, philosophic or metapsychological, taken by both the author and the characters in the play without the privileging of any one position over another, means, ultimately, that Albee's text refuses readers the refuge of certainty and leaves them with a vertiginous realization that no criteria are offered to determine the validity of any particular position. By this method, the reader is asked to consider the possibility that no position is always true or always false and that the "truth" may float instead between the two polarities, always potentially both determined and indeterminate, fixed and transforming. Albee's play thus represents a *playing* with the truth of truth, and the value of value, and in this way approaches the structure of a Zen *koan* that purposely deconstructs familiar meanings in order to hint at intuitions that are lost the moment language is used to describe them. As one commentator stated: "Any attempt at categorically understanding or explaining experience, Albee implies, is always already a kind of performative fiction, a creative attempt to represent the unrepresentable" (Bottoms, 2000, p. 14).

Although Albee was unimpressed with psychoanalysis and disagreed with some of its basic premises (Avery, 1973), still the theme of redemption in *Virginia Woolf* echoes a major thrust in the traditional psychoanalytic approach to treatment. In *Mourning and Melancholia* (1917), Freud argued melancholia is the result of the replacement of awareness of the *truth* about object-loss with the *fiction* that the loss did not occur. This replacement is accomplished via an identification with the lost object—a maneuver that preserves it, seemingly alive, within the ego. Freud's ineluctable implication is that the path to psychological health requires the abandonment of the fiction that there was no loss associated with the object. In so far as *Virginia Woolf* advocates redemption through giving up illusions, then, it also represents the traditional psychoanalytic perspective that truth and illusion are differentiable, and that there is more value in truth. Albee's juxtaposition, however, of the theme of redemption against themes of uncertainty and indeterminacy places the traditional psychoanalytic perspective into a specifically postmodern context, with the consequence that it no longer can retain its grounding in absolutist concepts of truth and reality—but neither has it lost all of its usefulness.

We began by considering whether *Virginia Woolf* simplistically advocates seeking truth as the path to redemption, or nihilistically asserts there are no truths, and we have found it asserts both and neither. To make use of this seemingly contradictory or paradoxical proposition, the reader is required to perform a kind of transcendence—out of absolutist convictions of either truth or no-truth, and into a more flexible position from which particular truths may be recognized for their value, but may also be left behind, and other alternatives sought, when their indeterminacy becomes too erosive. This perspective is reminiscent of Nietzsche's assertion that the overinvestment in truth as absolute and unchanging is a veiled attempt to deny the real nature of the world, which is instead marked by constant transformation, impermanence, perspectivality, and the "innocence of becoming" (Nietzsche, 1967, 1968, 1969). The reader is thus asked to assume a position honoring that perspectivality, and to be prepared to "overcome" the current truth in favor of newly emerging possibilities (Nietzsche, 1969).

A character in one of Albee's prior plays, *The Zoo Story*, seems to speak directly to the paradoxical method Albee employs in *Virginia Woolf*. Neither kindness nor cruelty, the character Jerry says, when separate and independent of each other, have any effect beyond themselves; but when the two are combined into a single, paradoxical stance, then learning can occur (Albee, 1960). In *Virginia Woolf*, the audience is treated both with the kindness of being provided a theme of redemption that can be grasped and understood, and the cruelty, reminiscent of Artaud's principles of the Theatre of Cruelty (Artaud, 1958), of having all of their preconceptions assaulted. In his interview in 1985, Albee addresses precisely this point:

> If one approaches the theater in a state of innocence, sober, without preconceptions, and willing to participate; if they are willing to have the status quo assaulted; if they are willing to understand that the theater is a live and dangerous experience—and therefore a *life-giving force*—then perhaps they are approaching the theater in an ideal state and that's the audience I wish I were writing for. (quoted in Roudané, 1990, p. 48)

THE SON-MYTH

One of the implications of Freud's theory of melancholia is, once the melancholic attempts to replace the reality of loss with the fiction that no loss has occurred, the lost object, as it is held in the melancholic's mind, must be scrubbed free of the aggression that would have been aimed at it had its loss been fully grasped. This cleansing of aggression from the lost object helps to sustain the illusion that no loss occurred because it eliminates any evidence the object was injurious or hurtful. The object is thus placed in a protective envelope in the mind, a kind of reliquary in which it remains idealized and unchanging, immune from the ebb and flow of emotions occurring in the remainder of the self. But the aggression that would have been felt toward the object cannot be suppressed and remains in the self. To keep it from sullying the idealized object, it therefore must be re-aimed—and the most compelling substitute target is the melancholic himself. By redirecting aggression toward himself, the melancholic succeeds both in avoiding "the necessity of openly expressing their hostility against the loved ones" and in taking revenge upon the original object "by a circuitous path of self punishment" (Freud, 1917, p. 251).

In *Virginia Woolf* the son invented by George and Martha bears all the trademarks of an idealized object ("So beautiful; so wise. . . . Beautiful, wise, perfect," says Martha), and an ideal ally. As an ally, the son is treated like a personal god, appealed to, through the invention of stories about him, for support of whatever point one partner tries to make against the other (George, for example, claims that as a child the son was sick because he couldn't stand Martha "breaking into his bedroom with your kimono flying," while Martha claims he was sick because "George makes everybody sick"). In neither case, however, is the son, or more to the point his *absence*, the target of either partner's anger; instead, he remains free of all emotions *about* him, except for the most positive emotions of love and veneration.

Moreover, in seeming confirmation of Freud's theory, George and Martha's idealization of their son originates in a history of losses that were so painful they had to be suppressed. Albee, in 1965, was explicit in affirming this interpretation: George and Martha, he said, are "only occasionally" confused about the reality of the son illusion, but their confusion reaches a peak "when the awful loss and lack that made the creation of the symbol essential becomes overwhelming—like when they're drunk, for example. Or when they're terribly tired" (Flanagan, 1988, p. 59).

What is the loss George and Martha have found to be so painful? As might be expected, the play abounds with losses, both in the past and the present. The most obvious is that George and Martha have been unable to have a child, which has had a devastating impact on all aspects of their relationship. But each has also experienced personal losses, and the son-myth functions as a salve against those as well. Martha, for example, is a discontented housewife who didn't reach her desired level of achievement, whose mother died when she was a child, whose father didn't care about her and who lives in "a dump" with her "bog" of a husband. Her life, in sum, lies in a "stranglehold of nothingness" (Stenz, 1978, p. 41) over which the shadows of loneliness and disappointment have been cast. George, on the other hand, is a self-loathing professor who may have been the youth who killed his parents (and may have *wished* to kill them), who receives no support from his wife or father-in-law, who has rejected the petty values of the academy but has found nothing of more value in which to invest himself and who is full of noble visions, but also capable of viciousness and tedium, as Martha persistently points out.

These are far from the only losses alluded to in the play, but in each case, the son-myth soothes and distracts George and Martha from acknowledging the reality of those losses, and thereby prevents them from being angry with or working through any of the pain or grief they've had to suffer. The pain Martha feels after George "kills" the son in the final act illustrates the extent to which the son-myth has blocked their access to real emotions. Prior to that scene, Martha's dependence on the son was so compelling that she had lost the capacity to distinguish truth from fiction, and with it the ability to feel the pain of the actual absence of a son. George's insistence that Martha face reality about their son releases, in a flood of emotion, all the pain, anger, despair and remorse that had been dammed up behind the idealized son's image.

Indeed, the many emotional responses George and Martha might have had toward the injuries and disappointments in their lives were fettered by their need to preserve the son as an ideal object. Far from being available to be metabolized and worked through, those emotions have instead found substitute targets—George and Martha themselves—just as Freud's theory would have predicted. This is why George and Martha continuously, until the exorcism of the son-myth, aim withering condemnations at each other. Although each has injured the other, the full, terrifying intensity of their accusations can only be understood in terms of the accumulation of years of uncon-fronted injuries from multiple sources. Each loss in their lives is thus present in the son-myth in a repressed form; the reality of the loss is both known and subverted via the myth, so the original target of the accusations is forgotten, but the accusations themselves are preserved and re-aimed at the couple, even at the expense of their belief in their own value, or in the value of their marriage.

Albee's telling of the story to this point fits nicely within the structure outlined by Freud in *Mourning and Melancholia*. Equally consistent with Freud's views, and with the traditional aims of psychoanalysis, is George's recognition that the time has come to destroy the son, reorient themselves toward their painful losses, and re-aim their aggressions. If this were where *Virginia Woolf* ended, it would have been interpreted, since its first publica-tion, as essentially a confirmation of the Freudian narrative.

But *Virginia Woolf* does not end here, primarily because of Albee's refu-sal to privilege any of the multiple perspectives he presents within its pages. Albee's writing has been described, for good reason, as being "less interested in linear dramaturgy than in a kind of musical circularity, in theme and variation" (Bottoms, 2000, p. 88). More to the point, Albee's writing consists of a series of variations around a theme that, if it exists, cannot be found by either the characters or the audience. Just as the audience hears, for example, or thinks they hear, a resolution of the tensions surrounding the son-myth, Albee once again pulls the rug out from under them and asks whether they can be sure this should count as a resolution.

The deepest way Albee raises this question is through his subtle but omnipresent infusions of uncertainty about illusion v. truth throughout the play. In the son-myth, these uncertainties surround even the "factual" events that contributed to its formation. The most unquestioned fact in the play, for example, is that George and Martha were unable to have a child. Because Albee, though, has constructed the entire play so as to create, in both his characters and his audience, the "dangerous experience" of the contraposi-tion of truth v. uncertainty, even George's insistence that the son does not exist necessarily elicits disorienting feelings of ambivalence in both the audi-ence and the characters. Prior to the final scene, when Martha was still portrayed as fervently believing in the son-myth, it was a simple matter for the audience to conclude she was committing the kinds of errors cited by Nietzsche: refusal of ambiguity, clinging to certainties, and ignoring confus-ing evidence to the contrary. By the time George advocates "killing" the illusion in favor of the truth, however, the audience has become conditioned to the indeterminacies inherent in this stance as well. Albee's construction of the final scenes contributes substantially to this effect: although the exorcism of the son takes place at dawn, symbolizing the value of a new embrace of truth, what is more emotionally compelling is the intimate tenderness with which George and Martha then treat each other, as well as their uncertainty that this is the "right" course. As Bottoms has pointed out, the weight that the play, in its entirety, brings to bear on the issue of truth v. illusion calls any truth (including, I would add, the truth of the son's nonexistence) into as much question as the illusions that surround it:

> For Albee, it seems, acknowledging that one has created illusions for oneself, and then continuing to live by them is not an act of bad faith but a necessary form of self-invention, a rejection of the essentialist assumption that there is a "true self" to be faithful *to*. It is simply to admit that one's take on the world is necessarily performative, that we are composed of the roles we play, the lines we improvise for ourselves. The stripping away of such illusions will not, therefore, necessarily result in the revelation of some hidden layer of underlying truth. It is as likely that another provisional arrangement of fictions will have to be negotiated. (2000, p. 13)

Through the long, dark night of the play, Albee has succeeded in creating a particularly postmodern perspective toward every nuance in the final scenes. No longer can George and Martha's belief in their son-myth be regarded, without question, as an ill-conceived strategy for coping with loss. But their search for what's real can also not be claimed to be without benefit. To assume either would be to imply that Albee had endorsed either a positivistic faith in truth or a nihilistic destruction of truth. Instead, through his juxtaposition of opposing perspectives throughout the play, he steadfastly refuses to endorse either.

Through his intricate maneuverings between the two polarities of truth and illusion, Albee has constructed for the audience a position remarkably similar to that of a therapist who acknowledges the influence of the two Others: the intrapsychic and the relational unconscious. The arena of interaction these two Others create is both decentered and indeterminate, and recognizing it as a foundation of the therapeutic relationship means that the therapist must both protect the patient from the imposition of rigid and unyielding truths (whether born out of the patient's need or their therapist's "natural authoritarian tendencies"—Bollas, 2002, p. 36), and provide the conditions under which the patient may gain emotional nutrition from discovering something real about themselves. Such a therapist must always wait for and help their patients give birth to the clarifying truths—arising from the field between them—that will be of use for some measure of redemption. But if those truths are either overvalued or undervalued, the therapy runs the risk of suppressing the free, transformative expression of the patient's idiomatic way of being—both with him or herself and in relationship with the therapist. The analyst, Ogden says, quoting a poem by Ammons (1986, p. 61), is "not so much looking for the shape/ as being available/ to any shape that may be/ summoning itself/ through me/ from the self not mine but ours" (Ogden,

2001, p. 13). When conducted according to these intuitions, therapy becomes an art of liberation, and the materials for this art include the therapist's role in helping the patient establish a new communicative pathway to their unconscious, and a new understanding of its role in both creating and eclipsing truth. In this way, therapy becomes every bit as much a "life-giving force" as Albee wanted his plays to be.

DOUG AND CAROL REVISITED

The evolving succession of Doug's lies continued for the better part of two years, as he, Carol, and I continued to try to understand them. Over the course of those two years, though, a different style of interaction among the three of us emerged. Subtle at first, the shift in style centered on a growing curiosity in the couple about how, together, they reinforced Doug's lying. After considering many possible motivations for his contributions, we began to settle into a view of Doug that harmonized with most of the data at hand. He was not motivated primarily by anger, although that was certainly present, acutely at times. Rather, his main motivation had to do with an internal imperative, originating in the demands made by both his mother and father that he always present himself with certainty and clarity. Under the rule of this internal imperative, ambiguity, ambivalence, and uncertainty created an intense anxiety and Doug early on trained himself to suppress any of his emotions or desires that didn't fit the clarified picture he felt required to present.

The anxieties Doug felt about his emotional ambiguities created an essentially obsessive-compulsive process in which he fastidiously snipped away at the parts of himself he couldn't present with clarity. We couldn't say these parts became unconscious, but they were consigned to an encapsulated space in his mind to which he remained persistently inattentive. Nevertheless, they still remained active within him and, at times, determined his actions. The reality, for example, about the videogame he bought for his son was that he simultaneously felt it was *both* detrimental and innocent. Because this was not acceptable to his conscious mind, and because he had told Carol he wouldn't buy the game, purchasing it was almost as much of a surprise to him as it was to Carol.

As our work deepened, the three of us began to realize Doug's anxieties mirrored Carol's. Raised in a hyper-religious family, who collectively were terrified of being judged by the community, Carol many times witnessed her father's wrath at her older sisters and brothers who had, at least in his eyes, embarrassed the family. From these examples, Carol developed a strategy of never straying beyond the bounds of what her father found acceptable. Although this contained the problem of his anger and helped her feel safe, it also created a constraint in her personality that she, at times, secretly wished she could escape. When she met Doug, she unconsciously recognized that his patterns offered her an opportunity to live out, by proxy, some of the more suppressed parts of her personality.

The hidden value Doug brought to his relationship with Carol was thus his intermittent lack of self-restraint, even though he lied about it afterwards. His actions, like his refusal to attend church services, both represented and enacted parts of Carol's desires she had long placed under lock and key. As the couple absorbed this new perspective on Carol, they realized Doug's lies were not only motivated by his fears of ambiguity, but also by Carol's suppressed needs for liberation from her strict internal regime. Carol, they agreed, located her "bad girl" desires in Doug, and he unwittingly fulfilled them through his long string of misbehaviors and prevarications.

Doug also located something in Carol. He sensed that the obsessive monitor he had established in himself was faulty, and he needed a partner who reinforced his attempts to control his behavior. Carol, having internalized her wrathful and controlling father, was a perfect candidate: Doug could use the constraints in her personality as an ally in his battles with the unacceptable parts of himself. Thus, Doug and Carol used parts of the other's inner lives to attempt to solve problems each carried since childhood. And the near-identical anxiety they felt about disappointing a demanding parent created the unconscious field in which these exchanges took place.

As time went on, Doug and Carol became intrigued by the ways their unconscious lives blended. With each new lie revealed by Doug, they began to analyze, with decreasing input from me, how each had contributed to creating the conditions that necessitated the lie, and their joint analysis clearly became a new-found pleasure between them. Although their analyses followed the basic pattern outlined above, each analysis had its own character, and they shared satisfaction in discovering the specific events, both conscious and unconscious, that led to each lie.

It was at this time that Doug revealed his Big Lie. Near the end of a session they found particularly fascinating and pleasurable, he told Carol that before they married he fathered a daughter out of wedlock, with whom he had re-established contact several years earlier. This new truth devastated Carol and created a crisis in their relationship that threatened its very existence. But over the ensuing weeks, she and Doug were able to re-establish the newer style of interaction they had developed. They explored the barricades, created in both by the individual and the shared dimensions of their unconsciouses, which prevented Doug from telling Carol of his daughter; and they faced, with discomfort, the benefits each had received from keeping the daughter secret. Ultimately, they reached an accommodation even with the painful fact of his having a daughter, and they each accepted responsibility for its having remained hidden. Our therapy ended shortly after Carol asked to meet the daughter. The meeting was successful, if still filled with discomforts and anxieties. But they now felt they had the tools necessary to face them.

The work Doug and Carol accomplished in nearly three years of couple therapy illustrates the value of teaching our patients a *method* of relating to the conscious and unconscious parts of themselves and their partners. When we terminated, Doug and Carol possessed no cut and dried explanations—referring to enduring truths about themselves—for the difficulties between them. Instead, they had an appreciation for the process of discovering those explanations. This struggle, in which they were able to find unexpected pleasure, created a more solid foundation for their relationship, and allowed them to survive the blow of Doug's Big Lie. No longer did they seek the truth of Doug's lies in a fatal flaw within either him or Carol. Instead, they saw his lies as an integral part of the fabric of a relationship they had consciously and unconsciously woven together.

The quest for truth, in a postmodern world, is analogous to Odysseus's return to his Ithaka home in the poem by C. P. Cavafy: "Keep Ithaka always in mind. / Arriving there is what you're destined for. / But don't hurry the journey at all. . . . And if you find her poor, Ithaka won't have fooled you. Wise as you'll have become, and so experienced, / you'll have understood by then what an Ithaka means" (Cavafy, 1972, p. 19).

Bibliography

Abraham, K. (1924). A short study of the development of the libido, viewed in the light of mental disorders. In E. Jones (Ed.), *Selected papers of Karl Abraham M.D.* (D. Bryan and A. Strachey, Trans.) (pp. 418–501). London, England: Hogarth Press, 1949.

Abraham, N. (1975). The phantom of Hamlet or the sixth act *preceded by* the intermission of "truth." In N. T. Rand (Trans. and Ed.), *The shell and the kernel: Renewals of psychoanalysis, Vol. I* (pp. 187–205). Chicago, IL: University of Chicago Press, 1994.

Abraham, N. and Torok, M. (1975). "The lost object—me": Notes on endocryptic identification. In N. T. Rand (Trans. and Ed.), *The shell and the kernel: Renewals of psychoanalysis, Vol. I* (pp. 139–156). Chicago, IL: University of Chicago Press, 1994.

Abraham, N. and Torok, M. (1994). *The shell and the kernel: Renewals of psychoanalysis, Vol. I.* N. T. Rand (Trans. and Ed.). Chicago, IL: University of Chicago Press.

Aeschylus (1975). *The Oresteia.* (R. Fagles, Trans.). New York, NY: Penguin.

Aeschylus (1999). *The Oresteia.* (T. Hughes, Trans.). New York, NY: Farrar, Straus and Giroux.

Akhtar, S. (1995). A third individuation: Immigration, identity, and the psychoanalytic process. *Journal of the American Psychoanalytic Association, 43,* 1051-1084.

Albee, E. (1960). *The zoo story, the death of Bessie Smith, the sandbox: Three plays, introduced by the author.* New York, NY: Coward-McCann.

Albee, E. (1962). *Who's afraid of Virginia Woolf?* New York, NY: Atheneum.

Altman, N. (1995). *The analyst in the inner city.* Hillsdale, NJ: Analytic Press.

Ammons, A. R. (1986). Poetics. In *The selected poems.* New York, NY: Norton.

Amos, A. and Balfour, A. (2007). Couples psychotherapy: separateness or separation? An account of work with a couple entering later life. In R. Davenhill (Ed.), *Looking into later life: A psychoanalytic approach to depression and dementia in old age* (pp. 75–89). London, England: Karnac.

Aron, L. (1991). The patient's experience of the analyst's subjectivity. *Psychoanalytic Dialogues, 1,* 29–51.

Aron, L. (1996). *A meeting of minds.* Hillsdale, NJ: Analytic Press.

Artaud, A. (1958). *The theatre and its double.* (M. C. Richards, Trans.). New York, NY: Grove Press.

Avery, N. C. (1973). The exorcism of a tabooed wish: An analysis of *Who's Afraid of Virginia Woolf? Seminars in Psychiatry, 5*(3), 347–357.

Aviram, R. B. (2009). *The relational origins of prejudice: A convergence of psychoanalytic and social cognitive perspectives.* Lanham, MD: Jason Aronson.

Bach, S. (1985). *Narcissistic states and the therapeutic process.* Northvale, NJ: Jason Aronson.

Balint, E. (1993). Unconscious communications between husband and wife. In S. Ruszczynski (Ed.), *Psychotherapy with couples: Theory and practice at the Tavistock Institute of Marital Studies* (pp. 30–43). London, England: Karnac.

Balint, M. (1960). Primary narcissism or primary love. *Psychoanalytic Quarterly, 29*, 6–43.

Balint, M. (1965). *Primary love and psychoanalytic technique*. London, England: Tavistock.

Balint, M. (1979). *The basic fault: Therapeutic aspects of regression*. London/New York: Tavistock.

Bannister, K., and Pincus, L. (1965). *Shared phantasy in marital problems: Therapy in a four-person relationship*. London, England: Tavistock.

Baranger, M. (1993). The mind of the analyst: From listening to interpretation. *International Journal of Psychoanalysis, 74*, 15–24.

Barranger, M., and Baranger, W. (1966). Insight in the analytic situation. In R.E. Litman (Ed.), *Psychoanalysis in the Americas: Original contributions from the First Pan–American Congress for Psychoanalysis* (pp. 56–72). New York, NY: International Universities Press.

Baranger, M., Baranger, W. (2008). The analytic situation as a dynamic field. *International Journal of Psychoanalysis, 89*, 795–826.

Baranger, M., Baranger, W., and Mom, J. (1983). Process and non-process in analytic work. *International Journal of Psychoanalysis, 64*, 1–15.

Barnett, J. (1975). Narcissism and dependency in the obsessional–hysteric marriage. *Family Process, 11*, 75–83.

Bass, A. (2001a). Mental structure, psychic process, and analytic relations – How people change in analysis: Reply to commentaries. *Psychoanalytic Dialogues, 11*, 717–725.

Bass, A. (2001b). It takes one to know one; or, whose unconscious is it anyway?*Psychoanalytic Dialogues, 11*, 683–702.

Bass, A. (2003). "E" enactments in psychoanalysis: Another medium, another message. *Psychoanalytic Dialogues, 13*, 657–675.

Bass, A. (2009, April). *Mutual analysis reconsidered*. Presented at the International Psychotherapy Institute's Conference on The Therapeutic Relationship and the Dialogue of Unconsciousness, Rockville, MD.

Beebe, B. and Lachmann, F. M. (2002). *Infant research and adult treatment: Co-constructing interactions*. Hillsdale, NJ: Analytic Press.

Beebe, B., and Lachmann, F. M. (2003). The relational turn in psychoanalysis: A dyadic systems view from infant research. *Contemporary Psychoanalysis, 39*, 379–409.

Beebe, B., Lachmann, F. M., and Jaffe, J. (1997). Mother-infant interaction structures and presymbolic self and object representations. *Psychoanalytic Dialogues, 7*, 133–182.

Benjamin, J. (1988). *Bonds of love: Psychoanalysis, feminism, and the problem of domination*. New York, NY: Pantheon.

Benjamin, J. (1995). *Like subjects, love objects: Essays on recognition and sexual difference*. New Haven, CT: Yale University Press.

Benjamin, J. (1997). *Shadow of the other: Intersubjectivity and gender in psychoanalysis*. New York, NY: Routledge.

Bernet, R. (1996). The other in myself. In S. Critchley and P. Dews (Eds.), *Deconstructive subjectivities* (pp. 169–184). New York, NY: State University of New York Press.

Berry, J. W. (1997. Immigration, acculturation and adaptation. *Applied Psychology: An International Review, 39*, 5-68.

Billow, R. (2003). Relational variations of the 'Container–Contained.' *Contemporary Psychoanalysis, 39*, 27–50.

Billow, R. (2010). *Resistance, rebellion and refusal in groups: The 3 Rs*. London, England: Karnac.

Bion, W. R. (1961). *Experiences in groups*. London, England: Routledge.

Bion, W. R. (1962a). The psychoanalytic study of thinking. *International Journal of Psychoanalysis, 43*, 306–310.

Bion, W. R. (1962b). *Learning from experience*. London, England: Karnac.

Bion, W. R. (1963). *Elements of psycho-analysis*. London, England: Heinemann.

Bion, W. R. (1965). *Transformations*. London, England: Heinemann.

Bion, W. R. (1970). *Attention and interpretation*. London, England: Tavistock.

Bion, W. R. (1980). *Bion in New York and Sao Paolo.* (F. Bion, Ed.). Pertshire, Scotland: Clunie Press.

Blechner, M. J. (1992). Working in the countertransference. *Psychoanalytic Dialogues, 2,* 161–179.

Bodnar, S. (2004). Remember where you come from: Dissociative process in multicultural individuals. *Psychoanalytic Dialogues, 14*(5), 581–603.

Boesky, D. (1990). The psychoanalytic process and its components. *Psychoanalytic Quarterly, 59,* 550–584.

Boesky, D. (2000). Affect, language and communication: 41st IPA congress plenary session. *International Journal of Psychoanalysis, 81,* 257–262.

Bollas, C. 1983. Expressive uses of the countertransference. *Contemporary Psychoanalysis, 19,* 1–34.

Bollas, C. (1987). *The shadow of the object: Psychoanalysis of the unthought known.* New York, NY: Columbia University Press.

Bollas, C. (1992). *Being a character: Psychoanalysis and self experience.* New York, NY: Hill and Wang.

Bollas, C. (1995). *Cracking up: The work of unconscious experience.* London, England: Routledge.

Bollas, C. (2000). Architecture and the unconscious. *International Forum of Psychoanalysis, 9,* 28–42.

Bollas, C. (2002). *Free association.* Cambridge, England: Icon Books.

Bolognini, S. (2008). Reconsidering narcissism from a contemporary, complex psychoanalytic view. *International Forum of Psychoanalysis, 17,* 104–111.

Bolognini, S. and Séchaud, E. (2000). Affective self-disclosure by the analyst. *International Journal of Psychoanalysis, 81,* 164–165.

Bonovitz, C. (2006). The illusion of certainty in self-disclosure: Commentary on paper by Helen K. Gediman. *Psychoanalytic Dialogues, 16,* 293–304.

Bottoms, S. J. (2000). *Albee: Who's afraid of Virginia Woolf?* Cambridge, England: Cambridge University Press.

Bowlby, J. (1977). The making and breaking of affectional bonds. *British Journal of Psychiatry, 130,* 201–210.

Bromberg, P. M. (1995). Resistance, object-usage, and human relatedness. *Contemporary Psychoanalysis, 31,* 173.

Brookes, S. (1991). Bion's concept of containment in marital work. *Journal of Social Work Practice: Psychotherapeutic Approaches in Health, Welfare and the Community, 5*(2), 133–141.

Burch, B. and Jenkins, C. (1999). The interactive potential between individual therapy and couple therapy: An intersubjective paradigm. *Contemporary Psychoanalysis, 35,* 229–252.

Burke, W. F. (1992). Countertransference disclosure and the asymmetry/mutuality dilemma. *Psychoanalytic Dialogues, 2,* 241–271.

Carlisky, N. J. and de Eskenazi, C. K. (1997a). The turn-of-the-century social imaginary. In N. J. Carlisky (Ed.), *Living without a project: Psychoanalysis and the postmodern society* (pp. 21–28). Lanham, MD: University Press of America.

Carlisky, N. J. and de Eskenazi, C. K. (1997b). Discontent in psychoanalysis. In N. J. Carlisky (Ed.), *Living without a project: Psychoanalysis and the postmodern society* (pp. 9–20). Lanham, MD: University Press of America.

Cavafy, C. P. (1972). *Selected poems.* (E. Keeley and P. Sherrard, Trans.). Princeton, NJ: Princeton University Press.

Chessick, R. D. (1996). The application of postmodern thought to the clinical practice of psychoanalytic psychotherapy. *Journal of American Academy of Psychoanalysis, 24,* 385–407.

Cleavely, E. (1993). Relationships: Interaction, defences, and transformation. In S. Ruszczynski (Ed.), *Psychotherapy with couples: Theory and practice at the Tavistock Institute of Marital Studies* (pp. 55–69). London, England: Karnac.

Clulow, C. (1993). "Good-enough marriage." In C. Clulow (Ed.), *Rethinking marriage: Public and private perspectives.* London, England: Karnac.

Clulow, C. (2001). Attachment theory and the therapeutic frame. In C. Clulow (Ed.) *Adult attachment and couple psychotherapy: The 'secure base' in practice and research* (pp. 85–104). London, England: Brunner-Routledge.

Cohen, A. B. (2009). Many forms of culture. *American Psychologist, 64*(3), 194–204.

Cohn, J. and Beebe, B. (1990). Sampling interval affects time–series regression estimates of mother–infant influence. *Infant Behavior and Development, Abstracts Issue*, 13, 317.

Colman, W. (1993). Marriage as a psychological container. In S. Ruszczynski (Ed.), *Psychotherapy with couples: Theory and practice at the Tavistock Institute of Marital Studies* (pp. 70–96). London, England: Karnac.

Comas-Diaz, L. and Jacobsen, F. M. (1991). Ethnocultural transference and countertransference in the therapeutic dyad. *American Journal of Orthopsychiatry, 61(3)*, 392-402.

Compton, A. (1990). Psychoanalytic process. *Psychoanalytic Quarterly, 59*, 585–598.

Cooper, S. H. (1998). Analyst subjectivity, analyst disclosure, and the aims of psychoanalysis. *Psychoanalytic Quarterly, 67*, 379–406.

Cooper, S. H. (2003). The countertransference transformation of Oedipal idealization, mourning, and erotic masochism: Commentary on paper by Jody Messler Davies. *Psychoanalytic Dialogues, 13*, 29–39.

Cushman, P. (1990). Why the self is empty. *American Psychologist, 45*, 599–611.

Dalal, F. (2006). Racism: Processes of detachment, dehumanization, and hatred. *Psychoanalytic Quarterly, 75*, 131–161.

David, L., Seinfeld, J., Leopold, T. (Writers), and Cherones, T. (Director). (1991). The café (Television series episode). In L. Charles and J. Seinfeld (Producers), *Seinfeld*. New York, NY: National Broadcasting Corporation.

Davidson, L. (1988). Culture and psychoanalysis—From marginality to pluralism. *Contemporary Psychoanalysis, 24*, 74–90.

Davis, J. T. (2002). Countertranference temptation and the use of self-disclosure by psychotherapists in training: A discussion for beginning psychotherapists and their supervisors. *Psychoanalytic Psychology, 19*, 435–454.

de Bernardi, B. L. (2008). Introduction to the paper by Madeleine and Willy Baranger: The analytic situation as a dynamic field. *International Journal of Psychoanalysis, 89*, 773–784.

Debusscher, G. (1967). *Edward Albee: Tradition and renewal*. (A. Williams, Trans.). Brussels, Belgium: American Studies Center.

Deleuze, G. and Guattari, F. (1987). *A thousand plateaus: capitalism and schizophrenia*. (B. Massumi, Trans.). Minneapolis, MN and London, England: University of Minnesota Press.

Derrida, J. (1978). *Writing and difference*. (A. Bass, Trans.). Chicago, IL: University of Chicago Press.

Dicks, H. (1967). *Marital tensions: Clinical studies towards a psychological theory of interaction*. New York, NY: Basic Books.

Eagle, M. N. (2003). The postmodern turn in psychoanalysis: A critique. *Psychoanalytic Psychology, 20*, 411–424.

Ehrenberg, D. B. (1992). *The intimate edge*. New York, NY: Norton.

Ehrenberg, D. B. (1995). Self–disclosure: Therapeutic tool or indulgence?—countertransference disclosure. *Contemporary Psychoanalysis, 31*, 213–228.

Ehrlich, F. M., Zilbach, J. J., and Solomon, L. (1996). The transference field and communication among therapists. *Journal of the American Academy of Psychoanalysis, 24*, 675–690.

Elliott, A. and Spezzano, C. (1996). Psychoanalysis at its limits: Navigating the postmodern turn. *Psychoanalytic Quarterly, 65*, 52–83.

Faimberg, H. (1997). Misunderstanding and psychic truths. *International Journal of Psychoanalysis, 78*, 439–451.

Fairbairn, W. R. D. (1940). Schizoid factors in the personality. In *Psychoanalytic studies of the personality* (pp. 3–27). London, England: Routledge and Kegan Paul, 1952.

Fairbairn, W. R. D. (1941). A revised psychopathology of the psychoses and psychoneuroses. In *Psychoanalytic studies of the personality* (pp. 28–58). London, England: Routledge and Kegan Paul, 1952.

Fairbairn, W. R. D. (1943). The repression and the return of bad objects (with special reference to the 'War Neuroses'). In *Psychoanalytic studies of the personality* (pp. 59–81). London, England: Routledge and Kegan Paul, 1952.

Fairbairn, W. R. D. (1944). Endopsychic structure considered in terms of object-relationships. In *Psychoanalytic studies of the personality* (pp. 82–136). London, England: Routledge and Kegan Paul, 1952.

Fairbairn, W. R. D. (1946). Object-relationships and dynamic structure. In *Psychoanalytic studies of the personality* (pp. 137–151). London, England: Routledge and Kegan Paul, 1952.

Fairbairn, W. R. D. (1952). *Psychoanalytic studies of the personality*. London, England: Routledge and Kegan Paul.

Fairfield, S. (2001). Analyzing multiplicity: A postmodern perspective on some current psychoanalytic theories of subjectivity. *Psychoanalytic Dialogues, 11*, 221–251.

Fairfield, S., Layton, L., and Stack, C. (2002). Introduction: Culture and couch. In S. Fairfield, L. Layton, and C. Stack (Eds.) *Bringing the plague: Toward a postmodern psychoanalysis* (pp. 1–31). New York, NY: Other Press.

Farber, B. A. (2006). *Self-disclosure in psychotherapy*. New York, NY: Guilford.

Federn, P. (1928). Narcissism in the structure of the ego. *International Journal of Psychoanalysis, 9*, 401–419.

Feinsilver, D. B. (1989). Transitional relatedness, containment and the transference neurosis. *International Review of Psychoanalysis, 16*, 433–44.

Feinsilver, D. B. (1999). Counteridentification, comprehensive countertransference, and therapeutic action: Toward resolving the intrapsychic-interactional dichotomy. *Psychoanalytic Quarterly, 68*, 264–301.

Ferenczi, S. L. (1909). Introjection and transference. In *First contributions to psycho-analysis* (E. Jones, Trans.). (pp. 35–57). London, England: Hogarth Press and the Institute of Psycho-Analysis, 1952.

Ferro, A. (1999). *The bi-personal field: Experiences in child analysis*. London, England: Routledge.

Ferro, A. (2002). Some implications of Bion's thought: The waking dream and narrative derivatives. *International Journal of Psychoanalysis, 83*, 597–607.

Ferro, A. (2006a). Clinical implications of Bion's thought. *International Journal of Psychoanalysis, 87*, 989–1003.

Ferro, A. (2006b). Preliminary reflections on psychoanalysis and narratology. *Funzione Gamma, 17*. Retrieved from http://www.funzionegamma.edu/articles.asp?id=423andid_numero=34.

Ferro, A. (2007). Bion and the Field. Paper presented at the *The Bi-Personal Field in Psychotherapy*, a conference of the International Psychotherapy Institute, April 27–29, 2007. Bethesda, MD.

Feynman, R. P. (2005). Richard P. Feynman to the Editor of the California Tech, February 27, 1976. In M. Feynman (Ed.), *Perfectly reasonable deviations from the beaten track: The letters of Richard P. Feynman* (pp. 301–302). New York, NY: Basic Books.

Fine, R. (1978). Praise be to Freud, but watch the ammunition: A critical revision of the psychoanalytic theory of aggression. In G.D. Goldman and D.S. Milman (Eds.), *Psychoanalytic perspectives on aggression* (pp. 4–18). Dubuque, IA: Kendall/Hunt.

Fiscalini, J. (2004). *Coparticipant psychoanalysis: Toward a new theory of clinical inquiry*. New York, NY: Columbia University Press.

Fiske, A.P. (2002). Using individualism and collectivism to compare cultures—A critique of the validity and measurement of the constructs: Comment on Oyserman et al. (2002). *Psychological Bulletin, 128*, 78–88.

Flanagan, W. (1988). The art of theater IV: Edward Albee: An interview. In P. C. Kolin (Ed.), *Conversations with Edward Albee* (pp. 45–66). Jackson, MS: University Press of Mississippi.

Fliess, R. (1942). The metapsychology of the analyst. *Psychoanalytic Quarterly, 11*, 211–227.

Fogel, G. I., Tyson, P., Greenberg, J., McLaughlin, J. T., and Peyser, E. R. (1996). A classic revisited: Loewald on the therapeutic action of psychoanalysis. *Journal of the American Psychoanalytic Association, 44,* 863–924.

Fonagy, P., Gergely, G., Jurist, E., and Target, M. (2002). *Affect regulation, mentalization and the development of the self.* New York, NY: Other Press.

Frank, K. A. (1997). The role of the analyst's inadvertent self-revelations. *Psychoanalytic Dialogues, 7,* 281–314.

Frederickson, J. (2005). The problem of relationality. In J. Mills (Ed.), *Relational and intersubjective perspectives in psychoanalysis: A critique.* Lanham, MD: Jason Aronson/Rowman and Littlefield.

Frederickson, J. (2006). From blank screen to participant observer to co-participant: A review of *Coparticipant psychoanalysis: Toward a new theory of clinical inquiry* by John Fiscalini, Ph.D. New York: Columbia University Press, 2004, 242 pp. *Contemporary Psychoanalysis, 42,* 330–334.

Freud, A. (1979). The role of insight in psychoanalysis and psychotherapy-introduction. *Journal of the American Psychoanalytic Association, 27S,* 3–7.

Freud, S. (1911). Psycho-analytic notes upon an autobiographical account of a case of paranoia (dementia paranoides). *Standard Edition* 12:1–82.

Freud, S. (1912). Recommendations to physicians practicing psychoanalysis. *Standard Edition* 12:109–120.

Freud, S. (1914a). On narcissism: An introduction. *Standard Edition* 14:67–102.

Freud, S. (1914b). On the history of the psychoanalytic movement. *Standard Edition* 14:7–66.

Freud, S. (1915). The unconscious. *Standard Edition* 14:159–215.

Freud, S. (1917). Mourning and melancholia. *Standard Edition* 14:237–258.

Freud, S. (1919). Lines of advance in psycho-analytic therapy. *Standard Edition,* 17:157–168.

Freud, S. (1922). Group psychology and the analysis of the ego. *Standard Edition* 29:65–144.

Freud, S. (1923). The ego and the id. *Standard Edition* 19:1–66.

Freud, S. (1926). Inhibitions, symptoms and anxiety. *Standard Edition* 20: 75–176.

Freud, S. (1933). New introductory lectures on psycho-analysis. *Standard Edition* 12:1–182.

Frie, R. (1999). Psychoanalysis and the linguistic turn. *Contemporary Psychoanalysis, 35,* 673–697.

Frie, R. (2003). Introduction: Between modernism and postmodernism: rethinking psychological agency. In R. Frie (Ed.), *Understanding experience: Psychotherapy and postmodernism* (pp. 1-26). London, England: Routledge.

Friedman, L. (1962). *Virgin wives: A study of unconsummated marriages.* London, England: Tavistock.

Gabbard, G. O. (1995). Countertransference: The emerging common ground. *International Journal of Psychoanalysis, 76,* 475–485.

Gabbard, G.O. (1997). A reconsideration of objectivity in the analyst. *International Journal of Psychoanalysis, 78,* 15–26.

Garland, C. (1998). Thinking about trauma. In C. Garland (Ed.), *Understanding trauma: a psychoanalytical approach* (pp. 9–31). New York, NY: Routledge.

Garner, S. N., Kahane, C., and Sprengnether, M. (1985). *The (m)other tongue.* Ithaca, NY: Cornell University Press.

Garza-Guerrero, A. C. (1974). Culture shock: Its mourning and the vicissitudes of identity. *Journal of the American Psychoanalytic Association, 22,* 408-429.

Gediman, H. K. (2006). Facilitating analysis with implicit and explicit self-disclosures. *Psychoanalytic Dialogues, 16,* 241–262.

Gerhardt, J. Sweetnam, A. and Borton, L. (2003). The intersubjective turn in psychoanalysis: A comparison of contemporary theorists Part 3: Darlene Bregman Ehrenberg. *Psychoanalytic Dialogues, 13,* 533-577.

Gerson, M-J. (2001). The ritual of couples therapy: The subversion of autonomy. *Contemporary Psychoanalysis, 37,* 453–470.

Gerson, S. (1996). Neutrality, resistance, and self-disclosure in an intersubjective psychoanalysis. *Psychoanalytic Dialogues, 6,* 623–645.

Gerson, S. (1998). From disclosure to foreclosure: Reply to commentary. *Psychoanalytic Dialogues, 8*, 741–746.

Gerson, S. (2004). The relational unconscious: A core element of intersubjectivity, thirdness, and clinical process. *Psychoanalytic Quarterly, 73*, 63–98.

Gerson, S. (2006). The elusiveness of the relational unconscious: Commentary on paper by Juan Tubert-Oklander. *Psychoanalytic Dialogues, 16*(2), 217–225.

Gerson, S. (2009). When the third is dead: Memory, mourning, and witnessing in the aftermath of the holocaust. *International Journal of Psychoanalysis, 90*, 1341–1357.

Gilligan, C. (1982). *In a different voice: Psychological theory and women's development.* Cambridge, MA: Harvard University Press, 1982.

Girard, R. (1977). *Violence and the sacred.* (P. Gregory, Trans.). Baltimore, MD: Johns Hopkins University Press.

Glover, E. (1947). Basic mental concepts: Their clinical and theoretical value. *Psychoanalytic Quarterly , 16 ,* 482–506.

Goldberger, N. R. and Veroff, J. B. (Eds.). (1995). *The culture and psychology reader.* New York, NY: New York University Press.

Goretti, G. R. (2007). Projective identification: A theoretical investigation of the concept starting from "Some Notes on Schizoid Mechanisms.' *International Journal of Psychoanalysis, 88*, 387–405.

Gorkin, M. (1987). *The uses of countertransference.* Northvale, NJ: Jason Aronson.

Graller, J. L. (1981). Adjunctive marital therapy: A possible solution to the splittransference problem. *Annual of Pschyoanalysis, 9*, 175–187.

Green, A. (1999). *The work of the negative.* (A. Weller, Trans.). London, England and New York, NY: Free Association Books.

Green, A. (2002). A dual conception of narcissism: Positive and negative organizations. *Psychoanalytic Quarterly, 71*, 631–649.

Greenberg, J. (1991). *Oedipus and beyond: A clinical theory.* Cambridge, MA: Harvard University Press.

Greenberg, J. (1995). Self-disclosure: Is it psychoanalytic? *Contemporary Psychoanalysis, 31*, 193–205.

Greenberg, J. (1999). Analytic authority and analytic restraint. *Contemporary Psychoanalysis, 35*, 25–41.

Greenberg, J. and Mitchell, S. A. (1983). *Object relations in psychoanalytic theory.* Cambridge, MA: Harvard University Press.

Grinberg, L. (1962). On a specific aspect of countertransference due to the patient's projective identification. *International Journal of Psychoanalysis, 43*, 436–440.

Grinberg, L. (1969). New ideas: Conflict and evolution. *International Journal of Psychoanalysis, 50*, 517–528.

Grinberg, L., Sor, D., and De Bianchedi, E. T. (1977). *Introduction to the work of Bion.* NY, New York: Jason Aronson.

Grotstein, J. (1981). *Splitting and projective identification.* New York, NY: Jason Aronson.

Grotstein, J. (2000). *Who is the dreamer who dreams the dream?: A study of psychic presences.* Hillsdale, NJ: Analytic Press.

Grunberger, B. (1989). *New essays on narcissism.* (D. Macey, Trans. and Ed.). London, England: Free Association Books.

Guisinger, S. and Blatt, S. J. (1994). Individuality and relatedness: Evolution of a fundamental dialectic. *American Psychologist, 49*, 104–111.

Guntrip, H. (1961). *Personality structure and human interaction: The developing synthesis of psychodynamic theory.* London, England: Hogarth Press and the Institute of Psychoanalysis.

Guntrip, H. (1969). *Schizoid phenomena, object relations and the self.* New York, NY: International Universities Press.

Gussow, M. (1999). *Edward Albee: A singular journey: A biography.* New York, NY: Simon and Schuster.

Gutheil, T. G., and Gabbard, G. O. (1998). Misuses and misunderstandings of boundary theory in clinical and regulatory settings. *American Journal of Psychiatry, 155*, 409–414.

Hanly, C. (1998). Reflections on the analyst's self-disclosure. *Psychoanalytic Inquiry, 18*, 550–565.

Heaton, J. M. (2000). *Wittgenstein and psychoanalysis.* Cambridge, UK: Icon Books.

Heimann, P. (1950). On counter-transference. *International Journal of Psychoanalysis, 31*, 81–84.

Heimann, P. (1952). Certain functions of introjection and projection in early infancy. In Klein, M., Heimann, P., Isaacs, S., and Riviere, J. (Eds.), *Developments in Psycho-analysis* (pp. 122–168). London, England: Hogarth Press.

Heimann, P. (1956). Dynamics of transference interpretations. *International Journal of Psychoanalysis, 37*, 303–310.

Herron, W. G. (1995). Development of the ethnic unconscious. *Psychoanalytic Psychology, 12*, 521–532.

Hirsch, I. (1992). The value of naïve directness in countertransference work: Commentary on Mark Blechner's "Working in the Countertransference." *Psychoanalytic Dialogues, 2*, 191–203.

Hoffman, I. Z. (1983). The patient as interpreter of the analyst's experience. *Contemporary Psychoanalysis, 19*, 389–422.

Hoffman, I. Z. (1987). The value of uncertainty in psychoanalytic practice. *Contemporary Psychoanalysis, 23*, 205–214.

Hoffman, I. Z. (1991). Discussion: Toward a social-constructivist view of the psychoanalytic situation. *Psychoanalytic Dialogues, 1*, 74–105.

Hoffman, I. Z. (1994). Dialectical thinking and therapeutic action in the psychoanalytic process. *Psychoanalytic Quarterly, 63*, 187–218.

Hoffman, I. Z. (1996). The intimate and ironic authority of the psychoanalyst's presence. *Psychoanalytic Quarterly, 65*, 102–136.

Hoffman, I. Z. (2002). Toward a social-constructivist view of the psychoanalytic situation. In S. Fairfield, L. Layton, and C. Stack (Eds.), *Bringing the plague: Toward a postmodern psychoanalysis* (pp. 33–68). New York, NY: Other Press.

Holmes, J. (2001). *The search for the secure base: Attachment theory and psychotherapy.* East Sussex, England: Brunner-Routledge.

Jacobs, T. J. (1986). On countertransference enactments. *Journal of the American Psychoanalytic Association, 34*, 289–307.

Jacobs, T. J. (1991). *The use of the self: Countertransference and communication in the analytic situation.* Madison, CT: International Universities Press.

Jacobs, T. J. (1995). Discussion of Jay Greenberg's paper. *Contemporary Psychoanalysis, 31*, 237–245.

Jacobs, T. J. (2001). Reflections on the goals of psychoanalysis, the psychoanalytic process, and the process of change. *Psychoanalytic Quarterly, 70*, 149–181.

Jaffe, D. S. (1968). The mechanism of projection: Its dual role in object relations. *International Journal of Psychoanalysis, 49*, 662–677.

Javier, R. A. and Herron, W. G. (2002). Psychoanalysis and the disenfranchised: Countertransference issues. *Psychoanalytic Psychology, 19*, 149–166.

Javier, R. A. and Rendon, M. (1995). The ethnic unconscious and its role in transference, resistance, and countertransference: An introduction. *Psychoanalytic Psychology, 12*, 513–520.

Joseph, B. (1985). Transference: The Total Situation. *International Journal of Psychoanalysis, 66*, 447–454.

Kadyrov, I. (2002). Psychoanalysis across cultural and linguistic difference: Conceptual and technical issues. *International Journal of Psychoanalysis, 83*, 695–701.

Kakar, S. (1985). Psychoanalysis and non-western cultures. *International Review of Psychoanalysis, 12*, 441–448.

Kantrowitz, J. L. (1999). The role of the preconscious in psychoanalysis. *Journal of the American Psychoanalytic Association, 47*, 65–89.

Kernberg, O. F. (1975). *Borderline conditions and pathological narcissism.* New York, NY: Jason Aronson.

Kernberg, O. F. (1995). *Love relations: Normality and pathology.* New Haven, CT: Yale University Press.

Kernberg, O. F. (1996). The analyst's authority in the psychoanalytic situation. *Psychoanalytic Quarterly, 65,* 137–157.

Kernberg, O. F. (1997). The nature of interpretation: Intersubjectivity and the third position. *American Journal of Psychoanalysis, 57,* 297–312.

Kernberg, O. F. (2003). The management of affect storms in the psychoanalytic psychotherapy of borderline patients. *Journal of the American Psychoanalytic Association, 51,* 517–544.

Kernberg, O. F. (2007). The therapeutic action of psychoanalysis: Controversies and challenges. *Psychoanalytic Quarterly, 76S,* 1689–1723.

Kernberg, O. F., Yeomans, F. E., Clarkin, J. F., and Levy, K. N. (2008). Transference focused psychotherapy: Overview and update. *International Journal of Psychoanalysis, 89,* 601–620.

Klein, M. (1935). A contribution to the psychogenesis of manic-depressive states. In Money-Kyrle, R. (Ed.) *The writings of Melanie Klein, Vol. I: Love, guilt and reparation and other works 1921–1945* (pp. 262–289). New York, NY: Free Press, 1975.

Klein, M. (1946). Notes on some schizoid mechanisms. *International Journal of Psychoanalysis, 27,* 99–110.

Klein, M. (1948). On the theory of anxiety and guilt. In Money-Kyrle, R. (Ed.), *The writings of Melanie Klein, Vol. III: Envy and gratitude and other works 1946–1963* (pp. 25–42). New York, NY: Free Press, 1975.

Klein, M. (1952a). The origins of transference. *International Journal of Psychoanalysis, 33,* 433–438.

Klein, M. (1952b). Some theoretical conclusions regarding the emotional life of the infant. In Money–Kyrle, R. (Ed.), *The writings of Melanie Klein, Vol. III: Envy and gratitude and other works 1946–1963* (pp. 61–93). New York, NY: Free Press, 1975.

Klein, M. (1952c). The mutual influences in the development of ego and id. In Money-Kyrle, R. (Ed.), *The writings of Melanie Klein, Vol. III: Envy and gratitude and other works 1946–1963* (pp. 57–60). New York, NY: Free Press, 1975.

Klein, M. (1955). On identification. In Money-Kyrle, R. (Ed.), *The writings of Melanie Klein, Vol. III: Envy and gratitude and other works 1946–1963* (pp. 141–175). New York, NY: Free Press, 1975.

Klein, M. (1957). *Envy and gratitude.* London, England: Tavistock; New York, NY: Basic Books.

Klein, M. (1963a). Some reflections on 'The Oresteia.' In Money-Kyrle, R. (Ed.), *The writings of Melanie Klein, Vol. III: Envy and gratitude and other works 1946–1963* (pp. 275–299). New York, NY: Free Press, 1975.

Klein, M. (1963b). On the sense of loneliness. In Money-Kyrle, R. (Ed.), *The writings of Melanie Klein, Vol. III: Envy and Gratitude and other works 1946–1963* (pp. 300–313). New York, NY: The Free Press, 1975.

Kohut, H. (1971). *The analysis of the self.* New York: NY: International Universities Press.

Kohut, H. (1977). *The restoration of the self.* New York: NY: International Universities Press.

Kuchuck, S. (2009). Do ask, do tell?: Narcissistic need as a determinant of analyst self-disclosure. *Psychoanalytic Review, 96,* 1007–1024.

Kusserow, A. S. (1999). De-homogenizing American individualism: Socializing hard and soft individualism in Manhattan and Queens. *Ethos, 27,* 210–234.

Lachkar, J. (1992). *The narcissistic/borderline couple: A psychoanalytic perspective on marital treatment.* New York, NY: Brunner/Mazel.

Laing, R. D. (1962). *The self and others: Further studies in sanity and madness.* Chicago, IL: Quadrangle Books.

Langs, R. (1976). *The bipersonal field.* New York, NY: Jason Aronson.

Langs, R. (1981). Modes of 'cure' in psychoanalysis and psychoanalytic psychotherapy. *International Journal of Psychoanalysis, 62,* 199–214.

Laplanche, J. and Pontalis, J.B. (1973). *The language of psycho-analysis.* (D. Nicholson-Smith, Trans.). International Psycho-Analytical Library, 94:1–497. London, England: Hogarth Press and the Institute of Psycho-Analysis.

Layton, L. (2000). "Cultural hierarchies, splitting and the dynamic unconscious." *Journal for the Psychoanalysis of Culture and Society, 5*, 65–71.

Leary, K. (1997). Race, self-disclosure, and "forbidden talk": Race and ethnicity in contemporary clinical practice. *Psychoanalytic Quarterly, 66*, 163–189.

Levenson, E. A. (1996). Aspects of self-revelation and self-disclosure. *Contemporary Psychoanalysis, 32*, 237–248.

Levine, S. S. (2007). Nothing but the truth: Self-disclosure, self-revelation, and the persona of the analyst. *Journal of the American Psychoanalytic Assocation, 55*, 81–104.

Levine, L. (2009). Transformative aspects of our own analyses and their resonance in our work with our patients. *Psychoanalytic Dialogues, 19*, 454–462.

Little, M. (1951). Countertransference and the patient's response to it. *International Journal of Psychoanalysis, 32*, 32–40.

Loewald, H. W. (1980). *Papers on psychoanalysis*. New Haven, CT: Yale University Press.

Ludlam, M. (2007). Our attachment to "the couple in the mind." In M. Ludlam and V. Nyberg (Eds.), *Couple attachments: Theoretical and clinical studies*. London, England: Karnac.

Lyons, A. (1993). Husbands and wives: The mysterious choice. In S. Ruszczynski (Ed.), *Psychotherapy with couples: Theory and practice at the Tavistock Institute of Marital Studies* (pp. 44–54). London, England: Karnac.

Lyons-Ruth, K. (1999). The two-person unconscious: Intersubjective dialogue, enactive relational representation, and the emergence of new forms of relational organization. *Psychoanalytic Inquiry, 19*, 576–617.

Main, T. (1966). Mutual projection in a marriage. *Comprehensive Psychiatry, 7*, 432–449.

Malin, A. (1966). Projective identification in the therapeutic process. *International Journal of Psychoanalysis, 47*, 26–31.

Maltas, C. (1991). The dynamics of narcissism in marriage. *The Psychoanalytic Review, 78*, 567-581.

Maroda, K. (1991). *The power of countertransference*. Northvale, NJ: Jason Aronson.

Masterson, J. F. (1993). *The emerging self: A developmental self and object relations approach to the treatment of the closet narcissistic disorder of the self*. Philadelphia, PA: Brunner-Routledge.

Maugham, S. (1915). *Of human bondage*. New York, NY: Doubleday and Company.

McLaughlin, J. T. (1981). Transference, psychic reality and countertransference. *Psychoanalytic Quarterly, 50*, 639–664.

McLaughlin, J. T. (1991). Clinical and theoretical aspects of enactment. *Journal of the American Psychoanalytic Association, 39*, 595–614.

McLaughlin, J. T. (1998). Power, authority and influence in the analytic dyad. In O. Renik (Ed.), *Knowledge and authority in the psychoanalytic relationship* (pp.189–223). Northvale, NJ: Jason Aronson.

Meadow, P. W. (1977). The treatment of marital problems. *Modern Psychoanalysis, 2*, 15–34.

Mehta, P. (1998). The emergence, conflicts, and integration of the bicultural self: Psychoanalysis of an adolescent daughter of South-Asian immigrant parents. In S. Akhtar and S. Kramer (Eds.), *The colors of childhood* (pp. 129-167). Northvale, NJ: Jason Aronson.

Meissner, W. W. (1978). The conceptualization of marriage and family dynamics from a psychoanalytic perspective. In T. J. Paolino and B. S. McCrady (Eds.), *Marriage and marital therapy: Psychoanalytic, behavioral and systems theory perspectives* (pp. 25–88). New York, NY: Brunner/Mazel.

Meissner, W.W. (1980). A note on projective identification. *Journal of the American Psychoanalytic Association, 28*, 43–66.

Meissner, W. W. (2000). The self-as-relational in psychoanalysis: II. The self as related within the analytic process. *Psychoanalysis and Contemporary Thought, 23*, 205–247.

Meissner, W. W. (2002). The problem of self-disclosure in psychoanalysis. *Journal of the American Psychoanalytic Association, 50*, 827–867.

Meltzer, D. (1981). The Kleinian expansion of Freud's metapsychology. *International Journal of Psychoanalysis, 62*, 177–185.

Meltzer, D., Milana, G., Maiello, S., and Petrelli, D. (1982). The conceptual distinction between projective identification (Klein) and container-contained (Bion): Donald Meltzer (Oxford) with Guiliana Milana (Rome) Susanna Maiello (Rome) and Diomire Petrelli (Naples). *Journal of Child Psychotherapy, 8*, 185–202.

Menaker, E. (1990). Transference, countertransference, and therapeutic efficacy in relation to self-disclosure by the analyst. In G. Stricker and M. Fisher (Eds.), *Self-Disclosure in the therapeutic relationship* (pp. 103–115). New York, NY: Plenum Press.

Merleau-Ponty, M. (1962). *The phenomenology of perception.* C. Smith (Trans.). London, England: Routledge and Kegan Paul.

Miletic, M. J. (1998). Rethinking self-disclosure: An example of the clinical utility of the analyst's self-disclosing activities. *Psychoanalytic Inquiry, 18*, 580–600.

Mills, J. (2005). A critique of relational psychoanalysis. *Psychoanalytic Psychology, 22*(2), 155–188.

Mitchell, J. (1974). *Psychoanalysis and feminism.* New York: NY: Pantheon.

Mitchell, S. A. (1988). *Relational concepts in psychoanalysis: An integration.* Cambridge, MA: Harvard University Press.

Mitchell, S. A. (1993). Reply to Bachant and Richards. *Psychoanalytic Dialogues, 3,* 461–480.

Mitchell, S. A. (1995). Interaction in the Kleinian and interpersonal traditions. *Contemporary Psychoanalysis, 31,* 65–91.

Mitchell, S. A. (1997). *Influence and autonomy in psychoanalysis.* Hillsdale, NJ: Analytic Press.

Mitchell, S. A. (2000). *Relationality: From attachment to intersubjectivity.* Hillsdale, NJ: Analytic Press.

Mittelmann, B. (1944). Complementary neurotic reactions in intimate relationships. *Psychoanalytic Quarterly, 13,* 479–491.

Mittelmann, B. (1948). The concurrent analysis of married couples. *Psychoanalytic Quarterly, 17,* 182–197.

Money-Kyrle, R. E. (1951). *Psychoanalysis and politics: A contribution to the psychology of politics and morals.* New York: Norton.

Moore, R. (1999). *The creation of reality in psychoanalysis: A view of the contributions of Donald Spence, Roy Schafer, Robert Stolorow, Irwin Z. Hoffman, and beyond.* Hillsdale, NJ: The Analytic Press.

Morgan, M. (1995). The projective gridlock: A form of projective identification in couple relationships. In S. Ruszczynski and J. Fisher (Eds.), *Intrusiveness and intimacy in the couple* (pp. 33–48). London, England: Karnac.

Morgan, M. and Freedman, J. (2009). From fear of intimacy to perversion. In C. Clulow (Ed.), *Sex, attachment and couple therapy: Psychoanalytic perspectives* (pp. 185–198). London, England: Karnac.

Nadelson, C. C. (1978). Marital therapy from a psychoanalytic perspective. In T. J. Paolino and B. S. McCrady (Eds.), *Marriage and Marital Therapy: Psychoanalytic, Behavioral and Systems Theory Perspectives* (pp. 89–164). New York, NY: Brunner/Mazel.

Nahum, J. P. (2008). Forms of relational meaning: Issues in the relations between the implicit and reflective-verbal domains: Boston Change Process Study Group. *Psychoanalytic Dialogues , 18 ,* 125–148.

Nietzsche, F. (1967). *The will to power .* (W. Kauffman and R. J. Hollingdale, Trans.). New York, NY: Vintage.

Nietzsche, F. (1968). *Twilight of the idols* and *The antichrist .* (R. J. Hollingdale, Trans.). Baltimore, MD: Penguin.

Nietzsche, F. (1969). *Thus spoke Zarathustra: A book for everyone and no one .* (R. J. Hollingdale, Trans.). Baltimore, MD: Penguin Books.

Norenzayan, A., and Heine, S. J. (2005). Psychological universals: What are they and how can we know? *Psychological Bulletin, 131,* 763–784.

Oberndorf, C. P. (1938). Psychoanalysis of married couples. *Psychoanalytic Review, 25,* 453–475.

Ogden, T. H. (1979). On projective identification. *International Journal of Psychoanalysis, 60,* 357–373.

Ogden, T. H. (1982). *Projective Identification and Psychotherapeutic Technique.* New York, NY: Jason Aronson.

Ogden, T. H. (1983). The concept of internal object relations. *International Journal of Psycho-analysis*, *64*, 227–241.

Ogden, T. H. (1986). *Matrix of the mind: Object relations and the psychoanalytic dialogue*. Northvale, NJ: Jason Aronson.

Ogden, T. H. (1991). Analysing the matrix of transference. *International Journal of Psycho-analysis*, *72*, 593–605.

Ogden, T. H. (1992). Comments on transference and countertransference in the initial analytic meeting. *Psychoanalytic Inquiry*, *12*, 225–247.

Ogden, T. H. (1994a). *Subjects of analysis*. Northvale, NJ: Jason Aronson.

Ogden, T. H. (1994b). The analytic third: Working with intersubjective clinical facts. *International Journal of Psychoanalysis*, *75*, 3–19.

Ogden, T. H. (1996). Reconsidering three aspects of psychoanalytic technique. *International Journal of Psychoanalysis*, *77*, 883–899.

Ogden, T. H. (2001). *Conversations at the frontier of dreaming*. Northvale, NJ: Jason Aronson.

Ogden, T. H. (2004). The analytic third: Implications for psychoanalytic theory and technique. *Psychoanalytic Quarterly*, *73*, 167–195.

Orange, D. M., and Stolorow, R. D. (1998). Self-disclosure from the perspective of intersubjectivity theory. *Psychoanalytic Inquiry*, *18*, 530–537.

Orange, D. J., Atwood, G. E. and Stolorow, R. D. (1997). Working intersubjectively: Contextualism in psychoanalytic practice. Hillsdale, NJ: Analytic Press.

Pincus, L. (Ed.) (1960). *Marriage: Studies in emotional conflict and growth*. London, England: Methuen and Co.

Pizer, B. (2006). Risk and potential in analytic disclosure: Can the analyst make "the wrong thing" right? *Contemporary Psychoanalysis*, *42*, 31–40.

Pizer, B. and Pizer, S. A. (2006). "The gift of an apple or the twist of an arm": Negotiation in couples and couple therapy. *Psychoanalytic Dialogues*, *16*(1), 71–92.

Pizer, S.A. (2006). "Aerial kiss attack": Affect communication, demystification, and analytic self-disclosure. *Contemporary Psychoanalysis*, *42*, 41–45.

Poulton, J., Norman, C., and Stites, M. (2006). The analytic third and cotransference in couple therapy. In J. Scharff and D. Scharff (Eds.), *Treating relationships: New paradigms in couple and family therapy* (pp. 311–322). Lanham, MD: Jason Aronson/ Rowman and Littlefield.

Prochaska, J. and Prochaska, J. (1978). Twentieth century trends in marriage and marital therapy. In T. J. Paolino and B. S. McCrady (Eds.), *Marriage and marital therapy: Psycho-analytic, behavioral and systems theory perspectives* (pp. 1–24). New York, NY: Brunner/ Mazel.

Pulver, S. E. (1970). Narcissism—the term and the concept. *Journal of the American Psycho-analytic Association*, *18*, 319–341.

Racker, H. (1953). A contribution to the problem of counter-transference. *International Journal of Psychoanalysis*, *34*, 313–324.

Racker, H. (1957). The meaning and uses of countertransference. *Psychoanalytic Quarterly*, *26*, 303–357.

Racker, H. (1968). *Transference and countertransference*. New York, NY: International Universities Press.

Rand, N. T. (1994). Secrets and posterity: The theory of the transgenerational phantom: Editor's note. In N. T. Rand (Trans. and Ed.), *The shell and the kernal: Renewals of psycho-analysis, Vol. 1*. (pp. 165–169). Chicago, IL: University of Chicago Press.

Reich, A. (1951). On counter-transference. *International Journal of Psychoanalysis*, *32*, 25–31.

Reich, A. (1960). Further remarks on counter-transference. *International Journal of Psycho-analysis*, *41*, 389–395.

Reik, T. (1930). Final phases of belief found in religion and in obsessional neurosis—an introductory communication. *International Journal of Psychoanalysis*, *11*, 258–291.

Reisenberg-Malcom, R. (2001). Bion's theory of containment. In C. Bronstein (Ed.), *Kleinian theory: A contemporary perspective* (pp. 165–180). London, England: Whurr Publishers.

Renik, O. (1993). Technique in the light of the analyst's irreducible subjectivity. *Psychoanalytic Quarterly*, *62*, 553–571.

Renik, O. (1995). The ideal of the anonymous analyst and the problem of self-disclosure. *Psychoanalytic Quarterly*, *64*, 466–495.

Renik, O. (1996). The perils of neutrality. *Psychoanalytic Quarterly*, *65*, 495–517.

Renik, O. (1998a). Getting real in analysis. *Psychoanalytic Quarterly*, *67*, 566–593.

Renik, O. (1998b). The analyst's subjectivity and the analyst's objectivity. *The International Journal of Psychoanalysis*, *79*, 487–497.

Renik, O. (1999). Playing one's cards face up in analysis: An approach to the problem of self-disclosure. *Psychoanalytic Quarterly*, *68*, 521–539.

Renik, O. (2004). Intersubjectivity in psychoanalysis. *International Journal of Psychoanalysis*, *85*, 1053–1064.

Robertson, L. H. (2010). Mapping the self with units of culture. *Psychology*, *1*, 185–193.

Robbins, M. (1982). Narcissistic personality as a symbiotic character disorder. *International Journal of Psychoanalysis*, *63*, 457–473.

Rosenfeld, H. (1952). Transference-phenomena and transference-analysis in an acute catatonic schizophrenic patient. *International Journal of Psychoanalysis*, *33*, 457–464.

Rosenfeld, H. (1964). On the psychopathology of narcissism a clinical approach. *International Journal of Psychoanalysis*, *45*, 332–337.

Rosenfeld, H. (1987). *Impasse and interpretation: Therapeutic and anti-therapeutic factors in the psychoanalytic treatment of psychotic, borderline, and neurotic patients.* London, England: Routledge.

Rothstein, A. (1997). Introduction: Symposium: Aspects of self-revelation and self-disclosure: Analyst to patient the New York Psychoanalytic Society March 11, 1995. *Journal of Clinical Psychoanalysis*, *6*, 141-144.

Roudané, M. C. (1990). *Who's Afraid of Virginia Woolf?: Necessary fictions, terrifying realities.* Boston, MA: Twayne Publishers.

Ruszczynski, S. P. (1992). Notes towards a psychoanalytic understanding of the couple relationship. *Psychoanalytic Psychotherapy*, *6*, 33–48.

Ruszczynski, S. P. (1993). Thinking about and working with couples. In S. Ruszczynski (Ed.), *Psychotherapy with couples: Theory and practice at the Tavistock Institute of Marital Studies* (pp. 197–217). London, England: Karnac.

Sander, F. M. (1978). Marriage and the family in Freud's writings. *Journal of the American Academy of Psychoanalysis and Dynamic Psychiatry*, *6*, 157–174.

Sander, F. M. (2004). Psychoanalytic couple therapy: Classical style. *Psychoanalytic Inquiry*, *24*, 373–386.

Sandler, J. (1976). Countertransference and role-responsiveness. *International Review of Psychoanalysis*, *3*, 43–47.

Schafer, R. (2002). You can get here from there. *Psychoanalytic Inquiry*, *22*, 29–42.

Scharff, D. E., and Scharff, J. S. (1987). *Object relations family therapy.* Northvale, NJ: Jason Aronson.

Scharff, D. E., and Scharff, J. S. (1991). *Object relations couple therapy.* Northvale, NJ: Jason Aronson.

Scharff, D. E., and Scharff, J. S. (2011). *The interpersonal unconscious.* Lanham, MD: Jason Aronson.

Scharff, J. S. (1992). *Projective and introjective identification and the use of the therapist's self.* Northvale, NJ: Jason Aronson.

Scharff, J. S. (1995). Psychoanalytic marital therapy. In N. S. Jacobson and A. S. Gurman (Eds.), *Clinical handbook of couple therapy* (pp. 164–193). New York, NY: Guilford Press.

Scharff, J. S. and Scharff, D. E. (1992). *Scharff notes: A primer of object relations therapy.* Northvale, NJ: Jason Aronson.

Scharff, J. S. and Scharff, D. E. (1998). *Object relations individual therapy.* Northvale, NJ: Jason Aronson.

Scharff, J. S. and Scharff, D. E. (2005). *The primer of object relations* (2nd ed.). Northvale, NJ: Jason Aronson.

Searles, H. F. (1963). Transference psychosis in the psychotherapy of chronic schizophrenia. *International Journal of Psychoanalysis*, *44*, 249–281.

Segal, H. (1956). Depression in the schizophrenic. *International Journal of Psychoanalysis, 37,* 339–343.

Segal, H. (1964). *Introduction to the work of Melanie Klein.* London, England: Heinemann.

Segal, H. (1979). *Klein.* London, England: Karnac.

Shapiro, E. R., Shapiro, R. L., Zinner, J., and Berkowitz, D. A. (1977). The borderline ego and the working alliance: Indications for family and individual treatment in adolescence. *International Journal of Psychoanalysis, 58,* 77–87.

Shill, M. A. (2004). Analytic neutrality, anonymity, abstinence, and elective self-disclosure. *Journal of the American Psychoanalytic Association, 52,* 151–187.

Sholes, M. A. (2005). Letting it hang out a little: A self-psychological perspective on self-disclosure. *Psychoanalytic Perspectives, 3,* 99–113.

Shweder, R. (1990). Cultural psychology: What is it? In N. R. Goldberger and J. B. Veroff (Eds.), *The culture and psychology reader* (pp. 41–86). New York, NY: New York University Press, 1995.

Slipp, S. (1984). *Object relations: A dynamic bridge between individual and family treatment.* Northvale, NJ: Jason Aronson.

Smith, H. F. (1997). Resistance, enactment, and interpretation: A self-analytic study. *Psychoanalytic Inquiry, 17,* 13–30.

Snibbe, A. C., and Markus, H. R. (2005). You can't always get what you want: Educational attainment, agency, and choice. *Journal of Personality and Social Psychology, 88,* 703–720.

Spence, D. P. (1989). Narrative appeal vs. historical validity. *Contemporary Psychoanalysis, 25,* 517–523.

Spence, D. P. (1993). The hermeneutic turn: Soft science or loyal opposition? *Psychoanalytic Dialogues, 3,* 1–10.

Spezzano, C. (1993). *Affect in psychoanalysis: A clinical synthesis.* Hillsdale, NJ: Jason Aronson.

Spezzano, C. (1995). "Classical" versus "contemporary" theory—the differences that matter clinically. *Contemporary Psychoanalysis, 31,* 20–46.

Spezzano, C. (1996a). The three faces of two-person psychology: Development, ontology and epistemology. *Psychoanalytic Dialogues, 6,* 599–622.

Spezzano, C. (1996b). Toward an intrapsychic-intersubjective dialectic: Reply to commentary. *Psychoanalytic Dialogues, 6,* 675–688.

Stein, S. (1991). The influence of theory on the psychoanalyst's countertransference. *International Journal of Psychoanalysis, 72,* 325–334.

Steiner, J. (1994). Patient-centered and analyst-centered interpretations: Some implications of containment and countertransference. *Psychoanalytic Inquiry, 14,* 406–422.

Steiner, J. (2000). Containment, enactment and communication. *International Journal of Psychoanalysis, 81,* 245–255.

Stenz, A. M. (1978). *Edward Albee: The poet of loss.* The Hague, Netherlands: Mouton Publishers.

Stern, D. B. (1985). Psychoanalysis and truth: Current issues (a symposium)—Introduction: Some controversies regarding constructivism and psychoanalysis. *Contemporary Psychoanalysis, 21,* 201–207.

Stern, D. B. (1991). A philosophy for the embedded analyst—Gadamer's hermeneutics and the social paradigm of psychoanalysis. *Contemporary Psychoanalysis, 27,* 51–80.

Stern, D. B. (1996). The social construction of therapeutic action. *Psychoanalytic Inquiry, 16,* 265–293.

Stern, D. N., Sander, L. W., Nahum, J. P., Harrison, A. M., Lyons-Ruth, K., Morgan, A. C., Bruschweilerstern, N., and Tronick, E. Z. (1998). Non-interpretive mechanisms in psychoanalytic therapy: The 'Something More' than interpretation. *International Journal of Psychoanalysis, 79,* 903–921.

Stewart, R. H., Peters, T. C., Marsh, S., and Peters, M. J. (1975). An object-relations approach to psychotherapy with marital couples, families, and children. *Family Process, 14,* 161–178.

Stolorow, R. D. (1995). Introduction: Tensions between loyalism and expansionism in self psychology. *Progress in Self Psychology, 11,* xi–xvii.

Stolorow, R. D. (2001). What in the (experiential) world is an "internal couple"? *Psychoanalytic Inquiry, 21,* 530–535.

Stolorow, R. D., and Atwood, G. E. (1992). *Contexts of being: The intersubjective foundations of psychological life.* Hillsdale, NJ: Analytic Press.

Stolorow, R. D., Atwood, G. E., and Brandchaft, B. (Eds.) (1994). *The intersubjective perspective.* Northvale, NJ: Jason Aronson.

Stolorow, R. D., Brandchaft, B., and Atwood, G. E. (1987). *Psychoanalytic treatment: An intersubjective approach.* Hillsdale, NJ: Analytic Press.

Sue, S. and Zane, N. (1987). The role of culture and cultural techniques in psychotherapy. *American Psychologist, 42,* 37-45.

Sullivan, H. S. (1953). *The interpersonal theory of psychiatry.* H. S. Perry and M. L. Gawel (Eds.). New York, NY: Norton.

Symington, N. (1993). *Narcissism: A new theory.* London, England: Karnac.

Tansey, M. J., and Burke, W. F. (1989). *Understanding countertransference: From projective identification to empathy.* Hillsdale, NJ: Analytic Press.

Tarantelli, C. B. (2003). Life within death: Towards a metapsychology of catastrophic psychic trauma. *International Journal of Psychoanalysis, 84,* 915–928.

Thompson, A. G. (1960). Introduction. In L. Pincus (Ed.), *Marriage: Studies in emotional conflict and growth* (pp. 1–10). London, England: Methuen and Co.

Torok, M. (1968). The illness of mourning and the fantasy of the exquisite corpse. In N. T. Rand, Trans. and Ed.) *The shell and the kernel: Renewals of psychoanalysis, Vol. 1* (107–124). Chicago, IL: University of Chicago Press, 1994.

Torok, M. (1975). Story of fear: The symptoms of phobia—the return of the repressed or the return of the phantom? In N. T. Rand, (Trans. and Ed.) *The shell and the kernel: Renewals of psychoanalysis, Vol. 1* (pp. 177–186). Chicago, IL: University of Chicago Press, 1994.

Tower, L. E. (1956). Countertransference. *Journal of the American Psychoanalytic Association, 4,* 224–255.

Triandis, H. C. (2007). Culture and psychology: A history of the study of their relationships. In S. Kitayama and D. Cohen (Eds.), *Handbook of cultural psychology* (pp. 59–76). New York, NY: Guilford Press.

Tubert-Oklander, J. (2006a). I, thou, and us: Relationality and the interpretive process in clinical practice. *Psychoanalytic Dialogues, 16*(2), 199–216.

Tubert-Oklander, J. (2006b). On the inherent relationality of the unconscious: Reply to commentary. *Psychoanalytic Dialogues, 16*(2), 227–239.

Tubert-Oklander, J. (2006c). The individual, the group and society: Their psychoanalytic inquiry. *International Forum of Psychoanalysis, 15,* 146–150.

Tummala-Narra, P. (2004). Mothering in a foreign land. *American Journal of Psychoanalysis, 64,* 167-182.

Wachtel, P. L. (1986). From neutrality to personal revelation: Patterns of influence in the analytic relationship (a symposium)—On the limits of therapeutic neutrality. *Contemporary Psychoanalysis, 22,* 60–70.

Wallerstein, R. S. (1988). One psychoanalysis or many? *International Journal of Psychoanalysis, 69,* 5–21.

Walls, G. B. (2004). Toward a critical global psychoanalysis. *Psychoanalytic Dialogues, 14*(5), 605–634.

Waska, R. (2008). A Kleinian view of psychoanalytic couples therapy: Part 1. *Psychoanalytic Psychotherapy, 22,* 100–117.

White, C. (2004). Culture, influence and the 'I-ness' of me: Commentary on papers by Susan Bodnar, Gary B. Walls, and Steven Botticelli. *Psychoanalytic Dialogues, 14,* 653–691.

Willi, J. (1982). *Couples in collusion.* New York, NY: Jason Aronson, in collaboration with Hunter House.

Williams, P. (2001). Object relationships—symmetry and asymmetry: Commentary on paper by Anthony Bass. *Psychoanalytic Dialogues, 11,* 711–716.

Winnicott, D. W. (1949). Hate in the countertransference. *International Journal of Psychoanalysis, 30,* 69–74.

Winnicott, D. W. (1953). Transitional objects and transitional phenomena—A study of the first not-me possession. *International Journal of Psychoanalysis, 34,* 89–97.

Winnicott, D. W. (1960). The theory of the parent-infant relationship. *International Journal of Psychoanalysis, 41,* 585–595.

Winnicott, D. W. (1963). The development of the capacity for concern. In *The maturational processes and the facilitating environment: Studies in the theory of emotional development* (pp. 73–82). Madison, WI: International Universities Press, 1965.

Winnicott, D. W. (1971). *Playing and reality.* New York, NY: Basic Books.

Winnicott, D. W. (1989). *Psychoanalytic explorations.* C. Winnicott, R. Shepherd, and M. Davis (Eds.). Cambridge, MA: Harvard University Press.

Wittgenstein, L. (1969). *On certainty.* D. Paul and G. E. M. Anscombe (Trans.), G. E. M. Anscombe and G. H. von Wright (Eds.). New York, NY: Harper and Row.

Wolstein, B. (1983a). Transference and resistance as a psychic experience. *Contemporary Psychoanalysis, 19,* 276–294.

Wolstein, B. (1983b). The pluralism of perspectives on countertransference. *Contemporary Psychoanalysis, 19,* 506–521.

Wolstein, B. (1992). Resistance interlocked with countertransference—R. N. and Ferenczi, and American interpersonal relations. *Contemporary Psychoanalysis, 28,* 172–189.

Yassa, M. (2002). Nicolas Abraham and Maria Torok—the inner crypt. *Scandinavian Psychoanalytic Review, 25,* 82–91.

Zavattini, G. C. (1988). The other one of me, that is my other half: Reflections on projective identification. *Rivista di psicoanalisi, 34,* 348–374.

Zeddies, T. J. (2000). Within, outside, and in between: The relational unconscious. *Psychoanalytic Psychology, 17,* 467–487.

Zeddies, T. J. (2002a). More than just words: A hermeneutic view of language in psychoanalysis. *Psychoanalytic Psychology, 19,* 3–23.

Zeddies, T. J. (2002b). Behind, beneath, above, and beyond: The historical unconscious. *Journal of the American Academy of Psychoanalysis, 30,* 211–229.

Zeitner, R. M. (2012). *Self within marriage: The foundation for lasting relationships.* New York, NY: Routledge.

Zinner, J. and Shapiro, R. (1972). Projective identification as a mode of perception and behavior in families of adolescents. *International Journal of Psychoanalysis, 53,* 523–530.

Zwiebel, R. (2004). The third position: Reflections about the internal analytic working process. *Psychoanalytic Quarterly, 73,* 215–265.

Author Index

Subject Index

aggression, 4, 35, 48, 64–65, 68, 69, 72, 102, 109–110, 113, 115–119, 120–121, 125, 137, 153, 155

alterity. *See* otherness

asymmetry, 16, 20, 63, 70

authority, 15, 18, 20, 61, 62, 63, 70–72, 76

bipersonal field, 48

cases: Alan and Rachel, 130–133, 136–138, 139; Carl, 113–119; Carl and Sarah, 120–124; Cindy and Bob, 96–100, 103–106, 109–110; David and Laurie, 72–76; Doug and Carol, 141–142, 157–159; Gerald, 64–65, 67; George and Martha (from *Who's Afraid of Virginia Woolf?*), 147–151, 153–156; Mike and Lana, 44–45, 46–47, 49–52, 55–57; Olive and Shawn, 86–89; Rick and Nancy, 25–27, 29, 33–39; Tanya and Michael, 2, 7–10, 23–24

containment, 4, 7, 10–11, 38, 39, 41, 48, 51, 54, 67, 71, 89, 92, 94, 107; container-contained, 68; intrapsychic, 67, 69, 71; relational, 41, 67, 68–69, 71, 76

countertransference, 4, 6, 9, 16–17, 22, 29, 36, 40, 43, 53–54, 59–61, 65–67, 71, 75, 90, 92, 93, 129, 132; cultural, 136–138; enactments, 6, 7, 29, 30, 39,

54, 55, 59–60, 71, 75, 76, 80, 93, 144; therapist's analysis of, 40–41, 53–54, 61, 65, 67, 74

couples: containing skin, 42; direct heir to childhood relationships, 28; narcissistic, 79–94; as therapeutic institution, 38; types of narcissistic, 85

crypt, 95, 100–103

cultural theory, 127–128; and deconstructionism, 127; and relativism, 127; and universalism, 127; definition of culture, 133; developmental aspect, 134–135; dialectics, 128; diversity and liberation movements, 128; environmental aspect, 135–136

cultural third, 127, 129–130, 132, 136–138; treatment, 138–139

depressive position, 5, 83

desire, 2, 5, 11, 14, 28, 31–32, 72–75, 81, 88, 93, 95–100, 103–106, 141, 157–158; origin of legitimacy of, 107–110

dialectic, 14–16, 19–20, 128, 137, 144–146; active-passive, 16; intrapsychic-interpersonal, 19, 20, 144–146

disidentification. *See* identification

ego psychology, 13

About the Author

Dr. Poulton is a psychologist in private practice in Salt Lake City, and adjunct assistant professor in psychology and clinical instructor in psychiatry at the University of Utah. He is a member of the national faculty of the International Psychotherapy Institute (IPI), based in Washington, DC, and currently serves on IPI's Steering Committee and is the co-director of its Salt Lake City chapter. He is the coauthor of *Internalization: The Origin and Construction of Internal Reality* and the upcoming *LeConte Stewart: Masterworks* and has authored numerous articles and presentations on psychological treatment and theory. He is the 2007 recipient of the Norman S. Anderson Award, given annually to a mental health professional in Utah "who typifies distinguished service to community mental health through clinical, administrative, consultation, or training functions."

Lightning Source UK Ltd.
Milton Keynes UK
UKOW041531020413

208555UK00004B/25/P